RULAND'S PASTORAL THEOLOGY

Vol. III: Morality and the Social Order

MORALITY AND
THE SOCIAL ORDER

BY

Rev. LUDWIG RULAND, D.D.

PROFESSOR OF MORAL AND PASTORAL THEOLOGY
IN THE UNIVERSITY OF WÜRZBURG

ADAPTED INTO ENGLISH BY

The Rev. T. A. RATTLER, O.S.A.

EDITED BY

The Rev. NEWTON THOMPSON, S.T.D.

B. HERDER BOOK CO.
15 & 17 SOUTH BROADWAY, ST. LOUIS, MO.,
AND
33 QUEEN SQUARE, LONDON, W. C.
1942

IMPRIMI POTEST

New York, June 2, 1942

Athanasius Pape, O.S.A.

Vicarus Provincialis

NIHIL OBSTAT

Sti. Ludovici, die 23. Septembris, 1942

Wm. Fischer, S.T.D.

Censor Librorum

IMPRIMATUR

Sti. Ludovici, die 16. Octobris, 1942

✠ Joannes J. Glennon,

Archiepiscopus

Copyright 1942

B. HERDER BOOK CO.

Vail-Ballou Press, Inc., Binghamton and New York

Translator's Preface

THIS is the third and last volume of Ruland's *Pastoral Theology*. The problems discussed in it are of extreme importance and timeliness. Although many authors have written on these same subjects, the attentive reader of Ruland's work will not fail to recognize its theoretical and practical usefulness.

In offering this *Pastoral Theology* to the clergy at a time of gravest dangers, which threaten religion from all sides, we commend to the consideration of priests the following words of the learned and experienced author, which appear at the close of this book: "There is no more ignorant and inexperienced view than the belief that the times of supernatural faith, of religion, and need for priestly ministrations are past. No, they are not past; in the new era they are going to have a greater part than ever before."

T. A. RATTLER, O.S.A.

St. Rita's Monastery
Racine, Wisconsin

v

Contents

CONTENTS

I

Charity and Justice

LOVE OF NEIGHBOR

THE commandment of the love of God and neighbor includes, according to Christ's word, the whole pre-Christian revelation, the law and the prophets. In the same way the active concrete realization of the law of charity must be the supreme goal of the Church's work for souls.[1] Hence we must consider the problems of the love of neighbor. Man is by nature not a solitary but a social being, and as such is compelled to accommodate himself to the ways of orderly society. On the other hand, there is in man the natural instinct of self-defense and self-preservation which to a certain extent opposes his social inclinations. The reconciliation of these two forces is never complete and in the course of history has produced as many individual and group solutions as the variety of circumstances and the placing of emphasis on the one or the other attitude suggested.

Mutual social obligations are, then, a matter of the natural order, but also a very definite demand of the Christian religion. In the order of grace God has placed man again into a society where the love of God is practiced by an active love of neighbor (1 John 4:20) in the patient bearing of one another's burden (Gal. 6:2). The kingdom of God on earth is realized in a society which imposes obligations to be fulfilled by the practice of corresponding virtues.

The ultimate prerequisite for any social coherence is the mutual respect of men for each other's dignity as human persons and Christians. This respect is not the same as absolute equali-

---

[1] For a discussion of the duties toward God and self, see Ruland, *Foundations of Morality* (Herder, 1936).

zation. Nature has endowed individuals and nations with various gifts and talents. And men make such different use of their native faculties that differences of personal value cannot be gainsaid. But the basic dignity of human personality and supernatural calling cannot be denied to any human individual or race.

Wherever in the cultural history of man whole tribal groups were denied freedom and their standing as human beings, or where excessive differences of rank developed which led to the disregard of any social class, mankind has gone astray and has followed a course opposed to Christian truth. Besides these practical aberrations, are the errors of philosophers who called the masses of men evil or loathsome, and despised them as the Stoic did—*odi profanum vulgus et arceo*. Schopenhauer among the moderns says: "I became early tired of considering beings as my equals who in reality are not such. Nature is extremely parsimonious in producing real men." But also the Christian ascetic who swathes himself with too great horror at the wickedness of the world is not quite free from this taint. Unjust social distinctions grew up again at the end of the eighteenth century when, as a result of the fast developing industrialism, the belief sprang up that by an iron rule of the law of nature those necessarily rose up into a preferred social class who possessed the qualities for economic and industrial organization, while the great mass of men had but their labor to offer. And by paying for the worker's labor as for any impersonal article of merchandise, the employer was thought to acquit himself of all further social obligations. Liberalism regarded human society as merely an assemblage of individual competitors. Marxian socialism aims at atomizing society and fusing the isolated individuals into economic classes. Its theory of the dictatorship of the proletariat is the old standpoint of unjust class distinctions, but in the inverted order which raises up the formerly oppressed and makes them oppressors of their former masters.

However, the fact must not be overlooked that for the first time in history the modern world is attempting to build up a cultural society from which slavery and vassalism as accepted institutions are absent. Our admiration for Egypt's pyramids or the splendid architecture and sculpture of Greece and Rome, or even for the towering castles and gorgeous palaces of many former Christian rulers must not blind us to the fact that all these achievements have as their background the somber setting of slavery or similar conditions of enforced labor. On the other hand, Soviet Russia is at present carrying out its industrial five-year plans by the unpaid slave labor of the former bourgeoisie. Unfortunately mankind seems able to learn its social lessons only in the school of blood and tears. If the authors of the social utopias (Campanella and St. Thomas More) had been privileged to see their dreams realized on some little island in the ocean, mankind might have been spared the monstrous experiments of Marxism and Bolshevism. The modern world is faced with the tremendous problem of sharing, to a satisfactory degree, the achievements and goods of our highly developed civilization and culture among all members of society on the principle of the personal equality of all. The accomplishment of this task is the social problem of our day, and the realization that this cannot be done on the basis of class conflict is the first step of a better wisdom.

Mutual respect is the soil from which spring the two basic social virtues of justice and charity. God commands us to love our neighbor as ourself. The right love and respect for self, which are needed in the attainment of our own eternal and temporal end, are, then, the measure of our love of neighbor. In the exact determination of the equality of love for self and neighbor the two virtues of justice and love will always have to be taken into consideration. Justice will at times rightly suggest a falling short of exact, say, mathematical equality, while heroic charity will often abound far beyond the ordinary requirements.

Love of neighbor arises from the natural law, is more fully unfolded by divine revelation, and is perfected in the supernatural order of redemption. Historically, the friendly feeling of unity extended, first of all, to the members of the restricted societies of the family and the tribe while all beyond these limits were regarded as alien and hostile. The natural feeling of cosmopolitan love and affection for all has never been a reality but only a philosophical abstraction. Man's first social reaction is partly to cling to the naturally given environment for support and protection and partly to ward off dangers and encroachments.

An analysis of the various ways and degrees of intimacy in our relations to other persons appears to justify corresponding gradations of our active love of neighbor. We may mention the relations based on consanguinity and affinity, nationality and religious community, cultural traditions, professional occupation, and personal friendship. On the other hand, these special reasons of neighborly love involve a certain danger to the general obligation of charity, because men are prone to regulate their relations to others according to the benefit deriving therefrom, and to foster a love which demands sacrifices rather than a love that is ready to make sacrifices. Such behavior is, of course, the very opposite of true love. The history of man is a history of egotism. No race or state is free from this fault.

The commandment of charity was well known to the Jews (Lev. 19:18), but its observance was practically restricted to the members of their own race; and even there real love was much stifled by self-seeking and narrowness, as may be seen by the questions "Who is my neighbor?" and "How often shall my brother offend against me and I forgive him?" Charity is indeed a new commandment in the new dispensation, and a sign that marks the children of light. "Again a new commandment I write unto you: which thing is true, both in him and in you; because the darkness is passed, and the true light now shineth. He that saith he is in the light, and hateth his brother, is in darkness even until now. He that loveth his brother, abideth in the light, and there is no scandal in him" (1 John 2:8–10). The deepest foundation of the Christian love of neighbor is man's sonship of God through grace. We must love all men because all have God as their father, and Christ as their brother. This common condition of all men before God excludes and condemns every form of antagonism and fanaticism. God extends his good gifts to all alike (cf. Matt. 5:45; Acts 14:16 ff.). And we who equally share the fruits of God's patience and kindness are required to refrain from judging our neighbor and to think of penance for our own faults (Rom. 2:4 f.; 1 John 4:10 f.). Charity in the Christian spirit is indeed a new law; new in its manner of promulgation, in its contents and aim. It flows forth from the divine love of the Savior and is sustained by it and is communicated to those united with Him by grace. Thus man's divine sonship implies obligations in the service of the neighbor, for we are called upon to practice our love of God by loving our neighbor and so to work for the establishment of God's kingdom on earth. Thus it is clear that the Christian love of neighbor includes both his temporal and his eternal welfare.

The love of neighbor engages the whole man, his inner and outer faculties. He must sincerely wish (*amor affectivus*) and actively promote (*amor effectivus*) his neighbor's well-being. In the New Testament it is especially the writings of St. John and St. Paul that speak of charity. From them we learn that charity subjectively and objectively is a process of continual growth, never a finished state. Charity must lead to an ever greater knowledge of the truth, to penance and amendment.

Theology mentions three qualities of charity. It must be supernatural in its motive; universal in its scope so as to exclude no one; and both affective and effective in its manifestations. The Church has condemned the proposition that effective charity which positively excludes the appropriate affective disposition satisfies Christ's command. The religious motive must be ultimate and supreme but need not exist in pure culture, so to speak; it admits naturally good motives and insights. In practice, the actual exclusion of conscious selfishness may often have to be sufficient; but gradually the natural motives should be purified and inwardly transformed by religious considerations. Here lies an important problem of priestly work, requiring deep personal spirituality and patience.

The summit and crown of charity is the *love of enemies* which for this very reason is so difficult and rare, as are outstanding record performances in any other endeavor. The essence of enmity is best seen by contrasting it with love, which wishes for and effectively promotes the temporal and eternal well-being of another. Enmity consists in wishing evil to someone and working against his interests by thwarting his attainment to material or spiritual goods or his enjoyment of them. The chief root of enmity is the perverseness of the human heart, especially its proneness to jealousy which finds a fertile ground in the immoderate desire for possessions and external reputation. Another source of enmity is a lack of appreciation of the personal value of others and of the ways of divine providence. Persons who are unable to transcend the circle of their own ideas, purposes, and desires are the most likely to regard the ways, actions, and accomplishments of others as personal slights, unwarranted neglect, and malicious hindrances. Such, often very ridiculous, but at the same time always very painful and occasionally scandalous, failures are not confined to the unintellectual, but occur all too often among persons of high position in public affairs and in the field of learning. Occasions for friction of this sort are very likely to arise wherever persons must cooperate in the same work. Differences of methods are, then, considered deliberate obstruction and jealous rivalry; an unconscious awkwardness is construed as a well-aimed insult, and so on. Most of these things can be avoided by a definite effort at understanding the neighbor's objective position, his rights and duties; by generously allowing to others at least as many slips and blunders as we have to regret in our own conduct; and by convincing ourselves of the neighbor's decent dispositions through cultivating an unofficial friendly acquaintance on occasions which naturally present themselves. Fierce enmity breaks out at times between parents and adult children, and between relatives in general over matters of property and the like. The worst form of enmity is the persecution of others out of envy and vengeance under the pretense of zeal for religious truth.

By practicing the virtues opposed to the false attitudes that give rise to enmity we acquire the natural and supernatural disposition needed for the love of those who actually have done us wrong. In the community of the children of God redeemed by the blood of Christ there is no room for enmity and hatred. Even mere human highmindedness and generosity recognize as real trifles whatever may cause discord among men. And there is no human offense but vanishes into nothingness under the cross of Christ. Hence love of enemy is not a counsel but a command. We must wish well to those who are our enemies; we must be ready to forgive them and even to help them in need. We are not permitted to harm them even though they may have done us harm. There are people who believe they are entitled to inflict on their enemies as much damage as these have caused them, on the principle of secret compensation. This is, of course, a gross misunderstanding, for by secret compensation is meant the hidden restitution, under certain conditions, of unjustly sustained loss from him who violated strict justice, but not the infliction of harm on an enemy as an act of plain vengeance.

Love of enemy demands also that we do not exclude those ill disposed toward us from our prayers or general acts of helpfulness and signs of respect. The first indication of enmity usually consists in the refusal to greet another. On the other hand, readiness to greet another and the rendering of similar courtesies signalizes in the most inobtrusive manner one's readiness for reconciliation. By ignoring the signs of nascent enmity many a foolish quarrel can be nipped in the bud, even though the offended one may be the superior of the offender. No one lowers his dignity by his readiness for peace and conciliation, even at the expense of certain social proprieties. If, however, the offender continues in his conduct in a markedly offensive manner it is not necessary to show him signs of respect. Not infrequently both parties believe they are in the right. Generosity in taking the first step of conciliation is, also in such cases, not humiliating but much nobler than mere insistence on what one considers one's right. Objectively, the real offender has to make the first move toward conciliation. There is no obligation to show special respect for one's enemy; but it may be necessary to do so if by its refusal public scandal is given.

The obligation of loving our enemy does not forbid our invoking the law in order to restrain future attacks and violations of justice or to secure restitution of property and honor. This course of action may become a duty when the injury sustained, if left unchallenged, would reflect harmfully on all members of a profession which needs the confidence of the public or would render one's own work very difficult or impossible. However, in taking legal action we must be sure of our complete innocence if things are not to be made worse. Both as confessor and as spiritual adviser the priest may have frequent occasion to deal with enmities. This work requires much prudence and sympathy, but also firmness. When persons accuse themselves of the sin of hatred and enmity it may be well to discover whether they are troubled with recurring memories of past injuries that arouse also uncharitable sentiments. Such persons must be taught that these experiences are not sins as long as they oppose them and try to shake them off. The best remedy is to banish these memories as soon as they are consciously perceived and to present to the mind those reflections which in the past have proved apt to calm the emotions. Willful and obstinate persistence in the state of enmity renders worthy reception of the sacraments impossible.

Given the great variety in the different characters and other qualities of men, it is impossible that everyone should equally appeal to everyone else. In fact, often our spontaneous reaction to certain persons will be one of reserve and even aversion which would make close association with them a considerable burden. Such an attitude is not in conflict with the command of charity as long as we do not refuse those persons the ordinary attitude of respect and that practical kindness which the circumstances require.

We are not allowed to hate persons given over to vice and sin. We must love them as creatures of God who are called to be eternally united with Him; we must desire and pray for their conversion and salvation. But our attitude must never be such as to suggest approval of their sins and vices. This would be scandal. Besides our prayer for them, we may and at times must correct them. But this should be done only when there is a probability that some good will result from the fraternal correction, and only by those who on account of their special relationship or professional duty can influence such as do wrong. We must also help such persons when they are in need and when their proneness to vice is thereby not abetted. Special relations with them are not an obligation and must at times be avoided lest scandal be given. The priest will have to decide in each individual case what course of action is best. Certainly one of the greatest things priests can do is to bring a stray sheep back into the true fold of Christ. Real saints have in this respect accomplished deeds that are truly miraculous. It must not be forgotten that sometimes sinners show themselves vicious and most ungrateful toward the priest who takes special interest in their souls. Experience seems to indicate that neither pious zeal nor worldly proficiency is enough for such work. Both together with the addition of great personal sacrifices are the best means of reclaiming the lost sheep.

FRIENDSHIP

Friendship is a special kind of neighborly love. It has always been recognized and praised as a most valuable phase of personal relationship. It was reserved to the pansexualism of our day, a last consequence of materialistic medicine, to drag this beautiful blossom into the dust. In Ecclesiasticus we read: "A faithful friend is a strong defense: and he that hath found him, hath found a treasure. Nothing can be compared to a faithful friend, and no weight of gold and silver is able to countervail the good-ness of his fidelity. A faithful friend is the medicine of life and immortality: and they that fear the Lord, shall find him. He that feareth God, shall likewise have good friendship: because according to him shall his friend be" (6:14 ff.).

Friendship depends on a certain equality of station which renders possible the free exchange of mutual affection. The hero worship or any such one-sided admiration for older persons and attachment to them by young people—frequently observed as a passing phase of youthful development—cannot be called friendship. Friendship is a partial fruit of man's social nature which inclines him to unite with others. Such union based on the physical attraction of sexually different persons naturally leads to marriage. Pure friendship arises from the recognition of common spiritual interests the realization of which draws persons together with the bonds of emotional affection into the union of friendship. The spiritual interests must be, of course, morally good. As Cicero says: *Amicitia nisi inter bonos esse non potest.* The higher its motives, the higher the value of a friendship.

The esthetic attraction of bodily strength and beauty is not necessarily based on sexual difference; but by itself alone it is a source of danger and indicates the point where the warmth of friendship may burst into a flame of destructive fire. Con-scious eroticism is no friendship at all; as an unconscious ac-companiment it may be a source of enthusiastic strength but is likewise beset with dangers. Here we must say a word on the theory of friendship as unconscious sexuality. The fact that many emotions have an unconscious erotic tinge has caused some to explain the whole emotional life of man on the basis of sex, and friendship as hidden homosexuality. While the eight-eenth century and the beginning of the nineteenth were a time which reveled in exaggerated forms of over-enthusiastic friend-ship, the very idea of it became later so suspected that one could but blushingly profess friendship for any person and had to risk being looked upon as an abnormal case by so doing. It may be true that often relationships of an evidently sexual character were misnamed friendships. But false terminology does not justify slurs on the genuine value of true friendship. The whole question was much confused by the unwarranted alternative: friendship or normal sex-life. But this is an altogether false and misleading statement. Persons of a perfectly normal sex life have yet enough room and reasons for true and genuine friendship. The Old Testament shows us the beautiful example of friendship between David and Jonathan; but no one will be able to deny to David normal sexuality. Friendship is a historical fact which makes sense only apart from sex, besides or without sexual activity. As an explanation of the cases in which no eroticism and sex can be detected, the representatives of pansexualism invoke the theories of repression and sublimation. This method has proved helpful in a few instances but must be considered inadequate as a general principle. Repression may be accepted as an explanation only where its presence is directly perceived. But it is a criminal nuisance to suspect subconscious sexual motives where there is no indication of their presence. Of course, for those extreme Freudians who see in the dream of a train arriving in a railroad station a manifestation of sex, every human activity is hopelessly delivered up to sexual causes.

A much controverted question is whether there can exist pure and simple friendship between a man and a woman. The answer is that it will be a comparatively rare phenomenon, but it is not impossible. Of the highest moral value are those friendships which do not seek personal pleasure and satisfaction but spiritual advancement. The feeling of loneliness which often appears during the period of adolescence gives rise to a strong desire for sympathetic understanding and friendship. These friendships take, as a rule, a stormy course and do not last very long, like all other emotional phenomena of youth. The subconscious presence of erotic factors in such friendships is possible; therefore it will be well for the educator to watch them unobtrusively and, if necessary, separate the persons concerned. But it would be most improper and offensive to accomplish this separation by humiliating accusations of immorality and with indelicate publicity. Neither should any explanations of a psychological nature be offered.

Pessimists like Schopenhauer, Nietzsche, or Ibsen have denied the very possibility of friendship. The Scriptural word, "According to him shall his friend be" (Eccles. 6:17), explains their attitude most convincingly. As Christians we cannot deny the true value of friendship even if its occurrence were as rare as the discovery of a precious treasure. Of course, real friendship must not be expected wherever the word is used in the opening address on a letter or by a public speaker. True friendship meets its test according to the adage: a friend in need is a friend indeed. He who forsakes his friend in the hour of trouble or even seeks to build his own fortune on the ruins of his friend's misfortune never was a friend and desecrates the sacred word "friendship."

ORDER OF CHARITY

While the affective love will be more in evidence in our relation with those nearest to us and those most worthy of it because of their moral excellence, the effective love or helpful charity has its special place where our neighbor is in need. Hence the children, orphans, widows, the sick and weak, the prisoners, the mourning and dying, are in a special manner recommended to our charity. All these have a meaningful place in the order of God's providence, and we may be sure that their paths and ours will often meet in life, thus giving us an opportunity to become in some degree like unto God in love and mercy.

Charity through corporal and spiritual works of mercy is a glorious page in the history of the Church. Today it seems necessary to point out the sacrificial spirit and heroism needed in the care of the feeble-minded and insane from whose eyes never can come a look of grateful recognition. The renunciation of every material and spiritual recompense on earth for this work is the royal way of the cross in the imitation of Christ. However much we may be justified in rejoicing over exuberant health and strength, we should suffer an irreparable loss if we attempted to frustrate the heroism of those souls who are willing to serve mankind without any temporal gain and seemingly for no tangible purpose.

The right order of Christian charity demands that we subordinate the temporal to the eternal, the bodily to the spiritual, the lower to the higher. In practical life, the relief of bodily distress may at times have to be accomplished first. But corporal works of mercy done in the Christian spirit convey also a message of divine truth and grace both to the recipient and to the donor. It is the human person as a whole that is the child of God and the object of his love, and Christian charity seeks the good of the whole person according to the nature of the need that is to be supplied. Where this consideration is lost sight of, charity fails even though the amount and variety of help is multiplied. And, upon close inspection, it will be seen that assistance not based on real charity seeks but the control of the needy members of society for selfish ends. True charity is the fruit of Christianity and, where the Christian spirit is cut from underneath it, nothing remains but a degrading dole. The old pagan world did not know charity although it knew the dole which made the impoverished masses tools in the hands of the powerful. Philosophically, charity was despised as a moral weakness. But also in later times there were those who deprecated charity as a destructive passion. In our own day we must be careful lest powerful movements which are the secularist counterfeit of divine charity gain the upperhand and work for the destruction of the body and soul of our neighbor.

JUSTICE AND LAW

Love of neighbor is no doubt the most precious fruit growing out of mutual respect and esteem. But on account of its nature as an unbounded ideal, it is not sufficient to serve as the sole basis of human society; there is need of clearly defined laws that express the recognition of mutual equality. This is accomplished by the virtue of justice. Man as a social being feels an inward compulsion to live with others. Now in the most restricted society, the smallest family, the human reason cannot but perceive reciprocal interests and claims and the will must be ready to put the consequences into action: this is the origin of justice. Both justice and love are necessary elements of human society. But an essential difference is to be noted between them. Justice looks upon the neighbor as the other one different from the self; love sees in him a second self with whom one desires to be united. Love surrenders its own, justice gives to the other his due. St. Thomas' definition is: *Iustitia est virtus qua quis constanti voluntate ius suum unicuique tribuit.*

Now human reason tells us that, first of all, due to every person are those things which are required for the natural development and enjoyment of the common gifts of body and soul, as stated so well in the famous phrase of man's right to life, liberty, and the pursuit of happiness. In this respect, human society is a *societas aequalis.* But this supreme equality, which allows a man to find his own place in society according to his personal aptitudes and preferences within the frame of the impersonal circumstances of place and time and cultural condition, necessitates differences of social position and of individual rights (*societas inaequalis*). Liberty is thus seen to be no cure of social inequality. The conflicting claims resulting from this inequality and tending to become social inequalities, in the sense of injustices, must ever and again be harmonized so as to reestablish and maintain a satisfactory measure of equality.

Now the exact determination of the rights of any particular individual presents considerable difficulties and is exposed to the great danger of self-deception. Everywhere we find malcontents who complain that they are deprived of what is due them and that others hold unjust claims against them. Persons of normal intelligence who are stunted in the gifts of the body or for some reason have not attained to that place in society to which they aspire, are frequently tempted to assume an attitude of envy and resentment for the more fortunate ones and for society as a whole. In dealing with persons who surrender to this temptation, the priest will need much charity and patience to bring them to a point where their attitude fulfills, at least in a modest degree, the demands of the Christian religion.

Traditionally we speak of legal justice, which defines the obligatory contribution of the individual to the welfare of society according to the existing laws; of distributive justice, which regulates the actions of those in authority in assigning to the members of society the benefits and duties deriving from their social union; and of commutative justice, which requires that in the mutual claims of the individuals the strict measure of equal value be observed.

The obligation to practice justice is recognized by the natural reason and is frequently insisted upon in Sacred Scripture. But Christ's doctrine, especially in the Sermon on the Mount, goes beyond the natural demands of justice in several points, and it is not altogether easy to harmonize these demands of our Lord with the current conception of justice held also by the majority of Christians. Priests may frequently have to answer the objection that here there is a contradiction between Christian doctrine and practice. The Sermon on the Mount proposes many ideals the perfect attainment of which is not possible for all. On the way toward these ideals of Christian perfection, on a lower level but not opposed to them, are the demands of justice which represent the minimum requirements of Christian life. However, it would be unchristian to decline the ideal on principle or to refuse all striving for its attainment of set purpose. It certainly is not correct to say that the demands of Christian morality are satisfied by ideal moral impressions and sentiments while in practice we are free to follow the plain dictates of natural reason. For what good are lofty sentiments that do not make themselves felt in practical life; and of what value is a moral act that does not reflect an ideal motive? Here there is yet much room for further work in moral theology by way of penetrating analyses of the New Testament message. To be Christian, justice must not fall short of the demands of Christian self-love which forgoes every personal advantage to be had at the price of sin. But there is a higher degree of perfection where the standard of self-love passes into complete surrender to the spirit of Christ who gave His life for the salvation of all men.

Justice is a general moral demand; law is the precise definition of what is just in the concrete conditions of the universal and permanent order and in the actual variable circumstances. It is not the task of moral theology to expound the whole range of the law, but the law must never conflict with the demands of morality. Only such laws as are based on the moral order and agree with the ultimate end of man can claim obedience in conscience. The state is not the ultimate source of law, but must determine the concrete form of the particular legal ordinances in any given society according to the principles of morality. In this sense, law is the complex of norms and rules for the ordered life of society, which are considered by any particular cultural group as obligatory, regardless of whether they are written or handed on by oral tradition. The written codification of laws is so common among civilized states that it is almost felt to be of the essence of the law. But the written law, embodying always the experience of the past, loses, by this very fact, some of its applicability to the present and the future and may in time become an obstacle to the healthy functioning of human society. Hence the written law requires continual revision. Certain phases of the law cannot be written down at all, but must remain in the fluid state of judicial discretion such as we find in the institution of the court of equity, juvenile court, suspended sentence, probation, and the like.

The rightful claim of a person to an object is traditionally divided into *ius in re* and *ius ad rem;* the former denotes the actually existing dominion over an object; the latter is the rightful title to establish such a dominion over an object. The *ius in re* puts on all others the negative obligation of abstaining from encroachments, the *ius ad rem* obliges a limited number of persons to positive actions. The claim to one and the same object may involve both the *ius in re* and the *ius ad rem*. The owner of a coin may dispose of it according to his good pleasure. His *ius in re* obliges all others to refrain from interference as, for instance, by forcing a certain use of it or taking it away either secretly or violently. His *ius ad rem* entitles him to acquire objects and services offered for sale or hire in a commercial way. But objects not so exhibited need not be surrendered by their owners upon the presentation of the coin.

The theoretical aspects of the problem of law and right have of late again become of vital interest. Hence a brief statement of the salient points may be in place. By the natural law we mean the sum of those natural insights concerning right and wrong in social living, which reason perceives as necessary and unalterable truths. The natural law is, then, a part of the general moral law, i.e., that part which concerns the necessary conditions of human society. It is a part of the divinely ordained world order which ultimately reflects God's eternal wisdom and is thus intrinsically true and unchangeable. Many authors mean by natural law, not this social segment, but the whole natural moral order. The question whether or not St. Paul and the Fathers of the Church who spoke of the natural moral law were influenced in their doctrines and terminology by pagan philosophers, is an idle controversy. The idea of the origin of the natural moral order by divine ordination, often pantheistically conceived, was current in the world in which Christianity first entered. Truth remains truth, no matter by whom it is uttered, and has its source in God.

The natural law contains, of course, only the highest principles of moral right, and to these belongs the existence of legitimate authority. As St. Paul says: "There is no power but from God, and those that are, are ordained of God" (Rom. 13:1). Thus the positive human law, if issued by the legitimate authority and in agreement with the natural law and moral order, is mediately derived from divine authority. The human law is not in opposition to the natural law but is its amplification and detailed application. It may restate parts of the natural law, clarify its meaning, and regulate affairs cropping out of the most diverse concurrence of circumstances the connection of which with the natural law may perhaps be seen only by a long chain of inferential conclusions. However, the theory that the state is the source of all right is a most perverse error. In view of the divine ordination of human authority, many laws and decisions of the state in matters of seeming moral indifference receive a moral connotation.

Not all things belonging to the moral order can be the subject of human legislation. The moral order is not fully vindicated in this life. Not all its violations are atoned for on earth, but in the future life where the intrinsic futility of revolt against the author of the moral order will become manifest. The human legislator can enact only laws of such a sort that their execution can be supervised and enforced, and their violation can be detected and punished. It is not necessary that a state should be able to enforce its laws in every particular case and under all circumstances, but the possibility of doing so must lie within the sphere of the realities of the earthly society. It is not for the state to invoke the rewards and punishments of the world beyond. Hence the scope of earthly legislation is much smaller than the commands of the moral law.

Every law creates rights and obligations, but their becoming actual may frequently be limited or entirely nullified by willful violence or other obstructing circumstances. The reciprocity of right and obligation results in what is known as juridical order, which contains three elements: the possessor of a right (*subiectum iuris*), the contents of the right (*obiectum iuris*), and the title of the right (*titulus iuris*) or its rational basis. Man must make a morally good use of his rights because they are part of the general moral order without which there would exist no rights at all, except the right of brute force.

Only a personal being endowed with reason and free will can be the subject of rights, because only a person is able to recognize and claim a right. The ability to do this may be undeveloped, as in a child, or it may be disturbed, as with the insane. In the case of such inability a guardian is appointed to vindicate the rights instead of the incapable subject and for his benefit. Unborn children are not regarded as owners of rights; hence the difference between the crime of child murder and the sin against nascent life. A being which is naturally devoid of reason and free will cannot be the subject of rights. Thus animals have no rights in the strict sense of the word. This does not mean that the animal world is left without protection of the moral law, but that the relations between man and animal are to be seen and ordered from a moral angle different from that of right.[2]

Several persons who combine for the attainment of certain common purposes may became bearers of rights not as individuals but as a society known as a legal person. Since the protection of the rights of individuals and legal persons is of vital importance for the social peace and order, the state has the right to lay down certain conditions for the formation of legal persons. Only in this way is it possible to deal with societies as entities and with the assurance that agreements will be honored and enforced.

The contents of human rights concern first of all a person's life and health as the basis for the possession and enjoyment of any other goods. The basis of the bodily goods is the right to one's body; the basis of the spiritual goods is the right to the free use of one's spiritual faculties. Man's supernatural end gives him the right to be educated in the truths of religion and moral discipline. Existence and activity worthy of the human person demand also the right to recognition and to one's good name, as well as the right to private social association, first of all by entering upon marriage and raising a family, but also for recreational and protective purposes. The right to property is one of the most important and obvious requisites because man expresses his nature by work on and through the surrounding world of objects.

These rights belong not only to the adult person but also to

[2] This subject is discussed in Ruland, *Foundations of Morality*, pp. 360–78. Cf. also Roche, *These Animals of Ours*.

the child, whose development to maturity and gradually increasing claim to the actual exercise of its rights must not be impeded. Although the relationship between parent and child is unique in society, we cannot correctly say that it does not involve the question of right but of mere parental love and helpfulness. The child has undoubtedly a right to life and to the pursuit of its eternal salvation and likewise to such treatment and furtherance as the proper induction into human society requires. This implies, e.g., a certain amount of theoretical and practical education. A clear distinction between the parental duties of love and strict justice is impossible; neither is this possible in other human relationships where the issues of justice and charity are clearer.

The rights of the individual are not unlimited; they are bounded in many ways by the same or other rights of his fellow men. So true is this that right has been defined by someone as that condition in which the arbitrariness of one person can co-exist with the arbitrariness of another. This definition is not quite correct, for not all rights of our fellow men restrict our own. Despite the supremacy of the individual person, there have been recognized, at all times, certain limitations of the individual rights for the sake of the common good. The claims of the community have not been restricted to monetary contributions and to limitations in the use of property, but have touched such vital rights as the freedom to marry and have exacted the supreme sacrifice of the individual's life in the service of the community. But such limitations may be invoked only in cases of extreme necessity.

II

OUR NEIGHBOR'S SPIRITUAL GOOD

CARE FOR OUR NEIGHBOR'S SALVATION

ETERNAL salvation being the supreme end of man, there exists no higher duty of neighborly love than to help one another in the attainment of this end. To be sure, everyone must bear the main responsibility for his own salvation. Nobody can be saved against his will, but at the same time everybody needs some outside assistance in this sublime task. Hence men have mutual duties in regard to their spiritual good. The first duty is that of prayer for one another.

Another important obligation is that of *good example*. Instruction without deeds is sterile. Actions speak louder than words, as the old proverb has it. Example works not like a sudden gust of the wind that carries things along, but like the steady silent forces of nature. We cannot observe the growth of plants second by second; yet nothing is more plainly evident than the irresistible power at work in the earth's vegetation. Similar is the effect of example on our fellow men for good and for evil, silent but steady, building up or tearing down. Hence we are obliged to give good example for the spreading of the kingdom of God on earth.

"Let your light shine before men, that they may see your good works, and glorify your Father who is in heaven" (Matt. 5:16). Christ impressed on the apostles the great importance of good example, not only by explicitly teaching its necessity but also by the actual deed of washing their feet: "I have given you an example that as I have done to you, so you do also" (John 13:15). Likewise chapters 3 and 5 of the First Epistle of St. Peter contain much material on the question of good example,

21

where it is also pointed out that Christian women by their good example draw their pagan husbands to Christ.

The inner attitude with which a Christian, in all humility and sincerity, must give an example of striving after perfection, is stated in St. Paul's words: "Not as though I had already attained or were already perfect; but I follow after, if I may by any means apprehend, wherein I am also apprehended by Jesus Christ. Brethren, I do not count myself to have apprehended. But one thing I do: forgetting the things that are behind, and stretching forth myself to those that are before, I press toward the mark, to the prize of the supernal vocation of God in Christ Jesus" (Phil. 3:12 ff.).

The power of good example will be the greater, the less obtrusive its manner and the less calculated its intention. There may be occasions calling for an action purposely designed as a good example, e.g., the publicized subscription of a large sum for a good cause by an influential person by whose example others able to do likewise but less generous feel obligated to follow suit. But, as a rule, it would be wrong for a person in his actions to consider foremost the motive of good example. This would eventually lead to sheer pharisaism and comedy, and the effect would be the very opposite of that of the good example. Especially before young poeple such conduct would be most unfortunate because they would soon sense the artificiality and contrast it unfavorably with the lapses indicative of the reality behind the mask. Positions requiring, in certain essential matters, the continual giving of good example as the natural expression of the inner disposition, as, e.g., in the case of an educator, should not be accepted by persons who would find the obligation an unbearable burden. Occasional lapses in unessential matters by persons who from sincere inner conviction strive after perfection, do not detract from their good influence.

Good example need not be given in view of or for the benefit of any particular person or group of persons; its very existence exercises a certain influence. Every sacrifice or act of renunciation and mortification is a silent reminder to the intemperate and the libertine that temperance and continence are possible and actually practiced. In this lies the value of the temperance movement against the excessive use of alcoholic beverages. The great power of good example is seen also in the restlessness and opposition it arouses in those given to evil and vice. Nobody that craves the pleasures of the world is deprived of them by the fact that certain persons lead a life of retirement in chastity and continence. One should think that the lives of persons passed in the austerity of Christian discipline would be simply ignored by those not interested in such things. But this is not the case. The repeated attacks on such institutions as monasticism and celibacy show that the conscience of the world feels uneasy in the face of this reminder of man's supernatural vocation. The Church has officially recognized the power of good example by holding up to the world in the saints personalities who in the most diverse conditions of life have attained to perfection and received from God the eternal crown of victory.

Fraternal correction is another obligation of brotherly love enjoined by Sacred Scripture. In the striving after perfection, the Christian community should be so united as to exclude all disturbance of its peace by the sins and faults of any of its members. But when such have occurred, the erring member should be amended by admonition and consolation (1 Thess. 5:14) and, if this effort fails, association with the evildoer should be avoided (2 Thess. 3:6). In the correction of one's neighbor the following order should be observed. First, the sinner should be admonished under four eyes. If this proves futile, one or two trusted friends should make their influence felt. If even this effort should come to naught, the matter should be brought before the public tribunal of the Church in order that the sinner may realize the gravity of his situation, for after a third refusal to amend he is to be cut off from the community of the faithful. He is to be regarded as a pagan and publican (Matt. 18:15 ff.). St. Paul gives a similar instruction (2 Thess. 3:14 f.): "If any man obey

not our word by this epistle, note that man, and do not keep
company with him, that he may be ashamed. Yet do not esteem
him as an enemy, but admonish him as a brother."

Fraternal correction is a Christian duty because Christians
are united by the bond of spiritual solidarity and are obliged to
preserve the neighbor from grave peril of the soul as much as
from serious harm of the body. "We beseech you, brethren, rebuke the unquiet, . . . support the weak, be patient toward
all men" (1 Thess. 5:14). But the fraternal correction must
proceed from a spirit of true love and the humble realization of
one's own weakness. "Brethren, if a man be overtaken by any
fault, you, who are spiritual, instruct such a one in the spirit
of meekness, considering thyself, lest thou also be tempted. Bear
ye one another's burdens; and so you shall fulfill the law of
Christ" (Gal. 6:1 f.).

For fraternal correction as an act of charity, moral theology
has set forth three guiding principles. The first condition is
res gravis, i.e., a real and immediate grave danger to the spiritual
welfare of the neighbor, as it would be intolerable to have one's
life pried into and criticized for unimportant matters. Secondly,
the importance and urgency of the matter must be certainly
known, not merely by rumor, gossip, or even calumny: *notitia
certa*. Thirdly, there must be sufficient probability of success:
spes eventus. This last condition will probably not often be
realized among the laity, particularly in the cities, unless they
are attached to one another by some special social bonds. In our
Western world, in continental Europe perhaps more than any-
where else, the religious and moral conduct of the individual is
considered so much a private affair that warnings by any private
person are felt as an unwarranted interference and they are
rejected and resented. The *spes eventus* is thus practically nil.
We may definitely say that the duty of fraternal correction
hardly ever exists between individuals who by merely external
contingencies happen to be acquainted with each other. Only a
most tactful and self-disciplined person will be able to perceive
the fitness of a corrective remark under such circumstances.

Very different is the case of persons who by their position as superiors, teachers, or pastors of souls are obliged to care for the spiritual welfare of their neighbors. They will have to warn, admonish, advise, and correct their charges, privately or publicly as prudence and charity indicate. The prudent and spiritually alive superior will appropriately suggest considerations and ways of conduct which are apt to prevent the development of critical situations that otherwise might arise. He will correct in the best suitable manner faults and abuses which actually exist. In speaking against such from the pulpit, as the priest may have occasion to do, it would be fruitless to harp on the wickedness of the world in general, but it would be a very unfortunate blunder to be so specific as to expose individuals. Such a procedure would be certain to preclude the amendment of the sinner. Equally odious would be comparisons with other parishes. Lastly, the rebuke must not be made in terms which condemn sins and sinners beyond redemption, but possible and edifying ways of amendment must be pointed out.

Fraternal correction among the members of the clergy requires special consideration. The sudden change by which the newly ordained priests are transferred from a life of closely supervised discipline to the freedom and honored position of actual sacerdotal work, is a severe test of spiritual maturity and character. The young priest is generally assigned to the post of assistant to an older priest who is to guide him not only in his work but also in the adjustment of his character. In his youthful enthusiasm and zeal the young priest may easily regard the more moderate ways of his superior as negligence. The situation will be ideal if the zeal of the young and the experience of the older priest, made wise by the alternation of success and failure, meet in common understanding. A correction, when this seems necessary, need not always be given in the form of an open rebuke; there are milder forms of correction and guidance. It would be very impolite, uncharitable, and sinful for an older priest to show his displeasure with his assistant by unfriendliness and an attitude of coolness.

In some cases, fortunately rare, the young priest may have as his superior a man who, at least in some respects, falls short of what is to be expected of a priest. In less important matters silent toleration and forbearance will be best. Offensive criticism of the older priest's rubrical peculiarities would be in bad taste. In more important matters, correction of the older priest by the younger has little chance of success and need not be considered obligatory. If the question is not so important and urgent as to warrant a report to the higher superior, the young priest should seek confidential advice from other experienced and serious-minded priests. Such advice cannot be given on the basis of mysteriously veiled hypotheses but only upon the concrete account of the actual case. Priests who, soon after their ordination, obtain positions in which they are independent easily run the risk of contracting peculiar and harmful habits which it would be an act of charity to correct at an early stage. In general, all priests should be painstaking in the examination of their manners, policies, ambitions, and recreations, and welcome truly fraternal corrections lest their conduct be a scandal and stumbling block instead of a divinely inspired help to souls on their way to heaven.

Another form of dealing with a delinquent fellow man is denunciation to the competent authorities for legal action. Evidently recourse to this form of correction should be employed only when all other means have been tried and have failed to prevent a person from doing serious harm to another. The duty of denunciation by persons not officially engaged in watching the public order, exists only when their action is needed to save important moral goods for another person or to ward off serious damage from him. E.g., he who learns of an impending attack on the life or security of someone is obliged to forestall it by timely denunciation. Also serious moral abuses must be so stopped or prevented. The mistreatment of children is often brought to the attention of the court by outsiders who happen to know of it. Whoever takes the step of public denunciation must first conscientiously ascertain the truth of the matter. He

must realize the consequences of this action for the other person
and for himself.

An utterly detestable phenomenon of social life is the *anonymous letter*. Everyone is agreed that it is a most cowardly and
despicable deed to attack the good name of another person out
of the darkness of anonymity. But the deplorable fact is that
such attacks frequently happen. A considerable part of the
blame must be lodged with those who pay attention to such communications and act on them. If for once there were observed the
consistent and general practice of completely ignoring anonymous information both in public and in private life, this social
evil would soon come to an end.

The *publication in the press* of real or supposed faults of individuals is another modern means of attack and defense. This
may be done anonymously if the responsible editor is willing to
assume the consequences. Mere personal grievances should not
be aired in this way unless the writer signs his name, because
there exists the great danger that innocent persons may be suspected of writing the unsigned letter, thus causing endless quarrels and enmity. But, as a rule, personal matters should not
come before the public, which, apart from scandal mongers and
gossips, has no real interest in them. Decent-minded persons always regret such unpleasant spectacles forced on them by spiteful and morbid people. Public abuses and evil conditions which
could easily be removed but are neglected may, through press
publicity, be brought to the attention of the citizens, who may
then demand that appropriate action be taken.

TOLERANCE

Although this section chiefly concerns religious tolerance, it
will be helpful to introduce the subject with some general remarks of a psychological and historical nature. Tolerance means
admission on sufferance, and refers mostly to views, beliefs, and
practices in the field of religion, philosophy, and politics. Tolerance implies a certain disapproval. In the words of St. Augus-

tine: *Tolerantia non est nisi in malis*. It is unlikely that all men should ever agree in all things, and so a certain amount of tolerance was always necessary. But in certain essential matters social harmony demanded the sacrifice of personal likes and preferences. The more primitive and natural a people was, the more forcibly it insisted on the unity of belief and practice in religion and politics, these being always closely united. Tolerance is not only the slowly and painfully gained result of civilization; it is to a certain extent a phenomenon of decadence. All vital forces in politics, art, and religion are intolerant. The periods of history which felt strong in the development of their own artistic expression and their style, changed and destroyed without much regard the products of the preceding centuries. It was at a time which lacked an original style of its own that men began to preserve and conserve.

In restricting our discussion to religion it is well to consider briefly the impact of religion on public and private life. Religion, first of all, teaches doctrines that transcend the sphere of natural knowledge and thus demand faith. The stronger the authority for the truth of one's religious convictions is, the less can one recognize opposite religious views as of equal value. Every religion must be intolerant in matters of dogma. Now, the more a person is convinced of the truth of his religion and recognizes its supreme importance over all other social interests and motives, the more emphatically he will feel the need of the same belief as the common ground of a healthy social community; i.e., he will tend to be intolerant also in civic matters.

In former times the state, in all its external functions, was intimately bound up with certain religious beliefs and practices. Many of the pagan gods had a national character, and the true God of Christianity likewise was formerly so consciously and deliberately recalled and invoked in every act of the state that the state itself had a religious character. We know that at one time dogmatic controversies, e.g., the procession of the Holy Ghost from the Father and the Son, so stirred all classes of

Christian society that the vendors and buyers on the market place of Constantinople were divided along religious lines.

All religion is connected with morality. Even though some pagan religions had no moral codes—among the ancient Greeks the ethical questions belonged to the field of philosophy—every belief in gods involves the belief in moral retribution and thus requires morality of action. In the Old and New Testaments the connection between religion and morality is explicit and far-reaching. Despite the many dogmatic differences among the Christian sects, the moral demands were, with most of them, practically the same, at least until recently, so that Christian ethics served as a basis for the development of civic and political tolerance.

In the third form of religious expression (i.e., public worship), society and the state desire the most agreement and unity. The external forms of solemn public acts effect a deep impression of significant experience. In former times a public act without a religious ceremony was inconceivable, and therefore public worship became a source of civic and political intolerance. The ancient Romans were dogmatically very tolerant and admitted the gods of defeated nations into the pantheon as long as the Roman gods retained the first places. So room would have been made for Christ, but after Jupiter Capitolinus. In public worship, however, the Romans insisted on the observance of their traditional rites. It is here that the Christians faced difficulties which led to their persecution.

After the disappearance of paganism the Roman state and its medieval successor were in the same measure insistent on orthodoxy in Christian belief and ceremonial as the pagan state had insisted before in the matter of public worship. The juridical state and Church grew side by side, the state serving the Church as its secular arm. Opposition to Islam as their common enemy was for centuries the bond uniting the different races and nations of the Christian Middle Ages. Whoever, therefore, placed himself in opposition to the doctrine of the Church knew that by this act he jeopardized also his status as a citizen. The bloody wars in connection with the Protestant Revolt made no contribution toward religious toleration. Not only the adherents to the old and new religion were opposed to each other, but also the members of the various sects were intolerant of one another. The intolerance of the times is well illustrated by the principle *cuius regio eius religio.*

It is indeed true that exceptions were made in the case of outstanding men whose learning and other accomplishments were so highly esteemed that their religious views were overlooked. Thus several Popes were patrons of Leonardo da Vinci, who most likely did not excel in the depth of his faith, and many a scholar enjoyed the patronage of princes despite their differences of religion. In all this the course of history took an important turn in the seventeenth century. Higher education and scholarship ceased to be the special property of churchmen. Scholarship became secular in the field of jurisprudence, philosophy, medicine, and the natural sciences. The question of difference of religion began to lose its importance in social life. Civic toleration led to discussions of political tolerance. The first to establish complete tolerance was Joseph II of Austria in 1781. Next came the United States in 1787. Gradually tolerance was made a general principle in all nations although painful restrictions and disabilities have remained here and there, and new ones are likewise cropping up. Neither does the legal recognition of the equality of all religions in the state remove inveterate prejudices, which at times give rise to serious inequalities and intolerance.

As a result of this brief historical review we come to the conclusion that dogmatic tolerance is impossible for a religion which is convinced of the truth of its doctrines. This does not mean that attacks must be made on any other religious bodies. The forms, requirements, and aims of our civilization are so multifarious and intricate that civic toleration, i.e., the peaceful and sincerely sympathetic cooperation with members of other faiths in the service of one's people and nation, is easily possible, and has actually become a matter of course. Though we can understand the violent attitude of more robust and naïve times, we do not want it to return. Religion has become for us not less valuable than it was for those who were ready to crush its opponents and to suffer a similar fate at the latter's hands. Religion has been raised to a higher sphere, where it is not touched by the trifles of everyday life. We recall that the religious division is several hundred years old and that the individual person's religious affiliation is *de facto* largely a matter of being born into this or that denomination. Instead of stirring up past quarrels and bitterness, we prefer to think of the religious elements our separated brethren have in common with us. Of course, religious and moral errors which are being propagated in direct violation of the law of God and in opposition to His revelation must be refuted, and resisted where they are urged as matters of legislation. But this can be done on the basis of natural reason and experience. The actual work of regaining those outside the Church can be and is being done in a way that should not give offense to anyone. After all, religion is a matter of personal conviction which non-Catholics can be helped to acquire only by sympathetic instruction which they desire or willingly accept. Taunts and reproaches serve no good purpose. So there is no danger of social disturbance to be feared from the work of leading the erring back to the truth and grace of God. The feasibility of such work has been and is being demonstrated splendidly in the United States by such undertakings as missions and many other activities, lay and clerical, for non-Catholics in the cities and rural districts. The methods of the work are so well set forth in the clerical magazines that there is no need to describe them here.

Interesting but equally thorny is the problem of the union of Catholics by themselves in professional and civic organizations. Such organizations have existed and do exist in certain countries, although they vary considerably in their character and aims. The purpose of their formation, the defense of their economic and social rights, is not primarily religious but is connected with moral and religious issues like any other problem of life. The great question is whether or not this fact makes organizations along strictly religious lines necessary. In Germany the Catholics were unfortunately, by the unhappy circumstance of the Kulturkampf, forced to defend their rights in many respects by various civic-religious organizations. However, the prudence of such organizations in as many fields as were actually covered by them may be doubted. Perhaps it would have been better to make the Catholic influence strongly felt in the large and purely secular organizations. In America, where all these problems have become pressing at a much later date than in Europe, the Catholics have the advantage of being detached spectators of these things in other lands and of learning from their experiences. The best solution lies perhaps in the energetic and vital development of the various already existing organizations of Catholics, the strictly religious as well as the fraternal, and the wholehearted and enlightened cooperation of Catholics in all legitimate neutral organizations. If these are saturated with genuine Catholic thought and spirit, by the word and example and action of their members they will bear fruit for the benefit of society as a whole.

THE JEWISH QUESTION

One of the most difficult problems of practical tolerance is the Jewish question. For an objective view of the matter we must trace its historical development dispassionately and without prejudice. For the Christian it is, above all, imperative to distinguish between the chosen people before the advent of Christ, and their rejection after their refusal to accept the Messias. God's election of the Jewish race to preserve, despite many transgressions and aberrations, the belief in the one true God and the basic law of morality in the decalogue, and to bring forth the Redeemer of all men, is a mystery of the divine economy of salvation. Certainly neither political power nor cultural achievement nor any other outstanding qualities were the determining reasons, for God has chosen the weak to put to shame the strong (1 Cor. 1:27). The gospel was not to appear in the garb of wordly wisdom and philosophy. Neither were the Jews well liked by the other races who came in contact with them even in ancient times, as appears from occasional remarks of contemporary writers. E.g., the Roman Emperor Hadrian, who was well acquainted with the races in his Empire, preferred the rude Sarmatae to the prosperous Jews of Alexandria.

Historically the Jews have always been in the position of a race defending its existence in the face of almost overwhelming odds. They have succeeded by a remarkable tenacity which has not only its bad side but also its good side. Keen intelligence which may also be misused for destructive criticism, sobriety and industry, adaptability to varying conditions of life, devotion to the family and respect for parents, and charity toward the poor by which also many Christians have benefited: all these are undeniable traits of the Jewish race. As, according to experience, nowhere are the good qualities heaped up on the one side and the evil ones all on the other, it is senseless to deny the Semitic race their share of the former. This statement, however, does not forbid our recognizing in the Semitic race as a whole a temper which differs from that of the Aryan peoples. Anybody's attempt to reconcile his anti-Semitic prejudices with his admiration for the superhuman greatness of Christ or a recognition of Him as the divine Redeemer, by maintaining that Christ was not a Jew, is a puerile aberration of fanatical and emotional scholarship. The Catholic dogma, comprehending all the facts of history and revelation, shows in a superb manner, as only truth can do, that Christ belongs to all men even racially. Christ had a human mother of the house of David, but no human father, so that our Lord is not biologically the descendant of one particular race in the same sense as all other men are of theirs. By His supernatural origin and incarnation Christ belongs to no race at all, and it is only those that deny Christ's divinity who find any difficulty on this point. The divine blessing promised to the forefathers of the Jews has never deserted them; but by their rejection of Christ they have also drawn upon themselves the divine curse of being scattered throughout the world, where they are being felt and treated as an alien race.

Anti-Semitism as a formal doctrine is not found in the early Christian writings, but the practical attitude of the Christian world was not friendly. The unconverted Jew was not regarded as the venerable racial brother of Jesus and Mary, but as the descendant of those who crucified Christ and cried: "His blood be upon us, and upon our children" (Matt. 27:25). Hence it is not true to history that Christianity was always the friend and protector of the Jews, as some of late seem to claim and thus would make anti-Semitism a thing of recent origin. St. Ambrose, in one of his homilies, says: *Bonus ordo, ut vocaturus Gentes, et Judaeos iussurus interfici, qui noluerunt regnare supra se Christum* (Roman Breviary for August 25). The Jews were, indeed, guaranteed their right to life, property, and the exercise of their religion, but the enormous difference between the penances laid down in the medieval penitential books for the killing of a Christian and for the killing of a Jew points to a strange attitude of mind. At the time when the Christian world banded together to wrest the Holy Land from the hands of the infidels, there was aroused also a hatred against the Jews as the descendants of those who had demanded Christ's crucifixion. Upon payment of a special tax the emperors granted the Jews particular protection as to "servants of the imperial chamber," but under the difficult conditions of communication this protection from arbitrary treatment by local authorities may not have been very effective.

The opening of the thirteenth century marked the beginning of hard times for the Jews. A series of laws, for which the Church was also partly responsible, imposed upon them oppressive restrictions. Where their presence was permitted they had to live in separate quarters (ghetto) and were not allowed to use the baths of the Christians. A special dress, consisting of a pointed hood and a yellow ring in the garment, identified them even at a distance. Marriage and other social relations with the Christians were forbidden; they could hold no public office; they could not inherit from Christians or act as witnesses in court against Christians; Jewish physicians were forbidden to treat Christian patients; and other such restrictions were placed on them. On the last days of Holy Week they were forbidden to leave their houses or were even exposed to public mistreatment. From Nicholas III on they were obliged to listen to Christian sermons during Holy Week. The actual enforcement of these regulations ceased after a considerable lapse of time through contrary customs; they lasted in part till the beginning of the nineteenth century. In Spain it came to an especially violent clash between the Christians and the Jews and Arabs. There for the first time racially mixed marriages were stigmatized as a contamination of the blood. Even the lower clerics and other servants of the Church had to prove the absence of Jewish blood through four generations of their ancestry. The biographer of St. John of God, e.g., regrets that the name of the saint's mother is not known, but he is satisfied that *utriusque sanguis a Judaeorum commixtionis ignominia purissimus fuit.*

Since the Jews were barred from farming and the crafts, they were forced into retail trade as well as the pawn and loan business where their special talents brought them great success. The commercial success of the Jews was also furthered by the law of the Church forbidding Christians to take interest on loans. This prohibition had indeed noble motives. Those who sought to obtain loans were regarded as persons in distress, which was not to be made the occasion of gain for the creditor. The consideration that the lender of money limits his own economic opportunities by allowing someone else to work with his property, that the interest payment is a forcible reminder of returning the principal to the creditor, and that loans are made not only as a help in need but also for the purpose of business expansion: these reflections only gradually emerged from the simple economic life of the Middle Ages. The non-baptized Jew, not being subject to the law of the Church, was allowed to take interest, while the Christian, fearing loss from loans to others, was not inclined to make loans. Thus the Jews became the lenders of money for the Christians and thereby often acquired considerable power. But here again lay a danger for the Jews. When mighty princes happened to be too deeply in debt, they frequently opened the safety valve of persecution of the Jews. By attributing to them such crimes as the desecration of sacred hosts or the poisoning of wells, the populace was often aroused to acts of violence against the Jews, and such acts were tolerated by the authorities. When in the middle of the fourteenth century the Black Death was raging, there resulted in many places persecutions of the Jews, who were held responsible for the disaster, partly by conscious and partly by unconscious prejudice. Neither did the Protestant Revolt bring an improvement of the condition of the Jews.

The Jewish race, being intellectually a highly talented people who considered themselves the bearers of a sacred and age-old tradition about the very destinies of the world, and proud of their past, could not but develop, under such repressive conditions and amid such humiliations, the attitude of resentment and antipathy. While externally forced into abject submission, they were inwardly filled with hatred and envy of all others and critically observant of all their weaknesses. In their language united with the peoples with whom they lived, they were nevertheless international by the ties that bound them to their brethren in other countries and they were interested in the welfare of their hosts only so far as thereby their own advantage was served. In mystic and religious longing they awaited, as orthodox Jews, the day of their liberation. Such was the frame of mind of the Jews when the period of the Enlightenment brought them freedom in a way they themselves had not expected. It is true that the Protestant movement of Pietism had a certain influence on the change of attitude toward the Jews, but this is in no way comparable to the power of the ideas of the Enlightenment. Free from all religious and ecclesiastical ties, and consciously disregarding all racial distinctions, the Enlightenment opened the way for the concept of the equality and fraternity of all mankind, as it had been proclaimed by the men of the revolutionary age and set forth in an undogmatic religion so graphically expressed in Lessing's famous story of the three rings. The Enlightenment brought recognition of the equality of the Jews, and the influence of the Revolution upon all political constitutions in Europe liberated them from their legal and political disabilities. The traditional sentiments toward the Jews did not disappear at once with the advent of the new laws; consequently the Jews still had difficulty in being admitted to certain positions of public administration or in the army. Those who joined any one of the Christian denominations did not suffer from this handicap; many were knighted after a change of their names. From among the learned professions the Jews preferred the work of the physician, lawyer, and writer. It is an undeniable fact that the Jews have to their credit great accomplishments in many fields of science and cultural endeavor.

At the time of the Enlightenment appeared also a new type of Jews, the reformed Jews, who turned away from observance of their religion and, as freethinkers and atheists, became the champions of all leftist and radical ideas. They have been not only enemies of monarchy and Christianity but in general have acted as a solvent of all national life. Thus they have sown the wind which was sure to be reaped as a storm. We may well say that the liberation of the Jews in the eighteenth and nineteenth centuries was too sudden and unprepared for a race that had been held in subjection for so long a time. The number of those who took up learned studies and professions was insignificant in comparison with those who followed the old accustomed course of business; but now they did this on the largest scale and with unhindered rapidity. The Napoleonic wars and the unhappy secularization offered immense opportunities for enrichment and capitalist expansion into every branch of the economic and cultural life of the nations, which was out of all proportion to their numerical strength. Farseeing and well-intentioned Jews saw and dreaded the dangers inherent in this development. Membership in the masonic lodges was another welcome means of influence on the economic and political life of the nations. The Jews were not only freely admitted to membership in masonry, but soon occupied important positions in it. Their greater wealth gave the Jews opportunities for higher education and correspondingly larger representation in the learned professions where, in executive positions, they favored members of their own race. Thus the Jews represent the paradox of a small racial minority—there are about twelve million Jews in the world [1]—that wields an extremely large power in the economic, social, and cultural life of the nations. It appears likewise that the influential Jews, with their wealth, effectively promoted movements which as a whole are destructive of religion, morals, and national welfare.

The presence of a Jewish question is felt not only by non-Jews but also by those Jews who are able to view life in the light of history and of human nature. Much has been written in the spirit of truth and conciliation, and it is not difficult to obtain that literature. But the realities, including the individual and group inclinations and ambitions as well as the political and international complications, seem more difficult to master than it is for sensible and well-intentioned people to conceive of a just and equitable solution. According to the clear word of the gospel, justice and charity are not to be kept within the narrow limits of nationality but must extend to all mankind. Furthermore, the good results of the Enlightenment and other similar movements—everywhere there is a grain of good as of truth—must not be undone. As Christians we must consider the Jews our brethren who, now by individual conversion, and in God's own time as a whole, will be engrafted on the good olive tree of God from which they have broken away by their unbelief (Rom. 11:33).

[1] The American Jewish Committee reckons this total at about sixteen million. [Tr.]

III

Sins Against Our Neighbor's Spiritual Good

CHARITY forbids any encroachment upon the spiritual life of our neighbor whereby he may be led into sin or given an occasion to endanger or lose his eternal salvation. The ways by which this happens may be various. The strongest interference is direct coercion. Since the essence of sin lies in a turning of the will from God, i.e., an act of the soul, physical coercion to commit sin is impossible. Anyone who is physically compelled to do an act which is in itself sinful but who withholds his consent, does not sin. But moral coercion is possible and occurs in many different ways. Moral coercion consists in a person's use of his dominance over another person with a view to forcing the latter's attitude of the will into a direction which it would not have taken otherwise. Often the person so influenced may not even be aware, or only slightly aware, of this encroachment from without. One of the most usual forms of coercion is the arousing of the affections of love and fear, especially the latter. Such fear may appear under various guises. Every relation of superior to subject and of social dependency can be abused for purposes of moral pressure; e.g., the relation of parents to their children, of a husband to his wife and sometimes the reverse, of employer to employee, business reasons, hopes of reward and promotion, and particularly the fear of slights, jibes, and reprimands. Perhaps the most dangerous form of moral coercion is flattery. The great peril of flattery lies in the insidious nature of its attack. The one assailed by it is often not aware of it and becomes its victim in matters in which he would resist any recognized form of attempted coercion. Practically all men are likely to swallow incredibly large doses of this poison, especially

those who consider themselves above all deception. Also peti-
tions and pleas for things which are wrong may be an undue
pressure on persons whose love and readiness to comply is
known; not because they feel inclined to do what is wrong but
because it is hard for them to resist the one who asks, e.g., the
husband or wife, a friend, a companion. Hence it is sinful to
ask of one's neighbor what he can do only by committing sin.
It is permissible, however, to request for serious reasons a thing
which is in itself good, but which we suspect will be rendered
by the person approached in a manner that is morally not quite
correct.

SCANDAL

We have spoken of the great power of example as a motive
of action. Thus bad example is the chief form of seduction
which leads our neighbor to the same or a similar transgression
as the one shown him or at least to a less faithful regard for
moral and religious duties. The word "scandal" is derived from
the Greek, where it means lasso, i.e., a rope with a noose which
is thrown over fleeing animals to capture them and throw them
to the ground. The idea of the *skandalon* is fraught with the
fearful impression of the unforeseen and of irresistible power.
The general use of the word "scandal" for a situation of disorder
or abuse which arouses the indignation and protest of men is
not correct. For this result of scandal is the very opposite to
that of bad example by which those who see it are led to evil
or at least to greater indifference toward moral goodness.

The pages of the Gospels and of St. Paul's letters contain
many references to the evil of scandal. Scandal, like wickedness
and sin, is there represented as permitted by God and fitted into
the divine plan of the world. In Luke 17:1 it is even foretold
as a necessary phenomenon, but it is also threatened with the
severest punishment (Matt. 18:6 ff.; Mark 9:42 ff.). In the
traditional definition of scandal as a *dictum vel factum minus
rectum praebens proximo occasionem spiritualis ruinae* the
words *minus rectum* are of special interest, for they indicate

that not only real sin but also something less correct or what appears to the ill-instructed as sinful may be a cause of scandal. St. Paul gives us an apt illustration in his discussion of the eating of meat which was sold in the market but was derived from animals sacrificed in pagan temples. To eat such meat was in itself an entirely indifferent matter, and the intelligent Christians knew this. But there were less intelligent members whose attitudes were more a matter of the emotions and who considered the eating of this meat a horrible thing which seemed to confuse their simple minds as to the real difference between Christianity and paganism. St. Paul, therefore, advises the well-instructed to abstain from such meat if by eating it they would cause spiritual harm to the weaker brethren. Even now the violation of the Friday abstinence, which is enjoined by a merely ecclesiastical law and in many instances dispensed with by the Church, is considered by some Catholics as a more grievous offense and source of scandal than the infraction of more important commands of God. And so it may be with many things according to the mentality of the people or their customs and traditions. The evil effect and guilt of scandal will be the greater the higher is the position of him who gives the bad example and the more he is obliged by his state in life to give a good example. The seriousness of the sin of scandal increases also with the gravity of the moral transgression and the number of those spiritually harmed.

The *scandalum pusillorum,* i.e., the moral perplexity caused to persons who are too simple-minded or whose moral and religious ideas are too much the reflex of their emotions to judge their neighbor's actions with objective discrimination, need not always be avoided, particularly if there are good reasons to perform the action which proves offensive to such people. Again a change of conditions or the lapse of time may alter situations so that what appeared offensive yesterday is the commonplace tomorrow. The gradual adoption of helpful devices of our mechanical civilization by the clergy and religious is largely a history of such scandals of the simple-minded. Then there are many things which only appear to be such scandals but in reality are attempts by some people to criticize and dominate affairs which are none of their business. In every community will be found persons with their own special notions of what is fit and correct, persons who seek to foist their own brand of righteousness on everyone else. Their hobby consists in being shocked, giving advice, and trying to obtain their goal by seemingly pious and charitable gifts. Priests must be careful lest they fall under the spell of such outside forces. Especially in matters of their official duty they must not yield to the over-simple element of their congregation to such an extent as to paralyze the carrying out of a proper program and cause disgust among the intelligent and active members of their flock. In most cases prudent and charitable diplomatic procedure will succeed in reconciling the objectors to at least benevolent passivity. Furthermore, no one is obliged to forgo forever his personal freedom or considerable advantages merely for the sake of avoiding the *scandalum pusillorum;* much less may the fulfillment of a duty be omitted out of this consideration.

What the proper conduct is in matters which may involve the scandal of the little ones cannot be decided in advance but must be left to the prudent discretion and tact of the individual. Sometimes also the character of a person may be a decisive factor. Some persons can, without offense, do things that would be regarded as shocking if done by others. Often it will be advisable and even necessary to let time prepare the scene for an action which, if done earlier, may cause unpleasant surprise. The exceptional and trusted leader may indeed walk ahead of his time and open the way for healthy development.

By *scandalum pharisaicum* is meant the intentionally vicious misconstruction of morally good and dutiful actions, such as the Pharisees placed on the words and deeds of Christ. It would be not only unwise but unjust to have regard for such an attitude; rather it must be opposed as Christ and the apostles opposed it. Cf. Luke, chap. 12; Acts 4:19; Gal. 2:3 ff.

COOPERATION

As we are not permitted to do evil, so we are not allowed to take part in the sins of others. On the other hand, we are not obliged to prevent every sinful deed of our neighbor unless we hold a position which demands action on our part for reasons of charity or even justice, e.g., because of special bonds of family relations or friendship or official duty. Cooperation is defined as *concursus ad actionem alterius principaliter agentis*. While in theory the problem of cooperation is an easy one, it presents vexing difficulties in practice. Cooperation is divided into formal and material participation in the act of another. Formal cooperation consists in sharing the evil intent of the principal agent. This may be done by commanding or counseling the other's act; by consenting to, taking part in, keeping silence about, or defending it; by not resisting it or not revealing it; by bribery. Non-resistance and failure to make it known do not generally apply, but only in special circumstances as noted above.

Formal cooperation in the sin of another person is never permitted, and whoever does so cooperate contracts the same guilt. Besides, it is a sin of scandal because it confirms the original sinner in his evil, and thirdly, it offends against the moral order by obstructing the building up of the kingdom of God and by increasing the influence of evil. Formal cooperation clearly known as such presents no difficulties for the moralist. But great difficulties are found in the appreciation of material cooperation and particularly of those border cases in which material assistance in the sin closely approaches formal cooperation or merges into it. The purely material cooperation is a morally good or at least indifferent act which is misused by someone for sinful purposes. In material cooperation the act which is *in se* permissible is performed without intending the evil use that may be made of it, although the latter may be suspected or even foreseen. The permissibility of such cooperation is based on the principle that we are not obliged to prevent the wrong of others by suffering grave inconvenience ourselves.

A few examples will be helpful. A manufacturer and distributor of objects which as a rule are being used for licit purposes need not trouble himself about possible abuse of them. The same rule applies to objects the handling of which involves danger and which are often used in the commission of crimes but generally are intended for legitimate purposes, e.g., weapons, poison. Here the problem of material cooperation becoming formal often arises. The points to be considered are (1) the gravity of the evil that may result from the cooperation, (2) the extent of the harm done by it, and (3) the closeness of the connection between the action and the cooperation. Cooperation by actions in themselves evil is never permitted. Moreover, the production and sale of articles that can have no morally good use, and the cooperation in their manufacture and sale, are illicit.

Although these directions are sufficient to solve all possible complications in principle, it may be well to set down a few characteristic solutions. Servants may render to their employers all those services commonly expected of persons in their position, without asking questions about the ultimate purpose of what they are requested to do, e.g., delivering letters and presents. Employees in the offices of business establishments who work entirely under the direction of superiors are not responsible for the content of letters, bills, ledgers, etc. To the extent, however, that they are independent in their work, e.g., as managers and department heads, their personal responsibility increases. But in enterprises essentially based on fraud, even such merely material cooperation may be excused only in cases of extreme necessity and only temporarily. In publishing houses and printing establishments in which good and bad material is being handled, only the directors and editors are responsible for the work done, but such workers as the typesetters and machine operators are not responsible. It may likewise be permitted to subscribe to immoral and irreligious publications, thereby supporting them financially, in order to be informed about the position of the enemy and to prepare the defense against their evil designs. Owners of large halls may rent them out for any meeting licensed by the public authorities, especially where there are many facilities to choose from. But if, by refusal to rent one's accommodations, an evil gathering will be prevented, this circumstance renders the otherwise material cooperation formal.

Catholic hospital sisters and nurses may have occasion to refuse, for reasons of conscience, to render assistance at operations which the Church disapproves. For such cases the sisters and nurses should, once and for all, come to an agreement with the physicians on the hospital staff, that they will not be asked to serve at an operation which conflicts with the dictates of their conscience. They may feel secure that this agreement will be respected. It would be intolerable, however, to settle in each case by argument the question whether a surgical operation is necessary or compatible with the religious views of the nurse.

TRUTHFULNESS

Speech as the ordinary means for the exchange of thought and as the basis of all social intercourse depends on the essential agreement between the spoken word and the idea of which the word is the common medium of recall and expression. Thus truthfulness is necessary even apart from moral considerations. As physical life is impossible in an atmosphere lacking oxygen, so the social body cannot live in an atmosphere from which truthfulness is absent. At earlier stages of human history, the social circles were narrower than they are now, being restricted to members of the same family or clan or tribe. At first the stranger was regarded as an enemy who had neither a right to the truth nor to the protection of his life and property. Since then all men have been drawn together sufficiently to consider themselves in principle and to a certain practical extent as one social community, certain exceptions being made in time of war.

The first and absolutely essential requirement of truthfulness, the fulfillment of which everyone has a right to expect, is the avoidance of lying and deception. But not all have the same right to the positive communication of our thoughts. Just as for some persons certain air may be too cold and sharp, so every truth may not be for all equally helpful and wholesome. Without turning it into a lie, many a truth will have to be properly shaped in order to fit the minds for which it is intended. Every communication must be adapted to the age and education of the recipient. Then, the deepest thoughts and sentiments of a person are felt and guarded as a sacred and inalienable possession. While we must reject the witticism that we have the gift of speech in order to hide our thoughts, it is nevertheless true that it is possible to manifest as well as to disguise or altogether hide the inner state of our mind. Sometimes we may feel more inclined to disclose what is in and on our mind, at other times we are less communicative. It is a quite general phenomenon that the peoples living in southern countries speak more freely than those in northern lands. Some races show their emotions in their whole demeanor, whereas the educated man of eastern Asia considers it proper to maintain always the same facial expression of a faint smile. The Homeric heroes shouted aloud in their pains; for the modern person it is more heroic to moderate his reaction to pain and grief.

For the Christian the duty of truthfulness has a still deeper foundation in the revealed truth that man is created to the image and likeness of God. God is eternal Truth. God has appeared to men in His divine Son, who declared that He is the Truth; and all men are called to live in the kingdom of truth and to adore God in spirit and in truth. The praises of truth and the duty of truthfulness are so many in Sacred Scripture that they cannot be enumerated here. We point out only such characteristic passages as the following: Zach. 8:16; 1 Pet. 2:1; Eph. 4:25; 6:14.

The duty of truthfulness is negative and positive. The negative duty forbids us to deceive our neighbor; this duty is universal and suffers no exception. The positive duty of stating the truth and the whole truth is by far less general and depends in many things on the circumstances. Rightful authority in the sphere of its competency is entitled to the full truth. The same may be said of persons who are united by the bonds of free contract or special reverence and confidence such as exist between parent and child, between married persons or the betrothed, between friends and partners in business. The priest should admonish young people who contemplate marriage to disclose to each other, in sincere honesty, the facts of their past, of their own health and that of their families, and other important matters. Also the relation between the home and school or other educational institution should not be one of secretive opposition but of helpful communication.

The extent to which we are obliged to give information to persons to whom we are not bound by any special social bonds, is hard to define. This will largely depend on the customs of the people among whom we are living. Distinction must also be made between duties of justice and of charity, between asked-for and unrequested information. We may never give an untruthful answer to a question; neither are we obliged to give an answer to each question. When confronted by curious and prying questions, we may consider ourselves in the state of defense. We are not obliged in justice to prevent others from making obvious mistakes if we are not asked for advice. But if we are able to do so without appreciable inconvenience to ourselves, it may become a duty of charity to give helpful information. If, e.g., we see a traveler whose destination we happen to know, boarding the wrong train, we should sin against charity by failing to point out his mistake to him.

THE KEEPING OF SECRETS

The moral order as well as society requires secrecy concerning certain of our private affairs or those of others. Everyone has the duty of procuring his own well-being and is thus entitled to secrecy about matters vital to him if thereby no harm comes to others and no existing duties are neglected. Modern laws generally recognize this right of the individual, e.g., by providing that neither a defendant nor a witness need answer questions that would incriminate him. Secrecy in matters about our neighbor is the basis of confidence. All forms of social collaboration depend on confidence both as a trust in the neighbor's sincerity and as a reliance on his secrecy in matters of common interest. Secrecy is also a necessity because on many occasions of life man feels the need of laying before others, for the purpose of actual help or advice, the most intimate affairs of his physical and spiritual experience. Even apart from this, life offers us many casual glimpses of our neighbor's condition which in the interest of society must not be made the subject of gossip and general discussion. The fact that all men have faults and weaknesses, and the danger that good intentions and plans may be thwarted, require a certain degree of secrecy; for also the good must slowly mature until it may openly display its fruit. It is almost grotesque to reveal to another, with the request of secrecy, things which ought to have been kept secret in the first place. The very request of secrecy is a confession of guilt, and a person who makes himself thus guilty has no right to impose a duty of secrecy on someone else in the same matter.

There is the distinction between the natural and the professional secret (*naturale* and *commissum*). Things that we have come to know about our neighbor by mere chance and that he wishes not to be broadcast because he would thereby be embarrassed or even harmed, constitute the object of the simple or natural secret. The keeping of such secrets is often more a question of tact and charity than of justice, especially if the other party exposed his secret through carelessness or thoughtlessness. Since the knowledge of other person's secrets may often prove an inner burden and a source of external embarrassment, prudence advises us to shun it. Gossips who are eager to initiate us in such secrets should be told that we are not interested in their tales. Secrets discovered by active investigation are known as *secreta extorta*. Investigation of this sort by the public authorities is justified in the interest of public safety, in order to prevent or punish crimes. Also parents, educators, married persons, and those preparing for marriage may, under certain circumstances, have the right to investigate the secrets of others which are of real importance to themselves. But, on the whole, educators should obtain the confidence of their charges and have recourse to secret information only in most exceptional cases, particularly when the young have grown to a maturer age. The same rule should be observed by other superiors and public officials. Former centuries may have held different views in this matter. Man has become more sensitive, and rightly so, in things pertaining to his personal freedom. Secret prying into the lives of others and such denunciation are justly regarded as unworthy and shameful.

Professional secrets have almost as many ramifications as there are commercial forms of service, although they are not all of the same stringency. So it is, e.g., not proper for domestics freely to reveal unusual features of their employers' private lives. Clerks in government offices as well as in the various communication services learn many things which must not be divulged. Physicians and lawyers are informed by their clients of the most intimate affairs which are mentioned to no one else. There is no doubt that in some special cases information derived from the physician's professional secret would be a blessing, but this advantage would be far outweighed by the harm resulting from such an action because it would tend to undermine the public's confidence. The strictest of all professional secrets is the seal of confession.[1] To prevent scruples and to safeguard his position before the public, the priest should discuss in the rectory office such problems as do not belong to confession. Although confidences received outside confession must be kept strict secrets, they do not involve the seal of confession.

[1] Its implications are discussed in Ruland, *Foundations of Morality,* pp. 136 ff.

FIDELITY

Fidelity is the counterpart of truthfulness; the latter refer-
ring to the agreement between thought and speech, the former
to the concord between action and the professed attitude of
the will. Fidelity is a sort of practical truthfulness and an
essential prerequisite of life in community. Sacred Scripture
praises the virtue of faithfulness and mentions it as a trait of
man's likeness to God (cf. Matt. 23:23). God being faithful
wills that all men should become like unto Him in the practice
of this virtue (cf. 1 Cor. 10:13; 2 Tim. 2:13). Hence unfaithfulness is counted among the pagan vices that should not be
found among the Christians (Rom. 1:29 ff.).

In a promise of fidelity the expressed word is intended, first, as
an outward manifestation of the will and, secondly, as a pledge.
This is the origin of the phrase: to give or pledge one's word.
To our neighbor we give our word as a security and means of
coercion, as it were. Since fidelity is a virtue of special prom-
inence in public life, where formerly only men appeared in
evidence, the pledge of fidelity or word of honor has come to
be known as a man's word. The expression refers to those whose
word bears weight, to the mature man who does not promise
lightly but pledges his word only after sober estimation of
the object and his own strength, and after due deliberation.
Women are neither denied the capacity for faithfulness nor excused from it. It is difficult to say whether the frequency with
which, in literature, women are reproached for unfaithfulness,
is on account of their greater emotional excitability. General
experience discloses as much unfaithfulness among men as
among women. However, not all resolutions we may happen to
utter before others are pledges that we are bound to fulfill. It
is not enough that the other person be a witness to our pronounced intentions. He must act as the recipient of our word
and pledge, and so be the partner of a sort of unilateral contract. It is clear that the breaking of one's plighted word is sinful.
In some cases the promise may not have been made in good

faith or it may be broken by infidelity through a change of mind. Further, promises made in bad faith, which thus are lies, do bind in conscience, and their breach adds the sin of faithlessness to the sin of lying.

To the question about whom we owe faithfulness to, the answer is the same as to the famous query: "Who is my neighbor?" We owe faithfulness to all men with whom life brings us into contact. Therefore we may never promise anything we cannot render. As regards children who are not yet perfect juridical partners of social relations, it is morally wrong and educationally an egregious blunder to make promises which one is not able or does not intend to fulfill. Promises extorted by unjust means and violence, e.g., by robbers, do not oblige. The gravity of a breach of faith depends on the seriousness of the object involved in the promise and the solemnity and other circumstances under which the promise was made. Frequently promises are made in the form of an oath. Faithlessness mostly involves also violations of justice and vice versa. This applies especially to infidelity in marriage as well as in the performance of one's professional duties.

As infidelity is sinful, it is a sin to induce others to be faithless. Usually it is temporal advantages, known as bribes, which are offered as an inducement to betray one's professional obligations. *Bribery* is the subject of an important chapter in public life and an indication of the inner moral condition. Bribery often springs from the unchecked desire of wealth or it is the result of the impoverishment of large sections of the population by unemployment or low wages. Since we cannot expect the general presence of a heroic spirit among men, adverse circumstances such as we have just mentioned must be considered in judging the transgressions of individuals and whole nations.

The question whether it is proper, by special little rewards, to incite a person to a more alert fulfillment of his duties, is of some interest. Objectively, all men are obliged to carry out their professional obligations always and with unvarying fidelity. But an old custom has it that persons in the lower branches of commercial services are given small donations, called tips, in addition to their regular pay. Though considered voluntary gifts, the tips have become in many places and services an institution regulated by official tariff rates. In itself the idea of the tip is a corruption of the conception of duty and thus of social life. The more the consciousness of the dignity of every honest work and of the equal value of every worker in human society gains ground, the more the institution of the tip must be considered an unworthy survival of a past view regarding the dignity of labor. It would be useless for an individual to defy this custom. Hence it is not sinful to give and accept tips. Improvement can come only from a deeper moral understanding of the nature of professional obligation, of work and its just reward.

IV

LYING

A LIE is the direct and most obvious opposite of truthfulness. For the purpose of clarifying the nature of lying, we shall base our discussion on the definition of a lie given by St. Augustine, who was the first of the ecclesiastical writers to deal at length with this problem and influenced decisively all later theories. The views of other Fathers of the Church will occupy us only in the question of the profitable or white lie. St. Augustine defines a lie as *falsa significatio cum voluntate fallendi*. This definition implies three things. First, the signification must be false, i.e., the conscious expression of thoughts disagreeing with one's inner conviction. Secondly, the word "signification" includes not only verbal utterances but gestures or any external comportment. E.g., a man who disguises himself as a woman lies without speaking a word and may accomplish special purposes just as by a spoken lie. Third, the words *cum voluntate fallendi* do not mean that the intention to deceive must be willed by a positive act. This intention is present in any conscious and willful use of such language or conduct as cannot but convey another meaning than that which the liar knows to be the right one.

Besides the literal meaning of words and phrases, these may have and often do have another meaning. Illustrations in point are the parable, riddle, allegory, irony, hyperbole, or metaphor, all of which are not statements in the ordinary sense, neither are they lies. In the realm of action we may mention the rich field of symbolism. Here belong also the various forms of courtesy, which will be discussed later.

The problem of the lie is an intricate and difficult study, which has been treated from various angles in monographs, but with-

out yielding a satisfactory result. Psychologically it seems helpful to apply to lying the modern conception of disease as the
condition of an organism at the limit of its normal adaptability,
without minimizing the moral issue or interpreting the lie as a
disease. Just as the body behaves smoothly as long as its normal balance is not disturbed, so man normally recognizes the
duty of truthfulness and practices it without conflict as long as
his well-being and pursuit of happiness are not adversely
touched. But when the admission of the truth entails certain inconveniences, he is likely to be inwardly upset and fails to adapt
himself to the difficulties of the new situation. The lie affords
momentary relief but no real and permanent adjustment. For
every conscious disregard of moral demands creates an inner
division of man's personality which manifests itself even in
physiological disturbance (irregular breathing, blushing, etc.),
except in the case of the most accomplished and hardened liar.

We can best study the psychological pattern of lying with
children. Apart from the babbling expressions of the child's
lively imagination (which has nothing to do with lying because
it is entirely aimless), the first denials by children of having
done something are principally instinctive acts of self-protection. Even when these occur together with a marked emotional
reaction they have, in early childhood, not yet the moral
quality of lying. As dreams are wish-fulfillments and the
images of the imagination are for the child the same as the
impressions of the real world, so in the child's thought and
speech the imaginatively saturated wishful thought replaces the
objective fact. Only where there is sufficient use of reason to
discern not only truth from falsehood but also the purpose to
be served by the denial of the truth in a particular case, is lying in the moral sense possible. Considering the average mental
alertness of our present society, we may say that lying, strictly
speaking, is possible from about the fourth year of age on. But
it cannot be denied that with some children there appears very
early a strong tendency to self-assertion, which may lead to

more or less consciously willed acts or also to hysterical behavior.

The naïveté of the child also appears in its lying. Naïveté is an immature disregard of the consequences of one's actions. Although a real lie aims at a consciously perceived end, the child's lies may be naïve inasmuch as the child sees only the most immediate consequence, i.e., escape from punishment, but overlooks all other complications. Again, the immaturity of a child in its moral judgments and decisions manifests itself in the very limited sorrow for its lies. The shame and regret shown depend very much on the success or its opposite and the emotional attitude toward the persons whom it loves or hates or fears. It cannot be denied that the bad example of adults is the cause of many lies among children. But even without this kind of seduction and scandal, childhood with its fear of the superior power of the grown-up, with its fears of punishment and shame and, at times, also through indolence and the desire of pleasure, offers many occasions for lying. At school age, the very acute contrast between the former life of the child in carefree play and the new order of restraint and responsible effort, puts the child's capacity for moral and emotional adaptation to a severe test. Lying is here often a sign of weakness and lack of stability in facing the new situation. A noteworthy factor in all this is also the promptness with which the decisions have to be made. Every rational judgment and responsible decision requires some time for its formation, unless by conscious practice a certain spontaneity has been acquired. This cannot be expected of the child, for whom all critical situations involve the element of suddenness which, in turn, entails almost necessarily a lack of balance in the form of lying.

The lies of children of school age, like all other childhood lies, are mostly defensive actions (excuses, pretended and hysterical illness) born of fear. With boys of a more mature age, lies may often be prompted by the desire to shield their friends from trouble, as an act of heroism or bravado. However, young people are not excessively mendacious. Adolescent boys at times cultivate a sort of fanaticism for truthfulness and despise lying as cowardice. Of course, youth must find some degree of reasonableness and justice in their adult superiors. Narrow-minded censoriousness and pedantry will always be answered and defeated by lying. Seldom does youth lie out of sheer malice, e.g., for revenge or the desire to do harm. The social condition of the children makes little difference in the matter of lying. Under the same circumstances the children of the rich lie just as the children of the poor. With progressing age, wanton lying becomes less frequent, leaving only the ordinary untruthful excuses to escape embarrassment. Adaptation to the realities of life and the sense of strength progress, unless the child is the unhappy member of a family given to a social behavior which the child is directed to conceal by lying.

The difference of the sexes is of some psychological interest in the question of lying. Women are said to have a more delicate sense for truth. And yet we are told that lies occur more often among women than among men. The reason is probably the greater emotional character of the women, which results in more frequent disturbances of the power of adaptation to the shifting circumstances of the moment. For the most part, the lies of women are also probably about trifles. The higher percentage of men involved in perjury convictions is probably on account of the much greater number of men who are called upon to take oaths, for public and professional life with its struggles and pitfalls is still largely a man's world.

Returning from these psychological considerations to the theological question of lying, we find that the Old Testament explicitly condemns lying in a court of law, as a means of harming one's neighbor and as religious hypocrisy. Yet there is no doubt that the general duty of truthfulness was taught and insisted upon. It is just as certain that the vice of lying was extremely widespread before Christ, as is proved by the great number of oaths in daily use and of curses against their violation.

Only where public confidence was completely undermined was it possible to require so many oaths. It is against this condition and the resultant abuse of the oath that Christ protested and insisted that for the Christian the simple "Yes" and "No" should have greater weight than the former oaths. Traditionally the distinction is made between lies as expressed by words (*faliloquium*), by signs (*simulatio*), and by conduct (*hypocrisis*).

Lying by word constitutes by far the greater problem for moral theology. It is divided into jocose, harmful, and white (excusing, professional, official) lies. The degree of its sinfulness depends on various factors. First of all, lying is not the expression of an instinctive impulse but an action which is provoked by an external motive and ulterior purpose. Hence the morality of the purpose has an influence on the gravity of the lie. Then, the lie may be intended to deceive one or more persons. It may violate the laws of charity or of justice, accordingly as the person lied to has a strict right to the truth or not. Every lie contains also an offense against the neighbor who is not regarded high enough to be told the truth. Lastly, all lying introduces some poison of distrust into human society. The sinfulness of the individual lie will have to be determined by viewing it from all these angles. Generally a lie which causes no harm is indeed sinful but not grievously so, unless a person who is to be looked up to by the public with reverence is exposed as a liar, and thus grave scandal is given. Jocose lies in the form of amusing stories are no lies at all; they are merely fiction. But jokes which cannot be recognized as such or which are made to embarrass persons, who, though in other respects intelligent and even outstanding, are easily taken in, may become sinful, even seriously, according to the inconvenience they may cause. Lies which inflict actual harm are always sinful and entail the obligation of restitution.

The question of the *white lie*, always a moot question among the moralists, is not yet satisfactorily settled. Pre-Christian philosophers dealt with the problem and declared that lies are permitted for the purpose of reassuring and sparing our neighbor and as a defense against evils. In view of some extremely rigorous theories of later moralists, there is some spice in Jean Jacques Rousseau's remark that the problem is decided "negatively in the books of moralists, where the strictest rigorism costs the author nothing; and positively in practical life, where the books of moralists are merely useless verbiage that cannot be put into practice." Undoubtedly there sometimes arise situations in which a person may honestly believe that the statement of the truth will cause harm out of all proportion to the good resulting from its denial. Accordingly early writers of the Church (e.g., Origen and St. John Chrysostom) declared this sort of lie permissible. St. Augustine's view, which influenced the later theories, was stricter, although he clearly perceived the difficulty of the problem. Cassian, who was well versed in questions of asceticism, says that there are "untruths which we utter as in need of atonement."

To understand the Augustinian position we must keep in mind the effects of lying. It is possible that the deception of our neighbor in some cases is not against charity, but it always disturbs the mutual confidence of men. The greater the number of such lies and the acquiescence in them, the more uncertainty enters into the body of society. It disturbs the human order and contradicts God, who is Truth. God's providence is often harsh toward us but never untrue or unfaithful; and He knows how to turn evil into good. It is here as with all tragic situations in life: the sorrow and pain of the individual is a source of good for many. It may be hard to hear from the physician that our condition is critical or even hopeless, but if we knew that no physician would ever reveal the seriousness of a patient's condition, we should feel still more disturbed by the uncertainty.

While denying the permissibility of the white lie, theologians nevertheless recognized the actual difficulties of life which they sought to avoid by teaching two ways out, namely, the use of amphibology or equivocation, and mental reservation. Equivocation is a mode of speech with two senses, only one of which is applicable to the situation. There is a beautiful example of this in Matt. 9:23 ff., where our Lord, in the face of the people's assertion that the daughter of Jairus was dead, and as the Master over life and death, truthfully declared: the girl sleeps. We are told that St. Athanasius, while fleeing from his enemies in a boat, was overtaken by them and, his identity not being known, was asked by them whether he knew where Athanasius was. He answered that he knew that Athanasius was not far from them. They, thinking that he was in a boat a little farther on, hurried after it and thus let Athanasius escape. Not many repetitions of such a happy solution will be found available. Certainly there are not many persons who possess that presence of mind and promptness of reply. Most people will seek an escape by a false statement. If anyone wishes to resort to an equivocation he must use the words in their conventional sense and according to the context. To do otherwise does not by a hair's breadth differ from a lie.

An illustration of mental reservation is the famous reply to inconvenient callers, namely, that the person asked for is not at home, that is, not at home for the visitor. This particular answer, as well as the negative answers to questions which solicit the betrayal of a professional secret, are generally recognized as polite refusals. Wherever higher interests appear to conflict with the demands of social intercourse, people commonly resort to the white lie because neither evasive answers nor equivocations will save the situation. Pure mental reservation (*restrictio pure mentalis*) has been condemned by the Church as equivalent to lying. The attempts of the older casuists to justify mental reservation and equivocation can no longer be considered valid. They had their value and use in former times when in court the accused were forced to make damaging statements against themselves, and when the casuists were bookish legists who delighted in hair-splitting distinctions. We render moral theology no service by denying all defects of its past. We now feel that the words must be used in a sense which is the commonly accepted one and fits the context of the question, but not in a sense which may hide in an obscure corner of a dictionary.

The white lie certainly represents no moral ideal, even where it is prompted by sympathy and kindness. These motives may be misdirected but yet well intended so that they may preclude sin in individual cases, as nobody commits sin who acts in good faith. No satisfactory argument for the outright licitness of the white lie has yet been put forward by moralists. Some modern students of ethics are of the opinion that the validity of certain moral qualities cannot be proved at all but is directly perceived. It may be here as with suicide, the immorality of which is immediately felt and yet not easily argued constructively. Thus it may be more useful to prove, not the objective and absolute licitness of the white lie, but the fact that in many instances it is, for subjective reasons, not a sin. To this end, not only speculative theological arguments, but also psychological and general human considerations must be examined.

The cases in which the question of the licitness of lying can be at all considered must be limited as far as possible. The lies resulting from embarrassment as well as the mendacious excuses in school may be understandable, but they remain moral faults. The subject of our investigation concerns mainly the situations where the answer to a question becomes difficult either because there is not sufficient time to formulate a well considered evasive reply, or where the question itself is felt to be an unjust intrusion upon one's private affairs but cannot be brusquely repulsed for higher considerations or reasons of courtesy. According to a general principle, the social duty of truthfulness exists only between those who are interrelated by social bonds and ceases where these bonds cease. E.g., in war there is place for the employment of ruses; the enemy who is fought with physical weapons cannot expect to be told the truth by his opponent. Just as nations may defend themselves, so the individual is permitted to use as much physical force as is required to repel the unjust attack (*moderamen inculpatae tutelae*). We do not seem to go wrong in applying the same principle to the attack or rather encroachment which an unjust question makes on our personal self. If physical self-defense were not permitted, our life would be freely exposed to violent aggression. If we had no right to defend ourselves against unjustified questioning, our very self and its social relations would be the prey of irresponsible curiosity and malice. Hence we may quite logically conclude that within the scope of such unwarranted encroachments upon our just personal interests and relations the rights and duties of social life cease, with the result that such deviations from the truth are licit to the extent required by self-protection. Undoubtedly the simple and effective repulse of every improper curiosity would be better. But in most cases this is just as impossible as the prompt handing over of every thief to the police.

As in the sudden exigencies of physical self-defense a person may easily and without moral guilt exceed the limits of what is strictly required, so it may happen here. And lies as acts of justified self-defense are possible. This is also admitted by the great moralist Vermeersch. Another argument, not for the theoretical licitness but for the practical sinlessness of defensive lies under certain conditions, may be derived from the transfer of the modern concept of disease to the mental situation of those who are suddenly forced to make a statement of possible important consequences, without sufficient time for reflection. The hasty view of the grave results on the one hand and the smallness and harmlessness of a possible lie on the other, may perplex a person to the extent that it becomes impossible for him to see and weigh the moral factors pro and con. What upon calm reflection would appear wrong, may be judged by the mentally perplexed and emotionally upset person as free from guilt. Thus a solution of this problem, not altogether unsatisfactory, may be obtained. The older traditional formulas appear not comprehensive enough.

Although in the actual time of war the ordinary social bonds are interrupted between opposing belligerents, and the conflicting parties cannot be expected to make truthful statements to each other, at least in regard to their strategy and other such factors vital in warfare, the obligation of truthfulness does not entirely cease, especially since the effects of war lies do not automatically stop at the conclusion of peace. But the modern progress in evil, on account of the widespread defection from the Christian religion, has produced a new form of vicious lying on a world-wide scale. It is the *propaganda lie*. Hundreds of millions of people are nowadays deliberately misinformed about events, purposes, intentions, possibilities, dangers, and hopes of national and international movements. Thus the masses are emotionally conditioned for hatred and violent action which may and does result in untold bloodshed and indescribable moral misery and material destruction. Ceaselessly alert vigilance, rigorous self-examination, prayer, and real sacrifices must be our weapon to defeat the horrors of this kind of lying.

In international *diplomacy*, truth is theoretically preferred to untruth because it is said that there is only one truth but so many possibilities of untruth that negotiations based on evasions of the truth could never result in an agreement. As a matter of fact, however, every diplomatic formula is a combination of truth and untruth. Even the most evident facts are being officially denied. No official denial can be accepted at its face value. Worse still are the official interpretations of treaties and other measures; they hardly differ from the lying about strategy in war to deceive the opponent. This being so, nobody believes them, and so they have become more and more like conventional forms of evasive speech. As a consequence, occasional sincerity may prove even a more effective deception and bring greater results.

In every society there are certain forms of politeness and *courtesy*. Genuine courtesy is not a mere external thing but is rooted in conscious respect, reverence, and love of our neighbor. For the purpose of those frequent contacts in society which do not aim at deliberate cooperation or intimate personal relations, men need certain formalities which facilitate their approach and parting. We cannot on every occasion open our hearts to those whom we meet, or solicit their sympathy with our lot in life or our mood of the moment. We need phrases which enable us to approach other persons respectfully and at the same time limit the contact to the minimum of what is necessary. Before we can enter into a more serious and intimate exchange of thought and confidence we must first become acquainted and be assured of each other's trustworthiness. But with many persons whom we meet in the complications of our life we are not able and do not wish to become familiar. For such meetings the forms of courtesy are sufficient. Such courtesy, to use an illustration from the science of optics, is like the setting of the lens at indefinite focus. Again, as machines need grease in order to function well, so human society needs the conventions of courtesy for the smooth functioning of its traffic. The faster the speed at which poeple meet and part, the more these conventions are needed. They are not the same everywhere but vary according to the character of the people and their particular conditions of life. However, they all agree in this, that the words and phrases used must not be taken in their strictest sense. Coins that pass through many hands lose their clear contours. So it is with the forms of courtesy. Their original meaning has become obscured and is not taken as a specially formulated message. Nevertheless they express in some way that general attitude of respect and charity we should have for all, and so their use is a perpetual reminder of our Christian duty toward one another. This is also true of the polite forms of turning away applicants for positions and the like. It is true that the general assurances of consideration at an opportune time must not be taken as binding promises; neither should they be mere lying devices disappointing others under the cloak of sympathy.

Perhaps in the past, truthfulness was not given the prominent position it should hold in the program of religious education. After so much time and effort has been devoted to the best possible methods of advising the young wholesomely about matters concerning purity, it might be well to accord the same attention to the virtue of truthfulness.

V

THE HONOR OF OUR NEIGHBOR

HONOR is one of the spiritual goods of man. For his life in society, man needs a certain amount of respect and recognition on the part of his fellow men by which they acknowledge in him that sum of qualities and moral values which is regarded as the normal basis of social collaboration. As all human conduct proceeds from within and is the manifestation of the disposition of the heart, evidently the honor and respect due our neighbor must find there a secure and warm dwelling place. It would not be enough simply to abstain from external violations of our neighbor's honor, while entertaining freely all sorts of unfounded evil thoughts about him. To do so would offend not only against truth but also against justice. Our duties in regard to the honor of our neighbor are positive and negative. The positive duties require that we have genuine regard for our neighbor; that we express this regard in the customary circumstances and forms, and defend his honor. But these obligations may be variously limited. The negative duties are much more extensive, forbidding, as they do, all internal and external offenses against our neighbor's honor by unfounded suspicion and rash judgment, by detraction, calumny, or insult.

Respect for the honor of our neighbor is not merely a demand of the natural law and justice; like the duty of truthfulness and fidelity, it is a consequence of our nature as an image of God and our vocation and elevation in Jesus Christ. Charity, the fundamental law of Christianity, requires us to recognize all good qualities of our neighbor and especially the fact that he is, like ourselves, a creature of God and a brother and heir of Christ. If, as St. Paul says (1 Cor., chap. 13), charity thinks no evil and does not envy, it is always ready to entertain and exhibit respect and honor for all men.

The manner of showing forth this honor will vary according to the social relations of persons as superiors and subjects, parents and children, or in the less defined contacts of equal and independent persons. And in pedagogy it is a fundamental law and the secret of success that the educator, notwithstanding his position of authority, entertains and shows honest respect and reverence for the child. Even the ancient Romans had the motto: *maxima debetur puero reverentia*. This is owed to the child as to one who is sent into the world by God and called to fulfill a divine mission, regardless of whether this will actually be accomplished. This reverence does not call for external acts of idolizing the child, but must be the mature inner conviction of the educator.

One of the most frequent ways of expressing respect for our neighbor is the *greeting*. Its psychological root is threefold: profession, benediction, and defense. In culturally less advanced society, the meeting of one person with another was not always devoid of danger. There was need of assurance about the friendly or hostile character of the contact. This required mutual recognition and the profession of peaceful intentions. Possible evil was feared not only from physical violence but also from demoniac influences which might be conjured up by curses, the evil eye, or other spells. Such possible perils had to be banished by exchanging words of comfort and blessing.

The words of greeting were usually accompanied and emphasized by expressive gestures; sometimes the gestures took the place of the words altogether. Such bodily movements, many of which are still observed, were the following: turning the face toward each other, standing still, waving the hand, bowing the head, touching the forehead with the hand, clasping each other's hand, embracing, kissing, touching the beard, and even spitting into each other's face. Uncovering the head is the first and most general form of greeting in the Western world. The ancient Greeks hailed one another with *chaire,* i.e., "Rejoice"; the practical Roman wished good health (*salve*). The meditative Oriental desires peace, which is also the scriptural greeting. The salutation in the official prayer service of the Church is the request of a blessing (*iube, domne, benedicere*), and the reply *Deus,* i.e., "Godspeed." Persons who are animated by a common spirit and devotion to a cause may express this in their greeting, according to the adage, "out of the fullness of the heart the mouth speaketh." Thus we have the religious greeting, "Praised be Jesus Christ," and the answer, "Now and forever." The watchwords and countersigns of persons engaged in patriotic and other movements derive from the same psychological source.

Greeting is the expression of courtesy and respect. The omission of the greeting and its appropriate reply, where they are to be expected, is an obvious offense to our neighbor. Priests, teachers, and others who occupy similar respected positions, at least in certain limited circles of society, must be careful lest they offend by failing to answer the greetings of their environment or by answering them in a negligent manner. The effects of such offenses have often much wider and more lasting consequences than might superficially appear. Individual and group grievances, real or imaginary, as also burdens and hardships, will thus be intensified and lead to violent and permanent harm to good and necessary institutions. The form of addressing persons belongs also here and requires the same attention.

The defense of our neighbor's honor may become a duty. Many persons experience a morbid satisfaction in making sport of the good name of others, or regard it as a matter of private pastime. Needless to say, this sort of conduct violates both justice and charity, and offends against the essential spirit of the Christian soul (cf. Rom. 12:9; 15:2; Phil. 4:5). In repulsing or restraining attacks on the honor of our neighbor, a prudent weighing of the circumstances is advisable. Direct contradiction is not always necessary; in many cases it is enough to give the conversation a different turn. Occasionally it may be our duty to leave the company as a more or less open protest.

SINS AGAINST THE HONOR OF OUR NEIGHBOR

There would be no external honor if there were no internal respect for our neighbor, the lack of which makes all outer exhibitions of courtesy sham and deception. As mentioned before, the internal sins in this regard are false suspicion and rash judgment. Sacred Scripture has frequent warnings against our condemning our neighbor. Two reasons justify these warnings. First, all men are sinful and in need of God's mercy. Secondly, we lack that breadth and depth of insight required for a just appraisal of our neighbor's culpability and intentions. All who hold positions involving the duty of judging others, are often obliged to admit their mistakes. Where no such duty exists, we should be glad that we are not obliged to determine the guilt of other people. Although the French proverb, *tout comprendre c'est tout pardonner* ("to understand all is to pardon all") is not quite correct, it contains much truth. The greater our experience in life, the less prone we will be to judge and condemn, remembering the word of the Gospel: "Judge not, that you may not be judged" (Matt. 7:1; Rom. 2:1; Jer. 4:12).

The least of the internal sins against the honor of our neighbor is *false suspicion,* i.e., the unfounded or insufficiently founded assumption of another person's sinfulness, which leads to the refusal of internal respect for that person. Some people are naturally inclined toward suspicion, as a result of their own, often unconscious, feeling of inferiority. Great and well-balanced characters are not suspicious. Often suspicion springs from the wickedness of our own heart. St. Ignatius Loyola says: "The man who suffers from vertigo thinks the whole world is whirling round; so is the suspicious man, believing that all others are evil." Suspicion may also become a mental attitude on account of senile fears of being slighted and restrained. This mentality may set in long before the oncoming of real old age. Such people feel offended and harmed even by the quite justified ambitions of their fellows. In matters of property they suspect dishonesty and theft on all sides; things which they have forgotten or mislaid are, they feel sure, stolen or maliciously kept from them. To the extent that such suspicions are the result of physical deterioration they lack moral responsibility although they are the source of much trouble. Hence in the homes for the aged where old poeple can pass their last years without work and cares, there is mostly not that peace and contentment which one should expect. The sinfulness of false suspicion depends on the degree of malice attributed to the neighbor without sufficient reason and the persistence with which such unfounded beliefs are retained. They may range from vague and faint moods and thoughts all the way to firm belief.

False suspicion as a firm belief and consciously retained conviction is *rash judgment*. Not every thought of a suspicious nature nor every inquiry into the cause of some evil, requiring the imagination of possible concrete situations, is sinful. If I enter my room and find the desk broken into, I do not sin by asking myself who may have done this. To profit by our less pleasant experiences with others, without making them, of course, an excuse for injustice and uncharitableness, is not a sin. Neither need we wait until we have been personally abused and exploited, but we may act on the prudent advice of those who have had sufficient experience. Most of the hard-luck stories which are regaled to priests for the purpose of obtaining at once large sums of money are swindles, and it is not sinful to suspect the persons who make such appeals until the truth of their claims has been proved.

Contumely or *insult* is one of the external sins against the honor of our neighbor. It consists in offending him by words or conduct in his physical or moral presence. By moral presence we mean not only the presence of his more or less immediate acquaintances, but that of the circle of the public which is his actual sphere of life. This sphere may be narrower or wider according to a person's position, profession, and the like. The widest publicity is given by insults that are printed in daily papers and periodicals, and by malicious reviews of scientific publications in professional magazines. The gravity of an insult increases with the importance of the event in connection with which it is made and the dignity of the person concerned. Men in certain professions as well as persons representing authority need a high degree of external respect, e.g., priests, teachers, judges, physicians. Hence it is not always a good policy if members of these social groups allow insults to go unpunished. The sinfulness of the insult is to be judged by the evil intent of the offender, his education and social standing, and similar circumstances; but not by its external form or the personal sensitiveness of the person offended. Insults may be extremely vicious and effective, yet so cautiously phrased that there is no basis for the legal indictment and conviction of the offender. Higher considerations and real charity may make just and honest reproaches a duty, even though they are painful to those at whom they are aimed.

Much more important is the question of *detraction* because of its frequency among the people. Detraction is the intentional revelation of the faults of others, their blunders, blameworthy deeds, and the like by which it can be foreseen that the reputation and good name of the persons concerned will be impaired. In some instances society has a right to be informed of the dangerous qualities of its members. But these instances are limited, and, except in case of urgent necessity, these revelations should be left to those who by their office are obliged to deal with these delicate problems. As a matter of fact, detraction is one of the most widely indulged sports wherever people meet in a social way. Conversation is an art and presupposes a fund of worth-while information and lively interests. Where these are present, conversation may become delightful recreation and an occasion for cultural education instead of destructive backbiting. Where this danger exists it is better to have harmless social games which make for happy contact and at the same time stimulate and relax the mind. Gossiping and detraction are an inveterate vice. The verse against it which St. Augustine wrote on the wall of his dining room was probably a quotation from the common lore of the popular Roman philosophy and is thus a witness to the ubiquitous presence of the gossip. The spreading of the faults of others is, in a way, a sign of self-deceit as we see in the parable of the Pharisee and the publican. The harm done by the wagging tongue is set forth in St. James' Epistle.

Detraction is the more sinful according as the intention is the more uncharitable and the harm done is the greater. Detraction seldom abides by the exact truth, but tends to add subjective color to the facts and exaggerate them so that it passes into calumny. Frequently those who speak thus about their neighbor are little qualified to judge his personality and his work. Regard for the honor of our neighbor does not require, however, that we avoid every reasonable judgment about others or never speak to anyone about their faults. We are allowed to speak about them to serious and prudent persons in order to avert harm; to obtain advice, help, or comfort; to free ourself from false suspicion. Comment by subjects and students about the real or supposed faults of their superiors and teachers is probably motivated, in most cases, by less justifiable reasons. It is also licit to mention the shortcomings of others if amendment can thus be hoped for.

We do not sin by speaking of the faults of completely unknown persons, if we do not supply details by which they may be identified. Likewise we do not sin by speaking about things that are already known either as facts or by legal judgment. Yet we are not permitted to say anything and everything about a person who has been sentenced in the law court for a misdeed. Such a one has not lost all right to a good reputation. Where the interests of the public are at stake, as in the case of swindlers, the spreading of information harmful to them is not only permitted but may be even a duty. On the other hand, the malicious denunciation of persons for whom we have a dislike, for the sake of revenge or mere gossiping, or from self-righteous conceit, is a despicable and sinful act. Detraction is greatly abetted by those who lend a willing ear to the gossip. Some persons who would not speak ill of their neighbors delight in such stories, show lively interest in them, and stimulate others to recount them. This is, of course, as much a sin as telling the scandalous stories. Mere passive conduct in the presence of talk derogatory to our neighbor's good name is usually not sinful. Silence which indicates lack of interest and approval may serve as an effective rebuke.

Derision, or mocking, is similar to the sin of insult, but uses the form of jesting. Jesting or joking consists in combining logically incompatible matters whereby a comical effect is produced. In derision the same effect is frequently produced by the use of exaggerations which also contain the element of the illogical. Jests at the expense of others may be quite harmless when their jocose character is so obvious that it cannot be missed by anyone and there is no malicious intention. But jests based on actual facts which even suggest illogical exaggerations may lose the jocose nature completely and become more cutting than outright insults. Often persons who offer insults to their neighbor are emotionally excited. This circumstance has an extenuating value and helps reconciliation. In derision, what wounds so deeply is the cool deliberation and display of superiority. The sinfulness of derision is to be measured by the degree of uncharitableness which inspired it and the extent of the violation of the neighbor's honor in view of the gravity of the reproach and the extent of the harm. Derision is particularly heartless if it is based on the defects, mental or physical, of others which are their unhappy lot in life. Children are especially cruel in this, and they must be taught at an early age how mean it is to ridicule others for defects and weaknesses which they cannot help.

Great harm is done by teachers who use ridicule in dealing with young people. These will more readily accept rough treatment than smarting ridicule, which is likely to shut the door to every further influence on the youthful mind. Sometimes young people so treated develop an attitude of opposition and spite against all social and religious authority. Another destructive and despicable way of disturbing the peace of society in the matter of honor and reputation is the reporting to people of the derogatory things which others have said about them. We all wish to have others speak well of us and are inclined to believe that others do so much more than is actually the case. It is good that we do not know all the things that are being said about us. But this good which makes for peace and happiness is destroyed by talebearing of this sort, which is always sinful. Only where it is necessary or helpful to warn a person against those who abuse his confidence may it be done without sin. As a rule, however, those who carry tales are either stupid gossips or people who devilishly delight in the spread of enmities and hatred.

Calumny or *libel* (*calumnia*) is the worst offense against the good name of our neighbor and consists in attributing to him untrue and invented faults. Calumny usually grows out of detraction by exaggeration and develops independently in the process of repetition. Calumny occurs in every conceivable situation of life and is one of the chief weapons in the struggle of individuals, social classes, and nations. It is a threefold sin. It offends against justice by despoiling the neighbor of his just reputation, against charity as the basic virtue of Christian society, and against truthfulness by telling the untruth. The gravity of the sin depends on the subjective malice of the calumniator, the objective evil attributed to the neighbor, and the extent of the consequent damage.

RESTITUTION OF HONOR

We must not only repent of the injury we have inflicted on our neighbor's honor but we must repair the harm done. However, restitution in this matter is extremely difficult and, in most cases, is not attempted. In spite of the difficulty involved in the restitution of honor, some efforts toward its accomplishment must be made. In the case of detraction, restitution cannot be made directly but must be achieved indirectly by excusing, as far as possible, the neighbor's faults and mentioning his good qualities. This last method is probably the better one because, by excusing his faults, we draw attention to them again. Rigid rules cannot be given in view of the complexity of the actual situations in which only good will and tact will find the right way. The offenses by insult and derision are the easiest to repair through asking the offended person's pardon and by mutual reconciliation. These need not always be sought in a formal manner, especially in the case of superior and subject, but through appropriate and opportune signs of respect and friendliness. Calumny obliges the offender to a retractation as public as was the offense. But here lies one of the greatest difficulties. Where the offenses against the neighbor's honor and good name entailed also economic damage, such as loss of position or of customers, these losses must also be repaired.

One factor in the healing of wounds caused by attacks on the neighbor's reputation—a factor that operates automatically, as it were—is the speed of modern life. What excites the curiosity and interest of the people today is forgotten and replaced by something else tomorrow. Restitution may be omitted (1) when no harm has been done, e.g., because the detractor or calumniator was not believed; (2) when the restitution would require an action that is physically or morally impossible, being out of all proportion to the original harm inflicted; (3) when the truth has already become known through other channels; (4) when the effort at restitution would be ineffective because its truth and sincerity would not be believed; (5) when the matter has been forgotten so that an attempt at restitution would make matters worse; (6) when the wronged party prefers to have the matter dropped.

To the obligation of repairing harm done, corresponds the duty of forgiveness and reconciliation on the part of the wronged person. Strictly speaking, only an offender who sincerely regrets his wrong action can be forgiven. In small violations of one's honor, the best settlement of the matter is to forget about it. Where grave consequences result from such offenses, one may be compelled, without prejudice to one's attitude of Christian charity, to insist on appropriate restitution and amends.

VI

Duties Toward Our Neighbor's Bodily Good

All real values of human life must be protected by the moral order. The highest temporal good is life itself because the enjoyment of all other temporal possessions depends on it and ends with it. For the Christian, life has an added value as a time and opportunity of preparation for eternity; a time of sowing, of struggle and decision, which will determine the condition of our existence after death. Hence it is not only a demand of the natural law but a revealed positive command to leave the life's span and vigor of our neighbor unimpaired for the accomplishment of his tasks. Nevertheless, just as reason clearly indicates the duty of respecting the bodily integrity of our neighbor, so it is also the universal conviction that, under particular circumstances, his life may be interfered with and even cut short.

The simplest case where interference with our neighbor's life appears fully justified is the necessity of *self-defense* against unjust aggression. Whoever does not respect the life of others but attacks it without justification, forfeits his right to undisturbed freedom and integrity. In attacking one person he endangers the interest of the social whole, and he who defends himself protects society at large. To warrant actual encroachments on the attacker's bodily integrity and life, his injurious action must be morally present, i.e., it must be already started or at least be about to begin in the shortest time. Preventive actions against foreseen but not yet started or immediaely impending attacks, do not justify the destruction of the life of another. Other means must be employed, which do not endanger the bodily life of the prospective offender. Where physical violence in self-defense is allowed, it must be limited to what is actually necessary (*moderamen inculpatae tutelae*).

Besides attempts on one's life, also attacks on something of high moral value, such as the integrity of bodily chastity and other valuable goods the loss of which could not be restored at all or only with extreme hardship, may be so repulsed.

Again, the necessities of a pioneer's life under precarious circumstances or of explorers or persons involved in shipwreck, and the like, may justify much more drastic measures of self-defense than would be permissible under ordinary conditions. What we are allowed in self-defense we are permitted also in the defense of our neighbor.

Self-defense of this sort always takes place under unexpected circumstances and demands quick action. Naturally the emotions are strongly aroused and the mind is perplexed. As a result the prescribed limits may easily be overstepped without moral guilt. It is a mistake to consider only the emotions of fear and fright in the actions of self-defense. Often just anger and rage over the attempt of a very mean and shameful attack (e.g., rape) may be the chief emotional incentive to vigorous counteraction.

MORALITY OF WAR

A just war is the self-defense of a nation against foreign encroachments upon its vital conditions of existence. To these belong not only the integrity of the nation's territory but all material and moral goods which are necessary for its well-being and the attainment of the purposes of the state. War is for the whole nation what self-defense is for the individual, the last and unavoidable means of self-preservation.

War is practically as old as humanity. The farther back we go in the history of man the more frequently we find wars among the many groups of clans and tribes. We may almost say that, as youth exercises itself in plays and games, so man in his early history exercised himself in war and strife. Long periods of war were unknown. Life was a continual warfare in which some groups grew stronger while others disappeared, being absorbed by those gaining ascendance. With the increase of civilization and culture there awoke also a more definite desire for peace, because the development of science and art as well as the crafts and trade require security from violent disturbance. Hence war, if it came, had to be kept away from a nation's frontiers or confined to the outlying districts, as was the case with the expanding empire of the Romans.

With the coming of philosophy and the discussion of ethical problems, the morality of war began to be questioned and debated. The Stoics were outspoken opponents of war without being able to prevent it. Christianity brought most important considerations in favor of peace; yet the Christian nations have continued waging war from the beginning until now. What is worse, while in former ages the theaters of war were greatly restricted, e.g., involving a few cities, they have gradually spread over large areas and are now likely to involve whole continents, even the entire globe. Whether, in view of this fearful prospect, a time will ever come when there will be no war, is very doubtful. Mankind is so divided into races and nations and spheres of interest that cooperation to the point of unselfish concessions in every dispute is as far from probable as the power of cultural and religious education to turn all individuals into saints.

In theory, every war which cannot be explained as self-defense must be called unjust. But, as in individual self-defense the defensive action in order to be effective may precede in time the actual aggression, so it may be in the total defense of a nation. Self-defense in war does not exclude the opening of hostilities. Moreover, preparation for war is not immoral. Lack of armament may invite attack from without, while mutual fear based on parity of armed strength acts as a wholesome check. As in private life so in the life of nations there may occur a gradual accumulation of grievances leading to a tension which almost automatically results in war. Both sides may see justice in their cause and ask for God's assistance. The contemporaries of modern wars will hardly ever have sufficient information at the time needed to pass an absolutely clear judgment on the righteousness of their own country's cause. Hence the view of the old moral theologians that a soldier could fight only in a just war is of no practical value nowadays. Formerly, when famous generals enlisted mercenaries in their armies wherever they could obtain them, a man would indeed have the obligation of examining the justice of the cause for which he was going to fight. Practically, however, the soldier's chief considerations were the leader's fame and the prospect of booty and pay. All this is now changed, except in the case of volunteers from neutral countries. But this exception is an important one in view of what has taken place in recent years. On the other hand, help to a nation forced to wage a war of self-defense is morally permitted similarly to the right of assistance to an individual in like circumstances. The principle of non-intervention is not observed in the actual conduct of the nations and is condemned by the Church.

The manner of warfare and the conceptions as to what practices are permissible have not been the same with all peoples and at all times. In general, it was the idea of former ages that it was morally licit to exterminate the enemy completely, and so war used to be extremely cruel and merciless. Not only in the actual battle was the enemy wounded and killed, but also the non-combatants and all their possessions fell into the hands of the victors and were liable to be destroyed. The prisoners were killed or mutilated, frequently their eyesight was destroyed. Such were the wars that we read of in the earliest pagan records, the Old Testament, and the history of the Middle Ages. Slavery, which deprived men of all freedom and degraded them to the status of chattels and merchandise, was born of this sort of warfare and was regarded as an institution of kindness in view of the conqueror's right to kill the vanquished. Superstition also contributed to the development of cruel and abominable war practices. Cannibalism may have originated thus, for as the superstitious belief that by eating certain parts of the dead enemy his power was passed on to the victor led to the eating of human flesh, it may have induced a more general desire for this sort of food. Also the wearing of certain parts of the dead enemy's body as a trophy, e.g., the scalp, is of the same superstitious origin. The fact that the aborigines of the newly discovered continents were pagans was sufficient reason for certain Christian conquerors to hunt them like wild game and claim their land and property.

Any search of Sacred Scripture for material either to justify or condemn war as such is wasted time. We may say that Sacred Scripture speaks of war as something that actually occurs in human society and draws from it various illustrations of the soul's combat against the enemies of faith and morals. Man's life on earth is called a warfare; the helmet, shield, and sword are mentioned as symbols of Christian virtues. If anything at all can be deduced from the Sacred Scripture, it is that war as a last resort is as licit as private self-defense. In considering the cautioning words of some of the Fathers of the Church, we must not forget that the state of their time was yet pagan, and that soldiering even in time of peace required participation in many pagan ceremonies which involved conflicts of conscience. Fidelity and obedience to the civil authorities and the defense of the Empire were always regarded as compatible with Christian principles. Not only have the Roman soldiers given to the Church many saints, they also spread the faith among the peoples of the border provinces.

As the Christian faith spread through Europe and became the officially recognized religion, the Church was able to exert her influence for the promotion of peace. The first efforts were directed toward the mitigation of the barbaric methods of warfare and the establishment of certain periods of armistice (*treuga Dei*). Clerics were freed from the obligation of military service and forbidden to carry arms. In emergencies, as, e.g., when the Huns ravaged the lands, monks would also take up armed defense, and the medieval monasteries were at the same time fortresses where in time of war the peasantry could find refuge. All other advances toward more humane aims and practices of war are due to the influence of the Christian spirit and the civilization based on it.

Distinction was made between the armed combatants who waged the war and the unarmed population of the enemy country. Complete extermination of the opponent was no longer regarded as the aim of the war, but the breaking of his power to resist. Consequently the disarmed prisoners were now treated with consideration and respect. At the same time, it is true, the human mind searched for new and more effective weapons. Despite this fact, the wars did not become more cruel or sanguinary than they were at the time when the soldiers faced each other armed with swords and cudgels. One of the bloodiest battles in history, with casualties that were not equaled until the First World War, was the slaughter of the Cimbri and Teutons at Vercellae in 101 B.C.

In the development of rules of international law after the Thirty Years War, several norms were set forth for the mitigation of the horrors of war. The spreading of poison and of disease germs in the enemy country as well as the use of poisoned arrows and the like, was outlawed. The provisions that savage fighters should not be employed against the armies of civilized countries, and that it should be unlawful to incite the enemy soldiers and civilians to insurrection and the breaking of their oath of allegiance, read almost like fairy tales in view of the events of the last few wars. An institution of real blessing was the Convention of Geneva, suggested by the physician Henry Dunart and adopted by a number of nations on August 22, 1864. According to this agreement, such non-combatants as clergymen, physicians, and nurses were to be protected from hostile action. Their identity was to be indicated by a ribbon with the sign of a red cross on a white background. Similarly all places used for the care of wounded soldiers were to be marked with the emblem of the red cross and thereby exempted from attack, requisitioning, or contributions by the enemy.

Unfortunately the provisions of the Geneva Convention lose a great deal of their value because the use of long-range fire arms, aiming as they do at unseen targets, makes frequent accidental harm to the Red Cross personnel and stations more and more unavoidable. In other respects, too, the modern weapons seem to bring back the former type of war, now known as total war, in which the whole population of warring countries is subjected to attacks by food blockade and bombardment from the air. Actually, the war industry in the interior of the country is equally as important for the successful waging of war as the army that uses the weapons at the front. We have here new problems which former moralists did not see. If the aim of war is to break the opponent's power and will of resistance, then the all-out attacks on military objectives seem to accomplish this purpose the more quickly and so spare those involved from prolonged suffering. Are attacks on civilian workers who are *immediately* and *directly* producing war material less moral than the maiming and killing of persons bearing arms? Should the powerful death-dealing weapons of our time be called more brutal than those of past ages? It would be rash to make categorical statements while a war is raging, which almost daily presents new and startling developments. It must suffice to suggest such points of view as will help us to rethink our Catholic principles in the light of our present conditions. Even if we cannot offer definite solutions, the serious reflection on these grave problems will give us a wisdom that refrains from emotional excesses and exerts a similar wholesome influence on the faithful. The wounding and killing of human beings are acts of crude violence, and these are the essential acts of war. In view of the wide extent of modern wars the total number of casualties suffered in them are proportionately not greater than in former wars.

There is no judge on earth who can decide all international disputes and enforce his decisions. But decisions must be reached and enforced here. The idea of the League of Nations for the settlement of all international litigations is an attractive ideal but well-nigh impossible of realization, and the idea of an international army to force recalcitrant states to accept its arbitrations is altogether utopian. Powerful states would never submit, and the action of the international army would only start a large-scale war of opposite coalitions. Things being in this world as they are, there will ever and again arise situations in which nations will have to resort to the last means of obtaining justice, and this means among men on this earth is no other than physical violence, war.

In view of its extremely destructive consequences, war must be regarded as a cruel and brutal enterprise, a most regrettable situation and an unfortunately necessary evil to be resorted to only for the gravest of reasons. We may, therefore, never place deeds of war above other great accomplishments; no nation should esteem the glories of war higher than the works of peace. An old Chinese sage has truly said: The most glorious victory is but the glowing reflection of a conflagration.

War is able to endanger and destroy moral values, and to build up and create them. In examining this aspect of war, we must distinguish between men in the battle front and men at home. The combatants are torn away from their accustomed surroundings and way of life. Evidently the individual's reaction to so important a change will vary according to his moral training and maturity. Although everyone's conscience as the immediate norm of good and bad is on the whole the same, the differences in the training and character strength of the individuals make for differences in their conduct. Furthermore, soldiers are obliged to carry out the acts of war, i.e., they are directed to destroy or damage as far as possible the enemy's life, possessions, shelter, and the like; all of which actions run directly counter to the soldier's education and conduct in peace.

Countless soldiers at first feel an inner revulsion and horror at these things, while later their sensibilities become somewhat blunted and indifferent. But there are also those in whom an evil demon awakes, and they do with garish delight what should be only a sad and tragic necessity. To this must be added the lack of time for calm deliberation; the paralyzing influence of the continual efforts at deceiving the enemy; often the powerful pressure of prolonged over-exertion and privation under which scarcely the last spark of self-preservation may continue to glow.

The moral strength of the soldier at the front is thus exposed to severe tests. He often runs the risk of acting without moral reflection, simply on the spur of the moment, i.e., in a manner unworthy of a rational being. His obligation to destroy values of all kinds, natural and cultural, of human lives and works, may so dispose him that he does not respect these things even where the laws of war require him to do so. The soldier is in danger of lapsing into a state of moral crudeness and cruelty, or at least indifference to suffering and destruction. The extreme of the privations may lead to the other extreme of uncontrolled indulgence and debauchery as a sort of compensation, whenever an occasion for this presents itself.

On the other hand, war is also a time which calls forth in many individuals unsuspected heroism for deeds of courage, generosity, and charity. This is all the more true now when the best sons of the nation go out for the defense of their fatherland. And the spirit of dutiful obedience, sacrifice, and comradeship bear beautiful fruit. Those at home are likewise inwardly chastened and turn to serious reflections, to sacrifices and works of mercy.

The good influences of war are in great danger of giving way to impatience, resentment, and revolt if the strain of war lasts too long. Every war is an evil, every war of long duration is an unspeakably great misfortune. Nevertheless, undesirable though war may be, that pacificism which has but words of cynism for genuine patriotism is no moral virtue, but a sign of moral degeneracy.

PATRIOTISM AS A MORAL VIRTUE

The concept of patriotism is so controversial a subject that we cannot begin its discussion with a definition. The theoretical study of the question of patriotism is not very old. But Paulsen's view, that the terms "patriot" and "patriotism" were first used by the Jacobins of the French Revolution, is incorrect. Apart from the numerous passages in the ancient classics, the first extensive study of this subject is found in Bolingbroke's *Spirit of Patriotism* (1735). Patriotism as a conscious human attitude is as old as history and was always regarded as a high moral good, although its concrete forms have not always been the same but differed rather widely. The chief obstacle preventing modern students from understanding the problem seems to be their unwillingness to admit any other patriotism but that applying to the modern national state. Thus it was possible to deny patriotism to the ancient Greeks, or to the French at the time of absolute monarchy, to the Prussians under Frederick the Great, to the Tyrolese under Andreas Hofer, and to the Austrians under the Hapsburgs as late as our own time. For the same reason it was said that patriotism was only a matter of sentiment devoid of every logical and ethical element; a historical necessity, but never a moral good and virtue.

There have been those who held a rather negative view of patriotism. Epicurus ridiculed the men of earlier times who had exerted themselves for their fatherland, and declared that death for one's country is ridiculous. He rejected participation in public affairs as an obstacle to personal happiness; but so did the Stoics of that time seek release from all such bonds, the home of the wise man being the whole world (cosmopolitanism). The attitude of the Stoics of the second century B.C. was, however, different. Cosmopolitanism has never faded entirely out of philosophy. In recent times it was especially Schopenhauer who looked upon national character as a defect, and explained national consciousness as individual shallowness. He was followed by Nietzsche, who speaks of national mania. His aversion to all things German, which went to grotesque extremes, was partly the result of his pathological development, his personal experiences—he thought the French understood him better than the Germans—as well as his unrestricted individualism which refused all social submission. "The state is the coldest of the cold monsters. Coldly comes this lie from its mouth: I am the state, I am the people. It is a bait for you, the all too many; a devilish trick has been invented for many, a horse of death clanging with the ornament of divine honors; yes, this death has been invented for many, praising itself as life." For Tolstoi patriotism is only a "stupid, immoral, unnatural, and dangerous sentiment." Fear of war drew this sharp condemnation of patriotism from Tolstoi, for a vigorous national consciousness will always be ready to defend the fatherland with all resources of physical power.

In his inaugural address at the University of Turin in 1851, Stanislao Mancini, professor of international law, analyzed the concept of patriotism and found the following elements. According to him, the most important and decisive element is a *moral* one, i.e., the consciousness of solidarity and the will to solidarity. Next comes a *geographic* element, the country; then a *national* one, the language; an *ethnological* one, the race; a *religious* one, the religion and denomination; a *traditional* one, the customs, usage, historical memories; a *juridical* one, the laws and social institutions; and a *political* element, the constitution.

The bond which ties the hearts of men to their fatherland is formed of many strands, and is, no doubt, strongest where all of these are present. But it is wrong to admit patriotism only where this is the case. The moral element of conscious and active solidarity may be of decisive importance. In point of time, it is not the first, but originates naturally where the other important factors concur. The basis of all patriotism is the love of home. The love of home is as old as humanity—whether people feel it consciously or not. Since youth is most impressionable, the love of home is naturally associated with the places and persons of one's early memories. With the clarity and force with which youthful impressions are received and persist, man comprehends and preserves the impressions of the local scene of his early life. The countryside, the parental home with those living there, the locality with its buildings, the companions of school and play, the customs and usages, the food, the amusements and celebrations: all these are seen as a whole and idealized by memory.

Homer remarks that the smoke at home is brighter than the light abroad. The love of home becomes the strongest of all sentiments when, because of separation, it turns into secret longing which, like a gnawing flame, is able to consume a person's vitality. As chaplain of military prisons and hospitals, the writer often had occasion to meet persons in fits of wild rage, who could not be controlled in any way by the attendants. Spiritual consolation would have been spurned. But these persons were always calmed and their hearts opened to further influence by conversations about their home-places and their youth. To the natural love of home there comes, in the years of mature age, the conscious will and striving to preserve and further the community of fellow nationals as circumscribed by the national boundaries and constitution, and the readiness to do so even at the price of personal sacrifices. Thus we arrive at the definition of patriotism as the "sacrificial devotion to country as defined by boundary line and constitution."

The frontiers need not embrace all persons of the same race and language, or such persons exclusively; in other words, there can exist true patriotism which is only local. This sort of patriotism we find in the history of classical Greece. True, Homer sings of the campaign of all Greeks against Troy. But no Greek poet of the historical time speaks of Greece as a common fatherland, there being as many fatherlands as there were separate city states. On the epitaph in honor of the Athenians who died in the battle of Tanagra, it is even said that they died for their fatherland against the Hellenes. Some of the other factors of patriotism mentioned above were not altogether lacking. There existed a certain feeling of the community of all Greeks against the barbarians, which during the Persian wars led to a short union by way of alliance. Religion produced the national sanctuaries of Olympia and Delphi. At the end of Greek independence, Socrates speaks even of a common fatherland of all Hellenes, but offended Greek sentiment by assigning the hegemony to the Macedonians.

Hellenism introduced Greek ways and the Greek language

into many lands, but it did not create the idea of a common Greek fatherland. Nevertheless we cannot accept the view of those who would deny to the ancient Greeks true patriotism. Their patriotism was simply not that of the modern unified race or nation. We find the same local or particular patriotism all through history up to very modern times. A most instructive example is the rising of the Tyrolese against the Bavarian rule imposed on them by Napoleon. The Bavarians and the Tyrolese are practically identical in race, language, religion, and customs.

The history of patriotism in ancient Rome is peculiar. We see there a pronounced political concept of patriotism. Rome is originally the *patria*, and no bond, legendary or historical, unites the various Italic tribes. The sword of Rome conquers the Italic soil and organizes the conquered territory into a political state. Rome remains *patria* but grants citizenship to the subdued tribes, so that gradually all become citizens of Rome. The local patriotism of Rome expands so that Cicero could say that everyone had two fatherlands, the one, the place of his birth (*unam naturae*), the other the ruling city (*alteram civitatis*). Thus a politico-national unity of Italy is achieved—*italum robur* (Horace)—Rome being no longer a geographic, but a political and national, concept. This political Rome combined with Greek thought and created a new uniform culture. Philosophy under the influence of Rome describes again the ideal state in which justice is the fundamental virtue. While Plato's ideal state was a utopian fiction, the cosmopolitan Stoics could point to the universal Rome as the realization of their philosophical ideal of the state. Active participation in the life of the state was a duty imposed by reason. The feeling of Roman patriotism reached its height at the time of Octavianus Augustus, who was honored with the title *pater patriae*. Love of the fatherland was consciously and purposely cultivated and sung of by the poets. The celebration of such heroes as Cato the Younger and of the Roman victories was regarded as a source of patriotic feeling. Virgil, indeed, praises the beauties of the land of Italy, but the far-flung Empire is regarded as the fatherland to which

Horace applies the famous words: *dulce et decorum est pro patria mori*. At this time a new power entered into the world, the Christian religion, and it is of special interest to see its attitude toward patriotism.

Christ passed over many earthly questions with silence. Concerning the state, however, He declared definitely: "Render unto Caesar the things that are Caesar's." The fulfillment of duties toward the state, not from fear, but as a matter of conscience, was taught insistently especially by St. Paul. But this did not imply patriotism, which indeed was made very hard for the Christians. Public offices, because of the many pagan ceremonies connected with them, were almost impossible for Christians. To this difficulty was added the increasing moral corruption which could not but fill the Christians with detestation of the world and the Roman Empire, in which they saw the embodiment of Satan's reign. The Christians felt that they had "no abiding city" in the world. The thought of transforming the world with the penetrating leaven of the divine word was as yet foreign to their mind. They were looking for the second advent of Christ and the end of the world. They could not love the kingdom of Satan. It would, therefore, be useless to search for manifestations of patriotism in early Christian literature. Minucius Felix, Lactantius, Tertullian, and Cyprian declined all participation of Christians in the Roman state. In Origen and Clement of Alexandria we find a few traces of a more generous view. Gradually a different attitude about military service gained ground. In the army we find many Christians, who thus helped to spread the faith in distant regions. St. Jerome, with words of sincere patriotism, laments the sack of Rome.

St. Augustine in a few places speaks directly of the virtue of patriotism. He reckons patriotism among the virtues that deserve our recognition also in the pagans, but that acquire much greater value in connection with supernatural religion. He defends military service and war when, in a letter to Nectarius, he expresses his satisfaction over the latter's devoted work for the state, and declares that he agrees with his view that there is no limit to one's services for the state. It is true that the *patria* here in question is not the Roman Empire, but the home town of Nectarius. However, it was not the fault of Christianity that patriotism in the Roman Empire became again local. The Roman state had become too large. The geographic unit, which is an indispensable factor in an effective concept of fatherland, had become unlimited and therefore intangible and unreal. The political unit, too, faded more into a mere fiction. The remembrance of the past glory was not strong enough to keep alive national consciousness in that great medley of races. The Empire decayed and was ripe for its destruction.

After the migration of the nations, the Germans contributed a new factor which in itself has no relation to patriotism, but still exerted a certain influence on its rebirth in Europe: i.e., vassal loyalty. Vassalage was a purely juridical institution, without reference to country, nation, or race. And yet there sprang from it a new type of patriotism which we may call dynastic. It was a mixture of love of home and vassal loyalty. Originally war between the vassals of the same feudal lord was not considered incompatible with their common status. As the authority and power of the crown increased, such occurrences began to be regarded as unbecoming. Philip the Fair of France took the first decisive step by forbidding his vassals all private feuds during a war of the crown. Thus originated a feeling of solidarity among the vassals of the crown, from which developed a dynastic patriotism focused on the ruling family. To be subjects of the same king was felt as a common bond. France of Louis XIV, and Prussia of Frederick the Great, are outstanding examples of dynastic patriotism.

The fiction of the old Roman Empire which had been revived in the Middle Ages was then even less apt to inspire patriotism than at the time of the last Roman emperors. The Christian religion was the force uniting Europe against Islam, its common enemy. Still the seeds of national unification were sown in the Middle Ages and took root despite the strong cosmopolitan trends of the time. Especially in the crusades we find episodes of rivalries and national particularism. At the big international universities the students formed colleges along national lines.

The growth of national consciousness did not progress equally in all countries. As early as the thirteenth century, the policy of the French kings was not only dynastic, but deliberately anti-German, i.e., French and national, while the German kings and emperors continued their international policies. The capture of the German imperial banner by Philip Augustus of France in the battle of Bouvines, and the beheading of the last Hohenstaufen by the Anjous in Naples, were the chief factors in the formation of a strong French national consciousness. In Italy the rivalry for lucrative public offices was the factor that stirred up a hatred of foreigners and thus prepared the ground for the development of national feeling. The same result is to be noted in all countries from the gradual appearance of national literatures. Humanism, although essentially international, helped the growth of national patriotism by recalling the great patriots of Greece and Rome, and aroused the desire for national greatness and independence. Germany's national unity was for a long time crushed by religious wars of a most ruthless kind. In France the step from dynastic to national patriotism was soon taken. In Bishop Fénelon's writings we find for the first time a distinction between the duties toward the king and those toward the country, the latter of which he considers higher and more important than the former.

The spirit of liberty which allows every citizen participation in the functions of the government was quick in producing a perfect kind of constitutional patriotism in England, Switzerland, and the United States. The citizens of these countries are proud of their liberal institutions and are actively interested in the problems of local and national administration. Anyone is considered a good citizen who disinterestedly works for the good of the country. There exists even the duty of opposition on the part of the minority in parliament. This is certainly a generous and mature view. The patriotism of Switzerland is of special interest because it is free from all desire for conquest but rejoices in the harmonious cooperation of several races during their centuries-old independence. The power of the American patriotism, which is capable of assimilating the immigrants from many countries and turning them into real Americans, seems to come out of the proud consciousness of being a new and successful way of government unburdened by the historical survivals of the European nations.

This short sketch may help us to understand the problems involved in patriotism. Unfortunately the name *patriot* is often abused, as when a political party arrogates that name to itself and denounces its honest opponents as unpatriotic. History shows that the most sanguinary revolutionists as well as hidebound reactionaries have called themselves patriots. This is a deplorable perversion.

Patriotism is not an inborn but an acquired quality of man, fostered by upbringing and education. The love of home is its natural basis. The first hostile feeling against strangers does not deserve to be called patriotism. Only the possession of a certain culture, together with the conscious appreciation of this culture and the common will to support and defend it by a politically circumscribed unit of population, is patriotism. It is altogether a mistake to call patriotism a sentiment. Patriotism is a virtue of the will which includes the cheerful and devoted readiness to serve the political community even at the cost of personal submission and sacrifice.

Such an attitude gives rise to as many demands and duties as lie in the nature of devoted attachment. We can mention only a few of them. In order to work for the welfare of the political community, a person must be a useful member of society, first of all by competent and faithful work in his profession or state of life. True patriotism requires service, not empty words, not pretense or demagoguery. But besides positive professional contributions to the common welfare, direct interest in the issues of public life is necessary. It is often tragic to find honest and competent persons who shun political activity. This is a cause of great harm to the state and to society. For if the good and capable citizens keep aloof, the field of politics becomes the prey of the charlatans and demagogues, and among the blind the magpie is king.

True patriotism demands also the help of all for the preservation of the foundation and source of the common good. Unfortunately great numbers of people regard as essential the accumulation of wealth and the advance of science and technical achievements, to the neglect of sound morality and religion. And yet Christ's words, "What doth it profit a man if he gain the whole world and suffer the loss of his own soul?" apply also to the welfare of nations. Finally, patriotism requires the defense of the state against the forces of disintegration, revolution, and sedition, and the maintenance of its honorable independence among the nations. In view of the imperfection of all human institutions, the inevitable last resort in such matters is war. In the sacrifice of one's life for one's country patriotism shows itself in its purest splendor. Life is the highest and dearest of all temporal goods, and is guarded by the powerful natural instinct of self-preservation. Hence the surrender of life in the interest of one's country is an incomparable moral act; it is and remains a powerful test of natural morality.

What is the relation between patriotism and cosmopolitanism? Does cosmopolitanism not seem to be the final stage of the ever-widening and more civilized conception of the fatherland? Does the Christian religion, which certainly is cosmopolitan, not demand this solution? In fact, history shows that the fatherlands of the different nations are continuously expanding. Furthermore, the areas of war have grown wider. War between cities is now quite impossible. Instead of war between individual nations, there have appeared wars between great alliances. Are we on the eve of a European United States, to be followed by a United States of the world?

By cosmopolitanism we mean an international attitude, a feeling of human solidarity above and beyond all barriers and boundaries. A certain measure of this feeling of community with mankind as a whole is found in every educated person, while uncivilized races lack it to the extent that even their ideas of God and religion are nationally limited, and consequently they believe in deities of the tribe, the clan, and the family. Advanced civilization allows us to recognize common human traits despite the differences of race, language, and customs. The cosmopolitan outlook can be attained only by philosophical abstraction. It is never derived from the general consciousness or nature of man, nor is it the result of a general development of human outlook, but originates in the minds of a few thinkers.

Religion, too, brings a certain cosmopolitanism to the attention of man as a doctrine from without. Christianity conceives of the whole creation and of mankind as a unit: all men are created in the image of God, destined for the same supernatural end, and subject to the same order of morality and grace. Here the religious doctrine ends. It does not do away with the differences of race on earth, but bridges them over on the plane of religion. The earthly varieties of nations are lifted up into the kingdom of Christ, who has said: "My kingdom is not of this world." Where religion has to assume concrete forms of organization, the national differences make themselves felt. The Catholic Church is the largest supranational religious organization, and many concrete details of her ecclesiastical life differ in the various countries. In these national concessions is seen the wisdom of the central authority of the Church.

The political cosmopolitanism, on the other hand, by political agitation and without regard for the economic and cultural conditions of the various nations, denies all differences and attempts to obscure them under a cloud of international literature. There is something unreal about this sort of cosmopolitanism. It is not born from the soul of the people, but is worked out at the desk with the artificial light of the study lamp. The modern means of communication have indeed brought the nations closer together and promoted the exchange of ideas. Thus many obstacles to international understanding have been removed or are likely to disappear in the future. But for any future civilization to obliterate the differences of race and language is as impossible as the leveling of the mountains and valleys of the earth into a uniform landscape. The peoples of the future will belong to different races and countries and will bear in their minds and bodies the marks of these differences. And it must be thus. All valuable literature and art has a national character, and this element is what gives it its universal worth. Whatever is primarily international is insipid and worthless, for the original and real must first be ground to atoms before it can be forced into an international mold of universal sameness.

Besides the simple condemnation of patriotism, we find in history several attempts to substitute higher and worldwide organizations. In the French Revolution the idea of the fatherland took on an entirely constitutional content according to which every like-minded person was regarded as a fellow citizen of the French people. A number of foreigners, e.g., Wilberforce, Washington, Klopstock, Schiller, Kosciusko, were made honorary citizens of France. In contrast to this harmless make-believe, from which the French soon recovered, a new and dangerous cosmopolitan abstraction has arisen: the disease of communism. Love of fatherland and people is to be replaced by love of the proletarian class. Membership in this class is supposed to become the bond of world-wide solidarity: "Proletarians of the world, unite!"

Communism advocates the union of the masses of all countries; of people who neither know each other nor are able to meet, except by delegates to congresses; of people who share nothing as a common possession except their belief that they belong to a uniform proletariat, which in fact differs profoundly from one country to another. The masses of all countries and centers of industry are asked to unite although they are one another's competitors in the world market and are disliked as immigrants. The masses of all countries are asked to feel as proletarians although by the attainment of their aims they cease to be such, and when in control of the government they must assume responsibility for all, not only for the proletarians. Communism is the most senseless but also most accursed form of cosmopolitanism which keeps people from positive cooperation with their fellow citizens.

There is an urgent need for recognizing the real value of patriotism. The law of Christian charity says: "Thou shalt love thy neighbor as thyself." And there is the moral axiom: charity begins at home. This applies also to nations. Only a nation of full value can contribute toward the peace and progress of all other nations and must, therefore, first realize its own self by working out its own welfare, security, and character. What well-ordered love of self is for the individual, patriotism is in the life of the nation. To keep it alive and guide its right development is a truly worthy task.

DUELING

In the societies of primitive culture, every individual, especially every man as the head of his family, was the guardian of his own life, honor, and possessions and also of those of his wife and children. Thus the ideas of ability and nobility were identical with the esteem for bodily strength and skill in the use of weapons. This mentality, in turn, fostered pleasure in combat and even a desire for it. The mental faculties began to be appreciated, at first by the recognition of the practical value of shrewdness. Division of labor as the result of the growth of society furthered the better appreciation of the works of the mind and cultural goods. The defense of self, of the family and its possessions, could be entrusted to society and its rulers for safekeeping and vindication. Weak members of society had no other means of defense. But large and small social groups and nations continued to settle their litigations by resorting to the use of arms. In those struggles, token combats of individuals representing the opposing groups occasionally took place. Besides historical instances (e.g., David and Goliath), we have notable examples in literature, such as Menelaus and Paris in the Iliad, the Horatii and the Curiatii in early Roman legend. Later the institution of private armed contests disappeared among the

Romans, and the writers who report such from foreign nations (Scipio and Tacitus on Spain and Germany respectively) call them a barbaric custom.

Among the Germans and Celts dueling served especially the purpose of judicial decision. This practice, as all trials by way of ordeals, is based on the belief that God will always sustain the just cause in such contests. Needless to say, this idea of God and divine Providence is not in agreement with Christian theology. Despite frequent condemnations and prohibitions by provincial councils, the Church succeeded only very slowly in abolishing or limiting this practice. We have an interesting story about the conflict between the Roman and the Mozarabic rites in Spain: the question was decided by a liturgical tournament duel between two champions, in which the knight representing the Roman rite was victorious.

The fact that religious precepts alone do not bring about moral reform in the face of inveterate racial or social customs or views, is well illustrated by the history of dueling. The knights did not at any time submit to the prohibition of their tournaments, neither did the privileged social classes at any time renounce their supposed right to settle quarrels and infractions of personal honor by private armed contest. The carrying of weapons was a jealously guarded privilege of the upper social classes. Since attendance at the university was possible only for the sons of the nobility and wealthy families of the city, university students were also privileged to carry weapons as a part of their regular dress. It is only natural that persons who go about armed should make use of their weapon on occasions. Quarrels by such privileged persons, which were fought to the end on the spot, arose in great number out of their social life. Social slights and discourtesies or interest in women, after copious indulgence of alcoholic drink, offered the usual excuses for quarreling. Thus the efforts to prevent the immediate violent settlement of these affairs by dilatory agreements and formalities must be regarded as curbs on this savage custom. This is the origin of the present-day duel, i.e., the private and prearranged combat of two individuals with deadly weapons. The right to such combat is claimed by those who consider themselves the spiritual heirs of the former privileged classes, i.e., military officers and university students. They form the class of those who are considered capable of rendering satisfaction especially in matters of personal honor. Dueling of this sort is in general restricted to the European continent. In the Latin countries it has become largely a formality which involves no real risk, whereas in Germany often it is still a genuine combat with tragic consequences. As a rule, pistols are used instead of swords.

The advocates of dueling advance a number of reasons to justify their position. They say that the realization that discourtesies may entail the duty of satisfaction at the risk of one's life helps to develop a more refined sense for the honor due to others and thus fosters respect, politeness, and self-restraint in social intercourse. Good breeding is indeed desirable for the whole of society, not only for the caste of officers and students. A proof that this goal can be reached by other methods is the English gentleman. It is a matter of national pride for the Englishman to show himself restrained, respectful, and helpful in his social contacts. National pride is certainly a higher motive and bears fruit in wider circles of society than the fear of the possibility of a duel. Besides, good manners should be for the Christian the fruit of genuine respect and charity for his neighbor.

Another argument asserts that the legal protection of a person's honor is unsatisfactory, even illusory, because the defense lawyers are legally in a position to air before the public the whole private life of the offended persons, entirely irrelevant matters, often odiously construed and distorted. This procedure results in fresh insults instead of satisfaction. Moreover, the penalties, mostly small fines, for gross insults or even slanders, are said to be too lenient. Many offenders gladly pay this price for socially damaging or ruining a disliked person. These complaints are largely true to the facts, but they do not justify dueling. Society as a whole, not merely a small privileged coterie, is entitled to the proper protection of personal honor.

Higher penalties, in very serious cases even imprisonment, must be imposed, and the freedom of the defense to heap fresh insult on the offended person must be carefully eliminated.

Again it is argued that the readiness to accept the challenge of a duel fosters personal courage and is an effective preparation for the solemn duty of defending one's country. Undoubtedly courage is required in presenting oneself for a duel. But it must also be emphasized that such challenges often are accepted against the dictates of the person's conscience and better judgment; their acceptance is the result of human respect and moral duress born of the fear of losing social prestige and even their livelihood. Sometimes participants have to be dragged to the place of dueling in a condition which is the very opposite of courage. That a person's attitude toward dueling has anything to do with courage on the battlefield is being refuted by the facts of contemporary warfare.

Honor is indeed a great good; but we must distinguish between internal and external honor. Only the external honor can be touched by an offender. Internal honor, which is ours before God and our conscience, is beyond the reach of attack. We must not forget that duels are sometimes demanded on the slightest provocations and under the influence of alcohol. No proportion exists between such trifles and the risk of one's life with the consequent loss to family and country. Since no one believes any longer that victory in duel necessarily attends the just cause, no atonement for the offense and no restitution of honor is accomplished. The only concession made to the wronged party is the privilege of firing the first shot. If both shots miss their intended victim, the offender leaves without retraction, apology, or reconciliation. If, as often happens, the wronged party is hit, he may die or become a lifelong cripple and lose his position in addition to the insult, while the offender may enjoy his health and obtain higher honors and lucrative positions.

A most serious objection to dueling concerns the civil authority which allows this form of self-vindication. In all civilized countries the defense of a person's honor is taken from the hands of the individual and entrusted to the public authority. A few groups, however, have continued to claim for their members the right to settle offenses against their honor by armed combat. Although the law of no country makes allowance for such a privilege, it has been and still is the practice of a number of governments to tacitly permit it. While the members of the other social classes are severely punished for killing or inflicting serious bodily harm, persons who in dueling commit the same crimes are subject to honorable military arrest which, as a rule, is greatly shortened through pardon. Here is an inequality of the law which is certain to undermine the general public's respect for the law.

On the one hand, the state forbids dueling; on the other hand, officers of the armed forces are obliged to accept the challenge under pain of being removed from their position and rank. Even Catholic rulers of former times, who professed to be faithful sons of the Church and assumed such titles as Apostolic Majesty and Most Christian King, cannot escape the charge of having maintained this inconsistent and immoral situation. There can be no doubt that dueling would have ceased in the academic circles if it had been abolished in the army. The Church has consistently condemned dueling. But the privileged classes, as long as they existed, gave little heed to the Church's prohibition. The ecclesiastical penalty inflicted on a person participating in any way in duels is excommunication, and refusal of ecclesiastical burial to those who die in duels.

The students' duels take place as part of the routine ritual of certain students' organizations in German universities, without personal animosity. They are fought in the manner of fencing matches, in which certain parts of the body—the cutting of which might cause serious results—are carefully protected. As a rule, these combats inflict rather harmless wounds in the face; the scars remain for life and are, so to speak, a badge of membership in the upper classes of society. Under suitable precautions, there is less danger here than in boxing or bull fights. Formerly they were not forbidden by the Church. Upon inquiries from Germany, they have been put in the same class with real duels, and the same penalties have been applied to them. In fact, they may justly be regarded as a preparation for dueling and a continuation of the spirit underlying it.

VII

PUNISHMENTS

CAPITAL PUNISHMENT

MANKIND holds to the general conviction that capital punishment is justified under certain conditions. The determination of the reasons underlying this conviction is, however, a difficult problem, especially in view of the opposition to capital punishment by legists and governments and in view of the reintroduction of this form of punishment after its abolition in certain countries. In studying the problem we must free ourselves from all accustomed notions, e.g., that premeditated murder justifies the death penalty, for history shows this to be the least frequent connection of crime and penalty.

We may be more or less correct in denying that the justice of the death penalty can be derived from its purpose alone. Still it must be possible to bring into harmony the justice and nature of the punishment, without excluding other decisive considerations. We should bear in mind that the application of the death penalty preceded rational reflection and scientific analysis about it, and that the views of its nature and purpose vary in different places and times. The idea of punishment presupposes moral responsibility. The criminal, it is felt, violates the established order of the law and society and therefore cannot be left undisturbed in the company of the law-abiding. He must feel that a breach of the law entails enough discomfort to nullify the profit sought by the evil deed. The fundamental idea is, then, retribution and atonement, and the publicity of the punishment results in the feeling of satisfaction that amends have been made for the violation of the right order.

If the person directly harmed by the breach of the right order inflicts the punishment in the name of society, this act becomes an act of revenge and is exposed to the grave danger of excess. Hence, early in the course of history, society deprived the interested ones of the right to exact the penalty and assigned this right to disinterested officials. Thus authority was entrusted with the guardianship of right and the execution of punishment. These two tasks in combination have given to the meaning of punishment the further character of a means of deterring potential criminals from evil deeds. The idea of atonement and that of deterrent are apt to suggest the necessity of capital punishment for the safeguarding of the common good. The question of what crimes deserve the death penalty has received various answers in the course of mankind's history. Almost every offense has, at some time and in some place, been subject to this extreme penalty.

A few factors which, under different circumstances, rendered crimes subject to the death penalty may be mentioned here. Where the state and the whole organization of society were based on religious conceptions, as was the case from the most ancient times through the Christian Middle Ages up to the modern era, offenses against the Divinity and the respective religious cult were considered deserving of the death penalty. All acts endangering the security of the state, e.g., treason, desertion, cowardice, sedition, and disobedience to the authorities, were likewise considered so. Where the sovereignty of the state centered in the person of the ruler, violation of his person or possessions belonged to the same category of crimes. Where the family was regarded united with the head in solidarity, it appeared just to inflict the death penalty on all members of the family if the father became guilty of a crime worthy of death. Among the Indo-European races with whom the caste system was strongly developed, it happened that the same crimes were punished with death in the case of low caste persons or slaves, but only with a fine in the case of persons of high caste. In emergencies, when the life or welfare of nations or certain groups may be gravely endangered by deeds which ordinarily are of less consequence, the death penalty has always been more freely applied.

The death penalty has been demanded in cases where, according to the conviction of society, the public good can be safeguarded against violations only by the death of the offender. With the ancient Babylonians it was a crime worthy of death to steal anything from the royal palace, to help a slave of the king to escape, and for persons in the service of a temple to visit a public tavern. In Zoroaster's code, the eating of ritually unclean food, the torturing of animals, and the giving of water to women with fever while confined in childbirth, were crimes punishable by death. The laws of Draco, which are so notorious for their severity, decreed the death penalty for the drinking of unmixed wine, for idleness, deception of the people by exaggerated election campaign promises, and public drunkenness of the highest officers of the state.

We need not wonder that under such conditions the number of death sentences was very high in times past. The Roman Emperor Caracalla is said to have passed 20,000 death sentences in a single year, A.D. 212. The Roman law was severe especially in its provisions for the defense of the state and the official religion. One law threatening the death penalty may be mentioned particularly because it later served as the basis for the persecution of the Christians. Caesar's law (*lex Iulia de maiestate*) decreed the death penalty for all violations of the state's sovereignty. Later this law was interpreted as extending to any refusal to recognize the quasi-divine character of the emperor (*numen imperatoris*). Its severity consisted not only in the threat of death but also in the exclusion of appeal from any judge's decision in this matter. Thus it was possible for local judges to send to death great masses of persons on the charge of *crimen laesae maiestatis*.

For the free Germans the crimes punishable with death were cowardice, treason, and sexual perversity. Murder was a matter of private revenge. In some parts of Europe, private revenge has existed up to recent years with the tacit permission of the governments concerned. Revenge was not only a right but a sacred duty incumbent on the family of the slain. The original motive for this institution is not mere revenge but the religious sacrifice of the murderer, without which the soul of the slain would not find rest. But since each new killing called for such revenge, there would have been no end of murder unless another way of settling these feuds was found. Sheer necessity brought about the custom of satisfying for the guilt of murder by the payment of a certain fine to the family of the slain. Thus we find the anomalous situation that, among peoples who inflicted the death penalty for a number of lesser crimes, murder was considered atoned for by the easy penalty of a fine.

In conformity with the general view of early mankind concerning the relation between harmful deeds and personal responsibility, anyone who happened to kill another was considered a murderer regardless of his intention. Aristotle was the first to set forth the principle that the penalty for harmful acts was to be measured, not according to the external event, but according to the intention. Unfortunately this insight was lost again in the confusion of the migration of the nations, with the result that in the penitential books and the court practice of the early Middle Ages the external deed and the internal guilt are again treated as unquestioned correlatives.

Of special importance for us is the attitude of Sacred Scripture and the Church. The Old Testament recognizes the death penalty for many crimes. We need not wonder at this fact since, in the transition of the Jews from nomadic existence to the more stable forms of life, only a very simple method of dealing with culprits was effective, and in older times the value of human life was not highly esteemed. Various sins of impurity and offenses against the monotheistic religion were punished with death; private revenge for murder was approved. If in reading the Old Testament we seem to feel that the death penalty is of positive divine institution, we must remember that the civil and divine legislation cannot be separated there and that these laws are for us *leges mortuae*. Christ made no explicit pronouncement on this subject. The interpretation of Christ's strong condemnation of scandal as an approval of the death penalty is not less erroneous than the interpretation of His attitude to the adulterous woman as an indication of His opposition to the death penalty. However, St. Paul's word that the civil authority carries the sword not in vain (Rom. 13:4), may rightly be accepted as an acknowledgment of the state's right to inflict the penalties used at that time, among which was the death penalty.

The Fathers of the Church are also silent on the matter. Christians are merely admonished not to attend the gladiatorial combats and public executions. St. Augustine insists that heretics should not be condemned to death; his reason is that they should have an opportunity to amend. Several bishops protested against the execution of the Donatist bishop Priscillian at Trier. With the increasing confusion and crudeness that was caused by the migration of the nations, the penalties for misdeeds became very harsh. The Church sought to mitigate the extreme severity by protecting the lives of many condemned persons who took refuge in the sacred places, and also by having the penalties altered into ecclesiastical penances, pilgrimages, pious foundations, and later by participation in the crusades. The saintly King Wenceslaus I of Bohemia (d. 1235) was, in sharp contrast to the ways of his time, an outstanding and unique opponent of the death penalty. But his reign was short and thus had no appreciable effect on the existing conditions. The unity of the Christian faith as the religion of the state was regarded as so great a public good that, with the rise of heresies, their originators and leaders were prosecuted and condemned to death by the authority of the state. When the doctrine of state absolutism prevailed, the life of the subjects was placed at the discretion of the highest state authority which mostly resided in the absolute prince, who recognized no superior on earth. This doctrine reached its height in the sixteenth century and culminated in the practice, fortunately applied only in Italy, of condemning persons to death secretly and entrusting their execution to hired murderers.

The controversies about the moral justification of the death penalty revolve around the purposes to be attained by it. As long as we uphold the freedom of the will, the first purpose must be retributive punishment. It is true that the physical punitive act cannot equal the moral act of delinquency. However, the public authority has only physical means at its disposal, and since the state, as the highest earthly authority, must be able to enforce its provisions for peace and order here on earth, we must be content with this imperfection. The death penalty is also employed as a deterrent. The objection is true, that no one can demonstrate in exact figures this effect of the death penalty and that gruesome public executions have blunted the sensibilities of the people and induced cruelty. But the cruelties of former times have also other causes, and nobody now advocates public executions. Furthermore, the knowledge that certain crimes which are intended for personal gain, are punished with death whereby the advantages sought are most definitely defeated, is doubtlessly a check on the propensities of criminally inclined persons. Even life terms in penal institutions leave some hope. Moreover, the natural fear of death, especially violent death, deters potential criminals from carrying out their evil designs. The Roman Catechism (chap. 6, quest. 4) speaks of the justice of the death penalty: *ut audacia et iniuriae supliciis repressa tuta sit hominum vita.*

Another purpose of the penalty is the culprit's amendment. The time for this is, indeed, shortened by the execution; but the certainty of imminent death is so overpowering an experience that many criminals are moved to seek their peace with God, whereas many imprisoned criminals never think of reforming. For the rest, amendment cannot be the first and foremost purpose of legal punishment, which is, as a rule, inflicted upon adult persons who are beyond the age of education.

The idea of the death penalty as a last means of defense for society against crime, appeals to those who do not recognize the validity of the other arguments. However, this latter argument accomplishes no more than the others, especially if we consider the element of moderation which must be proportioned to the need of self-defense. If we deny the value of capital punishment as a deterrent, it is hard to see why a well-ordered state should not be able to cope with crime by the penalty of life imprisonment. There is more weight in the argument that in certain cases the authority of the state must show its full supremacy against the criminal. For some goods of society are so essential that their absolute security must be assured even by the real threat of the supreme penalty.

The question of the manner in which capital punishment is inflicted is of minor importance. In early and less advanced societies, the severe law of strict proportion between crime and penalty (*lex talionis*) prevailed: an eye for an eye, and a tooth for a tooth. With the ancient Egyptians, who needed tremendous quantities of slave labor for their gigantic constructions, we find for the first time the commutation of the death penalty into forced labor for life. Up to recent times, executions were mostly very cruel; at present the quickest and least painful methods are being used. The agony suffered by condemned persons is the consequence of their sure knowledge of the approaching death.

Much as the right of the state to inflict capital punishment may be upheld, there exists no corresponding obligation of the state to make use of it. Governments may renounce the use of it completely or whenever such a change of policy may appear useful. Especially Christian governments will be inclined to do so, thus reflecting the divine attribute of mercy according to the words of Sacred Scripture: "As I live, saith the Lord God, I desire not the death of the wicked, but that the wicked turn from his way, and live" (Ezech. 33:11).

Not much need be said about the formerly controverted question, whether the Church possessed the *ius gladii* and thus had the right to decree the death penalty. Evidently the Church may do this when, in default of the state's authority, the Church vicariously fulfills the latter's tasks until civil authority is again able to function. However, we are here speak-

ing of the Church as a religious institution. Christ explicitly
declared that His kingdom was not of this world and refused to
invoke the means of defense used by the rulers of the earthly
society. The Church exists in the world but forms no part of
it. Its work is the spread of the Gospel, which is a message of
love and mercy. Just as Christ did not cast a stone upon the
adulterous woman, though He did not approve her sin, so
must His servants be the ministers of holiness and mercy.
Where society is endangered by bad example and false doctrine, the evildoers must be excluded (excommunicated), as
St. Paul excommunicated a sinner in Corinth; but there must
remain the possibility of a reconciliation for the repentant sinner. As late an author as Gratian (d. about 1160), the classic
compiler and interpreter of canon law, stated: "The Church
has only the spiritual sword; her task is not to kill, but to give
life." At the time of the Protestant Revolt, when the Protes-
tants (Calvin and England) invoked the powers of the state
in the settlement of religious disputes, there were also those
who claimed for the Church and the Pope the right to pass the
sentence of death (*tamquam in imperante et jubente*), which
was to be carried out by the state (*tamquam in exequente et
moto ab alio*).

The argument derived from the parable of the good seed
and the cockle in favor of the *ius gladii* of the Church, is an
unfortunate one because this parable forbids the tearing up of
the cockle until the final judgment by God. Suarez and other
theologians vigorously opposed the theory of the *ius gladii*,
which is upheld by hardly any theologian at present. The
prosecution, in former times, of heretics by the state, which
called upon the Church to render an official decision about the
orthodoxy of the accused, is a different thing. In those times
heretics were also enemies of the established social and civil
order. They knew that their opposition to the accepted state
religion would not be permitted. If they wished their innova-
tions to become permanent or even to replace the old religious
order, they had to assume more or less the role of political

revolutionaries, or at least make certain political claims. Most of the heresies that were repressed by the power of the state were in many respects diametrically opposed to the most vital concerns of natural society, even apart from theological considerations. These facts explain the intimate connection between religious and political revolutionary movements in former centuries. Sporadically movements of this kind appear here and there even now, e.g., the Mormons and at present Jehovah's Witnesses. Generally, however, in civilized countries religion has outgrown these extraneous excesses and serves as a wholesome moral force in the life of society, even though the number of heresies in theological matters is legion. But since these regard the spiritual and otherworldly concerns of men, civil toleration is possible and must be granted.

OTHER PENALTIES

If the state has the right to inflict the death penalty, it must possess also the right to impose lesser penalties for smaller infractions of the law in order to preserve and restore the balance of the social order. Equilibrium and balance are an essential condition of life in all its forms and hence must be found also in the life of society. It is a requirement of social self-preservation that disturbances of justice, which assigns to all their due, shall be removed and order be restored by the authority of the state. This is accomplished only by depriving the evildoer of some right and good which he must sacrifice, as it were, that the loss of equilibrium of the social order be restored. Thus the idea of reward and punishment enters as a factor into the life of society. The general reward of law-abiding persons is the enjoyment of the things that derive from the good order of society. For exceptional contributions to the welfare of society, there exist everywhere special rewards. The questions of punishment naturally require more attention on the part of society.

For us at present imprisonment comes first to mind when

we think of legal punishment. This was not always so. For thousands of years the commonly accepted penalty consisted of pains or mutilations inflicted on the body. These were often designed to penalize those parts of the body which had been used in the performance of the wrong. We consider such justice barbaric, although we must remark that several atrocious instruments of torture exhibited in some places have been proved to be not genuine, e.g., the so-called "iron virgin of Nuremberg." As a general punishment, imprisonment would have been hardly possible in former times. Imprisonment was preferred only when there was fear that the inflicting of the death penalty or some bodily punishment would invite serious reprisals by powerful persons. Captives were also held imprisoned as hostages or for the purposes of exchange or ransom. The prisons were mostly places of horror and led the incarcerated to a slow death. Usually the jailers were demoralized persons who added to the hardships of the prisoners, or relieved their condition, even to the point of gaiety and debauchery, in return for rich bribes. John Howard, an English philanthropist, exposed the evils of the old prison system in his book, *The State Prisons in England and Wales,* published in 1777, and thus started a movement which led to the modern prison reform.

From the eighteenth century on, practically all civilized countries abolished bodily punishments and, except for capital crimes, retained the penalties of imprisonment and fine. Although fines are keenly felt, especially when they are so high as to put the one fined into a definitely lower social class, still they are not regarded as sufficient punishment for more serious breaches of the law. We need not set forth the whole modern penal system, its merits and defects. It will always be a problem of practical administration to combine the severity and equality of the law for all with equity and leniency in individual cases. There will always be successes and failures. We should note that the many improvements of the penal system designed to ameliorate the sufferings of the convicts and to effect their rehabilitation in society, are very costly. Expenses for this cause have to be kept within limits, especially if they curtail the expenses of the state for other worthy causes in favor of the law-abiding citizens.

No human law can do justice to the great variety of situations in life, and there will always be occasion for a deeper penetration and reinterpretation of the legal principles. The freedom of the will, however, must always be recognized as the ultimate basis for all such discussions. But as early as the time of ancient Greece, the problem of crime has been considered from a different viewpoint. For instance, Plato wrote that crime was a disease that ought to be healed if possible; otherwise the affected person should be destroyed. In an interesting draft of a new Italian code, which has not yet become law, the conception of the criminal has been replaced by that of a harmful being. This view entails a new attitude of the state toward its non-social members. It appears to eliminate or at least to overlook the factor of the freedom of the will.

We cannot share the view that man is so lacking in freedom as to be without responsibility for his actions. However, the intensive psychological and medical study of criminals suggests that many of them should be regarded as a source of harm rather than as criminals. Our attitude toward simply harmful beings is different now from what it was centuries ago, when the moral estimation of a misdeed depended mostly on the external act. In the Middle Ages there were court actions even against animals. We are amused when we think that, in past times, intelligent persons seriously arraigned mice and vermin at the bar and condemned them in a ceremonious court procedure.

But this matter has a serious side. It shows that within a few centuries the moral and legal conceptions of the same people may be turned into its opposite. We see how much the human mind is liable to be distorted and weakened. If criminals are but irresponsible sources of social harm, their treatment will have to be different from that of responsible culprits. We are convinced that irrational animals which are destructive of the things we desire, may be killed and exterminated. If this principle were applied to all who have come in conflict with the law, they would not fare very well. The only alternative would be lifelong confinement because amendment could not be expected. This would bring no alleviation to most prisoners and would only tend to increase their number to staggering figures. Fortunately we know that most of those who at some time came in conflict with the law are responsible persons capable of amendment and actually do amend in a quite commendable manner. For those who refuse to reform or who are "born criminals," segregation from society has been provided by existing laws.

EDUCATION AND PUNISHMENT

All violations of right order are motivated by a desire for subjective gain regardless of its justice and propriety. Punishment is designed to teach the practical and painful lesson that disturbance of the right order does not pay. Young persons are in greater danger of yielding to temptations because they lack the rational insight and experience of the more mature persons and, much more than these, are exposed to the incitements of natural urges and instincts and to the attractions of the moment. Hence it is useful and morally permissible to have young people experience the necessary connection of guilt and atonement in an unmistakable manner. This is the purpose of punishment, especially corporal punishment, in education.

The punishment of the young also has the character of atonement, but is likewise intended as a deterrent and a stimulant for amendment. The painful experience remains in the memory as a serious reminder that influences future willful decisions. In the fostering of moral restraint from evil, lies the educative value of punishment. The psychological experience of punishment must therefore receive our chief attention. Although fear acts as a moral restraint, its effectiveness is limited. Fear is also the least worthy motive and is not suf-

ficient to produce the fruit of a mature moral character. Therefore punishment must be so meted out as to focus the attention
of the young on the idea of atonement and satisfaction.

Corporal punishment in the process of education and instruction is as old as mankind; and the simpler the people, the
more natural was its use as a factor in raising and teaching
the young. The Old Testament recommendation of the frequent use of the rod is in strict agreement with the ancient
pedagogical wisdom. In some languages there are even words
denoting instruction and beating which derive from the same
roots. With the Spartans corporal punishment served also the
purpose of hardening the young bodies for later endurance
and making them accustomed to pain. This situation prevailed
up to rather recent years. It was all the more natural since
adults also had to submit to corporal punishment without any
loss of honor. Even the soldiers, who are trained to honorable
performance of their duty, were formerly subject to such
treatment; in Germany up to 1848, in Austria up to 1866.

In the nineteenth century, psychology began rather in-
tensely to study the child. Childhood and youth were regarded
not merely as necessary stages of transition toward maturity,
but as distinct periods of life in their own right. Movements
were set afoot to replace corporal punishment, which was de-
nounced as crude and cruel, with purely spiritual influences.
An exaggerated psychiatry tried to ferret out all sorts of
disreputable motives and suspicious complexes both in the
teacher and in the pupil. Thus anyone advocating the reten-
tion of corporal punishment in the school laid himself open to
the suspicion of shameful perversions. The exaggerations of
this attitude are now gradually being recognized. We would
not wish to bring back into the schoolroom the severe punishments of former centuries, which made life indeed miserable
for many students. But even in those circumstances youth did
not allow its humor to be crushed. Each year in May the
students went out into the forest with gay singing to fetch

the rods, and this custom (*virgatum ire*) is the origin of the May celebrations in the schools. Also on All Fools' Day and other occasions this serious aspect of their school life was a traditional butt of jesting.

On the whole, we must agree that the former practice of corporal punishment was too severe. Wherever the purpose of atonement and amendment can be achieved by spiritual means, we gladly renounce the use of physical force. This view is not against the spirit of Sacred Scripture. The scriptural praise of severity in education implies the duty of parents and educators to break the evil will and obstinacy of children by all appropriate means, corporal punishment not excluded. Actually the latter has certain advantages: its performance is simple, and its meaning is easily understood. The humiliation and subjection involved can be an object lesson in the recognition of the authority of God, who has established the right order and human superiors. Of course, the older the children are, the less use should be made of corporal punishment. But there is no fixed rule. For wanton disturbance of class discipline and obdurate laziness, there may be but one remedy, the rod.

Corporal punishment must never be cruel, nor should it be mere make-believe. Young people have a healthy feeling for just severity and are not prone to be ensnared by the multifarious complexes of psychiatry. But the incident must always be closed with the end of the punishment. In the case of nervous children, one must be very careful. If they are to be punished, the penalty must be administered quickly, calmly, and without ostentation. There should never be a scene. Corporal punishment should never be meted out in a fit of anger or rage. Still a certain indignation at the misdeed must be manifest, for mere mechanical punishment which seems to lack all moral interest appears to young people as an injustice. Hence it is not commendable to have corporal punishment administered by servants. Mass scenes and theatrical setting should be avoided because they may cause permanent psychic damage

in those punished and in onlookers who are psychically abnormal. It is easier to retain corporal punishment than to bring
it back where it has been abolished. But harsh times may require it to be introduced again.

VIII

Duties Toward the Unborn Life

The destruction of unborn life by artificial miscarriage and other methods is discussed, from both the medical and the moral viewpoint, in Ruland, *Pastoral Medicine*. The number of abortions is very high and beyond the reach of statistics. Hence we cannot judge how many lives are nipped in the bud every year. In former years it was possible to appraise the morality of a community by the number of births out of wedlock. Everybody knows today that the small number of such births is no longer an indication of high morality.

Christian ethics condemns every form of direct killing of unborn life and thereby sets up a powerful protection of life. This inexorable position, the only guaranty for the completely defenseless life, is weakened as soon as exceptions are permitted. No reason, however plausible, can ever justify death-dealing interference with budding life. In many countries the laws do not go to such lengths, but admit the so-called indications for the interruption of pregnancy. It has been rightly pointed out that legal enactments cannot extend to the whole field of ethics, but must consider only those common interests which demand a public penalty in case of violation. However, the secular legislation in this matter cannot be justified as a result of the restrictions inherent in the nature of the state, but constitutes a departure from sound ethics.

STERILIZATION

The destruction of the power of generation by the removal or extirpation of the germ glands is as old as human history.

For a discussion of the medical aspect of the problem, consult Ruland, *Pastoral Medicine*. Catholic moral theology always condemned castration just as any other mutilation, except as a penalty for crime. In one point, however, the Church was not quite consistent, and some theologians were rather lenient. Since women were not admitted to church choirs, it often happened, especially in Italy, that the parents of boys with beautiful voices thought to preserve the youthful voices through castration in order to secure for them permanent lucrative positions. The Church, though never approving of this practice, admitted those singers to the choirs. Thus this practice was no doubt favored, as can be seen from the fact that Pius X's rigorous exclusion of such singers has caused castrations to cease. Most moralists had always rejected this procedure of parents on the ground that the preservation of a beautiful youthful voice was not a sufficient reason for doing what nature forbids. Others considered it permissible because beautiful song contributed to the public welfare (*bono communi*), and these persons were compensated for their bodily loss by well-paid positions. Even St. Alphonsus cites this lenient view as probable (*ut laudes Domini suavius canantur*) but considers the opposite opinion more probable. The Church did well in returning to an attitude which avoids even the semblance of tolerating or approving this abuse.

Our knowledge about these matters no longer permits us to obtain male soprano singers at the expense of the harm consequent upon castration. We have in mind not only the disturbances caused by the absence of the internal secretion in the biological and psychological constitution of man, but also the lasting feeling of inferiority forcibly inflicted upon the person so incapacitated.

Castration can be considered morally permissible only as an operation required for the cure of diseases. Much more important at the present time is another interference with the organs of generation, known as sterilization. Medical science has developed a method of birth prevention which does not require castration but prevents the union of the male seed and the female ovum. This is done by ligating or severing the seminal ducts of the male and by interrupting the tubes through which the female ovum passes into the uterus. The activity of the germ glands that produce the hormones necessary for the continuance of the sexual character and the undisturbed metabolism of the body, is thus preserved. The undesired secondary effects of castration are avoided. The *potentia coeundi* continues, and is even increased in the beginning. This fact has long been known as a result of the experience gained from operations on the prostate gland and has been partially used in Steinach's operation of rejuvenation. However, the claims that the *potentia coeundi* will be permanently preserved may yet prove a mistake. With the permanent occlusion of the outlets, the germ glands will sooner or later begin to atrophy.

Sterilization has become so important for us now because several states have enacted laws aimed at preventing the hereditary transmission of diseases and deterioration of the race by the use of this artificial method of sterilization. That bodily properties, both good and bad, are being propagated by heredity, was known at all times, and this knowledge was used for thousands of years in the breeding of animals and plants. As regards man, these things were certainly not entirely neglected, nevertheless they were largely overlooked, probably because the factors of education and environment were over-estimated and the mental diseases were looked upon as punishments for personal guilt or as the result of demoniac influences. Another reason was probably the lack of long-range observation as regards man with his longer span of life than that of animals, which could be observed for several generations. Furthermore, considerable hesitation was felt in applying to the human body the Mendelian laws of heredity, because this appeared incompatible with the dignity of man. The writer has in his possession an article from the science supplement of a leading Catholic paper of a little over forty years ago, which indignantly and under clear pleading with the authority of the Church rejects the idea of applying Mendel's laws to the bodily side of man's nature. Today we know that they do apply.

The spiritual, immortal soul is essentially different from the physical organism, but in this life all its activities express themselves through its corporal instrument as the organist shows his art by means of the organ, so that apparently the soul is not able to express itself at all or can do so only in a discordant manner if the body is defective. This does not mean that a robust body is an absolute requirement for a person in order that he may possess high spiritual values and mental gifts which will leave their stamp on all future civilization. A great mind may dwell in a feeble body, and a strong will may wrest great accomplishments from a sickly constitution. But these will always be exceptions. The general rule is: *mens sana in corpore sano*.

Favorable education and environment are able to arouse and cultivate good traits, but these possibilities are limited by the contingencies of heredity. Experience shows that after good beginnings some accident in later life often causes inherited defects to come to the fore; e.g., children of drunkards, taken out of their dangerous environment early in life, displayed good gifts of mind and character at first, but sometimes in later life so react that they end in alcoholism as their parents did. Heredity shows its inexorable working still more clearly as regards inborn feeblemindedness, epilepsy, St. Vitus's dance, and in the widespread diseases of schizophrenia and circular insanity. We call these disturbances mental only because they upset man's mental activity, but in reality they are diseases of the brain.

The idea that, in a certain sense, the soul is affected by the laws of heredity, not in its essence but by its contact with the body, may appear to us somewhat novel. Yet we must not therefore consider this view materialistic and mechanistic. Every age has its own task. We cannot reject the undeniable discoveries of the sciences because they force upon us new problems to be analyzed and resolved with the aid of old principles that have a direct and clear bearing on the questions under consideration. Of course the principles of Catholic ethics and the doctrinal decisions of the Church must remain our ultimate standards. Yet we are not thereby relieved of the duty to become well acquainted with the facts of present-day science and life, and to clarify their every aspect.

The progressive forces set off by new discoveries have never proceeded in an even and straight course, but have always shown irregular tendencies. So we need not wonder that the recent dynamic biological conception of life, which has passed from the places of scientific observation and theory into the mind of the masses, should rush forward to practical application that may appear hasty and immature. Let us first state, as an objective report, the view of those who advocate the artificial sterilization of the unfit; afterward we will examine the moral issue involved.

The alleged reasons in favor of sterilization are the following. Not only has the successful fight of modern medicine against epidemics as well as for the prevention and cure of disease extended the average span of human life, but psychiatry in particular has preserved the life of the insane and mentally defective for at least ten extra years with the corresponding additional possibility of propagating their own kind, a possibility amply used by those persons during the time of their permanent or temporary dismissal from custodial care. The healthy and responsible portions of the population limit the number of their children for economic and social reasons so that their families average at the most two children, whereas the diseased average three and four children. These figures are based on statistical observations in schools and other institutions. There can be no longer reasonable doubt about the hereditary transmission of feeblemindedness and insanity as well as of certain grave bodily defects. By reference to certain famous instances, it is shown that countless imbeciles and criminals stem from such unfortunate parents. E.g., in the often mentioned Kallikak family, there descended from one moronic couple, through 41 marriages, 222 children of whom 220 were feebleminded and only 2 normal.

At this rate of propagation of the mentally unfit and inferior, their number will increase to a point where the cost of caring for them will be greater than the expense for the education of the fit. Even now the number of days of hospitalization of the mentally unfit is more than half of the time spent in the care of all other types of disease. And since the science of eugenics is not supposed to limit itself to theory but to make its accomplishments available for the improvement and protection of the race, society has begun to take measures of concrete action. The fact that the very recent science of genetics has not yet produced fully certain results must not prevent us from making practical use of its findings. As a matter of fact, we must act at every stage of our knowledge; no biological measure is 100 per cent reliable. Such reliability can be obtained in no human enterprise, as we know from medicine, surgery, aviation, railroad transportation, to mention a few random illustrations. Yet we make rightful use of them, and it is their use which leads to their perfection. Such are the claims of the advocates of artificial sterilization.

Since 1920, thirteen states of the United States have introduced laws concerning sterilization. Many countries of Europe are considering similar legislation. Sweden has a law forbidding marriage to the insane and the feebleminded., Germany's law of 1933 for the prevention of hereditary diseases has attracted wide attention. It covers the following diseases: congenital feeblemindedness, schizophrenia, circular insanity, hereditary epilepsy, hereditary St. Vitus's dance, hereditary blindness and deafness, serious bodily malformation, grave alcoholism. All persons thus afflicted may be sterilized if that is requested by the person himself or by his legal guardian or by the health commissioner of the district. Medical practitioners are obliged to report patients of this type to the health commissioner under pain of fine. As to the inmates of hospitals and similar institutions, the director is empowered to file the request. The cases are to be decided by a court of one judge and two physicians. The court of appeal is similarly composed. The presence of the disease must be medically established beyond doubt. Once the court's decision is final, it must be carried out in a hospital licensed for this purpose. The operation is to be omitted in the case of those who, at their own expense, enter an institution which assumes full responsibility, and likewise of those not capable of begetting or such as, for any other reason, are permanently kept in a closed institution.

The mental defectives will scarcely feel the condition effected by this operation. As to serious alcoholics, sterilization may possibly be considered a just punishment for their recklessness and lack of self-discipline. Among the blind and deaf, however, there may be highminded persons who would regard artificial sterilization forced upon them as a serious violation of their personal integrity and suffer grievously in consequence. Now, while it is not our intention to insist much on minor defects of compulsory sterilization, we must mention some of them before viewing the matter from a higher standpoint. It is now known that the operation of sterilization is not at all as simple as some enthusiasts at first maintained. This is especially true of the operation on women. No better evidence is needed for this assertion than the fact that there exist as many as thirty different methods of this operation on the female organism, none of which gained exclusive recognition. Moreover, the treatment after the operation requires much more care and is by far more troublesome than was at first thought necessary. These defects may, of course, be lessened and perhaps eliminated with more practice.

A serious objection arises from the condition of sexuality after the operation of sterilization. After the operation the sexual urge and activity remain. But the sexual relation of sterilized persons is, from the standpoint of nature, mere sham, since its natural purpose is definitely thwarted. There does not seem to be any justification for the repeated assertion that sterilization leaves the normal sexual act unimpaired. The painted scene of a house on the stage is no house despite the illusion and despite the presence of a door through which the actors pass in and out. We have here evidently a violation of nature. Ethics must consider things in their ultimate setting where the order of nature stands out clearly; i.e., human actions are ethically good or evil in the light of ultimate principles. A small intermediate advantage cannot change the situation. An action or condition which does not meet the test of the highest norms of morality is not good and remains such regardless of some partial profit. What is not permissible under the natural law, cannot be right as a means of race improvement.

Furthermore, there is much reason to fear that the sterilized persons, precisely because they are known to be such, will constitute a grave danger to public health and morals. Extra-marital sex relations are known to be the result of unrestrained passion which disregards the natural purpose and order. Man as a rational creature is supposed to regulate his natural instincts according to the laws of morality and in the service of ethical purposes. For many passionate persons the fear of possible consequences is a check on their immorality since no method of birth prevention short of sterilization is completely certain. Sterilization offers this guaranty. It is, then, to be feared that the sterilized will become much sought partners by whom infections will be spread, and the hoped-for racial improvement will turn into its greatly increased opposite.

Lastly, it is only right to let it be known that nobody familiar with the problem deceives himself with the belief that the high aim of race improvement both as to number of births and the health of mind and body can be attained by the mere expedient of sterilizing the unfit. There is need of a general moral effort and improvement of society. This does not exclude the use of small helps so far as they are ethically admissible. But their use is liable to create a false security and so paralyze the greater forces. Many may feel satisfied that the sterilization of the unfit will soon be followed by a general improvement of society, and therefore will continue in their old ways. In reality, a profound moral change and in particular a genuine regeneration of the family are imperative.

The recent demand that the individual place the common good before his private pleasure much more than was hitherto the rule, is quite compatible with the moral principles of the Catholic Church, which never held up selfishness as a virtue, but rather has often been chided as backward in its demand of sacrifice and renunciation. The fundamental difference between the claims of the modern state and the Church lies in the Catholic teaching about the limitations of the state's power over the individual. The Christian religion admits great sacrifices of the individual for the common good, even the sacrifice of life; e.g., in recognizing the lawfulness of war and of the death penalty. St. Thomas declares explicitly (*Summa theol.*, IIa IIae, q. 47, a. 10): *bonum commune est melius quam bonum unius*. But this does not mean that the individual in every case must sacrifice his personal moral rights to the community.

In recent times the connection of the individual in the chain of the coming and going generations of men has been emphasized to an extraordinary degree. The future seems to receive more attention and to be regarded as more important than the actual present with its society of concrete men. Society with its inherent tendency of biological renewal is regarded as a higher physical organism which has claims upon the individual beyond those of the family. Galton, the founder of eugenics, gave his ideas a religious note. He explained the tendencies of eugenics as an expansion of charity to the coming generation.

Another argument of the sponsors of artificial sterilization holds that the continual degeneration of the race in consequence of the increase in the births of the unfit, creates a state of emergency which justifies interference by the civil authority. God, it is said, has left the arrangements of temporal affairs to man, who seeks to control floods and famines for the same reason. Since the individual dies while society or the people lives on, interference with the right of procreation for eugenic reasons is declared to be permissible, just as in former times cities and states forbade marriage to persons who had not sufficient income.

Before the encyclical *Casti connubii* there was also disagreement among Catholic moralists regarding the lawfulness of sterilization for eugenic reasons. The question was discussed mostly in periodicals of English-speaking countries because of the enactment of the first laws on this point in the United States. Some said that with psychopaths the sex instinct had lost its meaning and was only a relic of its normal existence. The authority of St. Thomas Aquinas was invoked, who compares insanity to impotence, and the socially harmful persons, including the insane, to creatures below the animals (*bruta animalia*). Hence defensive measures against them were said to be justified. Again the view of St. Thomas, that the purpose of the use of the sexual organs is the generation of children and their education (*finis usus genitalium membrorum est generatio et educatio prolis; De malo*, q. 15, a. 1), was alleged as a justification of sterilization in the interest of the common good, since this sort of propagating the race could not agree with the designs of God.

Even before the encyclical *Casti connubii,* other theologians held a stricter view. They argued that every man had an absolute right to the integrity of his body. The state, they said, exists for the benefit of men, but not vice versa. The organs of the body are directly related to man's personality, and the individual personality, it is said, has no other end than God. Hence only God has a direct right to interfere with the bodily integrity of man. There is no justification for putting the state in the same position with respect to the individual persons which is held by the body with respect to its separate members. It is to be left to God whether He decrees the continuation or the end of a race. Again, it was stated that it was wrong to conclude that persons unable to educate children were unjustified in begetting them, or that persons who had lost the right to use their bodily organs had also lost the right to possess them unimpaired.

Now, although not every one of these propositions needs to be called a doctrine of the Church, it is nevertheless true that the stricter view on the whole has received ecclesiastical approval. The papal encyclical of December 31, 1930, in clear and unmistakable language denies to the civil authority the power to take for eugenic reasons the faculty of begetting from the persons whose descendants are expected to be tainted with hereditary diseases. It is there pointed out that in the divine order the family is superior and more firmly established (*sanctior*) than the state. Men are born primarily, not for their time on earth, but for heaven and eternity. Any other explanation of the papal words is incorrect; hence no Catholic moral theology can teach the lawfulness of sterilization of persons suffering from hereditary disease. In answer to an inquiry (March 18, 1931), the Congregation of the Holy Office once more explicitly rejected all eugenic doctrines and measures which, in disregard of the natural, divine, and ecclesiastical laws, claim to strive for racial improvement. This was the only possible answer, for any human enterprise that disregards the natural, divine, and ecclesiastical laws, is wrong.

But this attitude of the Church is far from rejecting all eugenics. Whatever is good in the doctrine of eugenics will be preserved as will every other genuine accomplishment of science and culture. The studies in heredity throw a new light on the succession of human generations, which the great philosophers and theologians of the past did not have. The undeniable facts of biological heredity present new problems and duties to the conscience of the individual who contemplates the transmission of his inheritable biological constitution. As the papal encyclical says, we may have to dissuade many a diseased person from marrying. And a person whose conscience is alive will thereby be faced with a serious moral question which he cannot lightly dismiss.

The most important result of the explicit position of the Church is the necessity of a large-scale effort of eugenic reconstruction along moral and religious lines. The whole encyclical is a splendid document of real eugenics on the largest scale. The biological recovery of society and real racial improvement must be based on solid moral and religious regeneration. Fight against the abuse of alcohol and tobacco, fight against immorality and the consequent sexual diseases, re-establishment of purity in prenuptial life, strengthening of unity and fidelity in wedlock: such are the means and aims of Christian eugenics. If the healthy part of the population gives up artificial birth prevention, which is only the result of fear, narrow calculation, and the desire for luxuries, the percentage of the unfit will soon drop to a small number in comparison with the total population. A certain amount of imperfection and suffering is a necessary consequence of sin and cannot be banished from the world. In their humble and loving acceptance, man will grow strong in spirit, and learn and remember the true wisdom that we are not Promethean titans who can fetch from heaven the torch of the immortal flame.

IX

Special Sins Against the Lives of Others

The duty to respect the life and bodily integrity of our fellow man is violated by any act or any omission which is apt to disturb or destroy them. We need not discuss the fact that it is grievously sinful to destroy or seriously endanger the lives of others intentionally and without just reason. From the pastoral standpoint, more important is manslaughter, i.e., homicide in which responsibility is limited by certain psychological circumstances. As a rule, it is the result of a fit of rage or of panic or intoxication. These psychological disturbances involve a limitation of freedom. However, the culpable neglect of self-discipline or of precaution in the situation leading up to the criminal action may involve serious moral responsibility.

Here must be mentioned the crime of *child murder*. To the extent that an unmarried expectant mother foresees the future event as the beginning of a time of suffering and shame, there arises often an understandable despair. The certainty of the knowledge about the future, which is continually repressed by rationalizations, induces in many unmarried mothers the artificial condition of psychopathic self-deception. Under the stress of the excitement and physical pain at birth, especially if it is the first delivery, as is mostly the case, this self-delusion is liable to turn into a furious rage resulting in child murder. In such cases the benefit of mitigating circumstances cannot be denied to the unhappy woman. In other cases, however, the murder of the child is criminally planned and executed. In former times, when an unmarried woman or an obviously adulterous mother faced very serious penalties, even death, the institution of foundling homes, where secretly born children could be placed either without any knowledge as to their identity or under the protection of the professional secret, was of immense social importance which it has not yet entirely lost and probably never will lose.

The act of simply exposing a child differs little from outright murder. Another practice is more important, i.e., the giving of illegitimate children into the care of private persons for pay. The foster mothers often feel from the very outset that these children are a burden to their mothers and that their death would be a welcome relief. Besides, it is a fact of experience that the first payment for the care of the child is made at once but that subsequently the payments are less and less regular and eventually cease, sometimes with the fault of the mother and sometimes without it. The foster mother has thus a professional interest in the quick succession of new children under her care. In view of the further circumstance that practically all such children must be artificially fed, their mortality rate is very high. It is said to be 48 per cent, but statistics on this point are hard to obtain. Since under such conditions the deaths of these poor children for the most part pass unnoticed and even bring more or less advantage to the interested parties, the temptation is great to accelerate the course of nature by a little negligence in the care or a drink of brandy or the like. Some women engage in this traffic with children's lives also under the pretense of unselfish charity or under the legal form of adoption as a screen. Here, then, is an important field of pastoral vigilance, which unfortunately is full of much unpleasantness.

Special attention must be given to the problem of negligence in doing things which may easily end in "accidents" of a fatal or serious nature. As a rule, moralists treat this problem as the *voluntarium in causa*. This may easily give rise to the view that such negligence becomes culpable only when an accident actually occurs but may be overlooked as long as the negligence is favored by undeserved good fortune. In other words, there is the danger of misplacing the basis of the morality of criminal negligence from the inner human attitude, where it belongs, to the sphere of the external events. The sinfulness of the negligence is dependent on the degree of knowledge of the existing danger and the motives for omitting the necessary precautions. The number of the occasions in which we may sin through negligence against the bodily life of others increases with the progress of technical civilization which spreads its net over our whole life. We learn again that civilization does not make life easier, but creates new responsibilities.

As regards the knowledge involved in negligence, we must ask if and to what extent a person is obliged to be acquainted with certain things or situations. Those who practice professions affecting the safety of human lives are bound in conscience to possess the pertinent knowledge and abilities available at the respective time. The sin is already committed when such a person begins his practice after neglecting his training, not merely when a life has been sacrificed on account of his ignorance. The willful omission of safety devices recognized as necessary or prescribed by the authorities is sinful before any accident has occurred. The sin is the greater the baser are the motives for the omission. E.g., avarice induces more guilt than unreasonable confidence in an unreliable device or policy. The possibilities of sinful harm to the life and health of others are to be found throughout the system of our civilization: mining, agriculture, manufacture of merchandise, transportation of persons and goods, sports, the building trade, the various forms of medical service, etc. A physician, e.g., commits sin by performing, without urgent necessity, an operation for which he is not sufficiently skilled, even though the patient, because of his extraordinary strength, does not suffer serious harm from the defects such as doubling the time of narcosis required by a skilled surgeon, and the like.

Automobile traffic has become an especially great moral problem in view of the immense toll of life and of serious injuries. The driver of a motor vehicle must be sure of the good condition of his machine as well as of his knowledge of the rules to be observed and his competence in the handling of the car. Above all, the driver of a motor vehicle must not be under the influence of alcohol. Disregard of these essential requirements is always sinful, whether an accident occurs or not.

Most regrettable are the injuries to health and sometimes even deaths caused by foolish jokes and senseless wagers. Ever and again it happens that workers out of fun connect door handles and the like with charged electric wires. To touch these lightly with dry hands and with a knowledge of the situation may result only in a shock. But persons not so prepared may easily be killed. Quite unworthy of man are the frequent wagers about the consumption of extraordinary quantities of food and drink.

A wide field of offenses against the health and life of others is found in the sale of spoiled, adulterated, and short-weighted food. The motive of greed involved in these sins makes them particularly serious and hateful.

The great suffering caused by drunkards, which often leads to undernourishment and other physical harm in their families, should be an object of watchfulness on the part of the priest. Much tact and unflagging zeal are required.

The harm to the health of the members of their own families should be brought to the attention of drunkards. Similarly, it is important that acts of cruelty be prevented in the domestic circles. Such offenses often come to the attention of no one but the priest, and he should take all steps that are possible and advisable according to the nature of the case. Many troubles of this kind can now be handled efficiently through the services of the diocesan charities. Priests should, therefore, direct the persons in need of advice and help to the proper department or division in the diocesan charity office. Good advice and efficient steps by the charity offices are often worth much more than money grants which, after all, must be limited and are frequently spent without curing the evil.

EUTHANASIA

Along with the secularization of our civilization and of public life, there appear views concerning the value of human life and its protection which conflict with Christian morals. In Christian ethics, human life is sacred and may be surrendered only for the sake of higher goods. God is the master of our lives. Therefore Christian teaching condemns suicide and the violent ending of the supposedly worthless life of others. Since only gentle and painless methods of ending life are being advocated, the word "euthanasia," i.e., beautiful or easy death, has been coined.

The idea of euthanasia requires clarification as it is being used to mean the alleviation of the death struggle as well as the acceleration and direct causation of death. History shows that each of the three forms of euthanasia has been advocated and practiced at various periods and for the same reason as now, namely, on the ground of the alleged worthlessness of certain lives either for the individuals concerned or for society. But the problem of its moral justification has been just as much a point of controversial discussion. The Spartans cast their feeble children, upon their being declared such by a council of elders, into deep gorges. We do not know how many cultural values they thus destroyed. But one thing we do know, namely, that this race which was so much intent on physical fitness has left practically no trace in the history of mankind. The Spartans failed to build up a large empire and were not able to preserve their freedom any longer than the other Greek tribes. There exist even today nomadic peoples who kill their weak and old folk as hindrances in their travels. But again there are very primitive races who offer the most touching examples of care for the sick and the aged.

Man's view of death depends on his estimate of life. Whereas the Orientals, especially the western Asiatics, have an extraordinarily low appreciation of life and hence are rather impassive in the face of death, the fear of death is very great among the peoples of the West, who are more aggressive by nature and enjoy the living exercise of their powers and faculties.

For the Christian this life is merely a state of trial and wayfaring on the road to heaven. At the threshold of the next life stands death and God's judgment, deciding man's eternal salvation or reprobation. Life is thus of supreme importance for the Christian, and even more so the moment of death when wrongs in the sight of God may be righted. Hence we pray to God against sudden and unforeseen death. The Christian values the hour of his death as one of the most important and precious of his whole life, which he wishes to prepare for and live through with clear consciousness.

The advance of the technical civilization in the nineteenth century brought a materialistic view of life and an aversion to metaphysical religious thought. Men now either deny the immortality of the soul and the reality of heaven, or at least prefer a skeptical attitude as regards these truths, so as to be able not to burden the business of their earthly life with thoughts about them. Thus it has become characteristic of our time to banish and repress the thought of death. Death itself cannot be abolished, of course, but men seek to avoid the conscious experience of approaching death lest the thoughts repressed earlier in life surge forth and forcibly demand attention. For the voice of the soul may be stifled under the din of distractions, but it cannot be silenced. Thus an extreme dread of the hour of death has seized modern society, and many patients or their relatives request that the physician in no wise indicate the possibility of death, but let the dying person pass out of life in the state of unconsciousness. To make things worse, popular novelists have frightened the people with unnecessary terrors by their imaginary descriptions of death scenes which in reality are not so horrifying at all.

Grave diseases of any long duration diminish the resistance of the organism and thus most persons suffering from long and painful ailments die peacefully and without a struggle. We may recall here the peaceful death of most tubercular patients, whose end is such a contrast to the frequent fits of painful coughing and shortness of breath in the course of their illness. In other diseases the increasing weakness often dims the consciousness to such an extent that there is scarcely enough strength left for a death struggle. For the rest, a Christian who has attended to his earthly affairs and the concerns of his soul to the best of his ability need not forgo the benefit of sedatives which soothe the pain and fear which are the result of the defective functioning of vital organs. The physician may, then, administer pain-soothing, benumbing, and cramp-resolving opiates. Frequently these drugs will cause, not a shortening, but a prolongation, of life by dispelling restlessness, pain, cramps, and fears. A moderate dose of morphine has no harmful effect even on weak hearts. This sort of euthanasia, namely, the alleviation of pain during the approach of death, presents no moral problem.

Different is the question of hastening or causing death. As the materialistic attitude of modern society has produced a great fear of death, so it is also responsible for an extraordinary increase in the number of suicides. Persons who consider their own existence no longer desirable are even said to have a right to commit suicide. Attempts at suicide are not punished by law, except where these conflict with the rights of others. Here arises the question, what the physician should do when he is called to an unconscious person whose condition is the result of attempted suicide. Should he halt the development leading to death, against the will of the would-be suicide? Since suicide either is committed with deliberation, and then is gravely sinful, or is the result of some mental disturbance, there exists the Christian obligation of preventing an evil. But also physicians who are not guided by Christian ethics consider it still their natural duty to be faithful to the intentions of their profession in such cases and to save the lives of would-be suicides. Experience shows that at least a greater number of the persons so saved from death are grateful for this service and do not repeat their attempt. The writer has had some practical experience with would-be suicides and can assure those who have other views that the use of morphine does not always lead to peaceful sleep but may result in extreme excitement, especially if a lethal dose is taken.

Positive assistance in the act of suicide, desired by the person concerned, is treated quite leniently in the secular penal codes.

The best aide for such purposes is, of course, the physician. But the medical profession has signified neither the desire nor the willingness to be called upon to do this work. The literature on the subject has, however, grown extensive of late. We have been regaled with fictional descriptions of gorgeous halls in which those tired of life would, amid flowers and sweet music, inhale pleasant perfumes that result in sleep and death. The certainty of impending death would, of course, nullify completely the effect of those cheap arrangements. Medical science, no doubt, is in possession of drugs causing quick and painless death. Yet the state's toleration of the form of euthanasia just described, remains in the realm of fiction.

More serious is the propaganda of those who advocate a mild view of mercy killing or wish it to be declared legal. Even though we recognize the good intentions behind this movement, we cannot help but notice the one-sidedness of the reasons alleged. It does not seem just in a matter of such paramount importance simply to envisage a few points of immediate utility and ignore completely the wider implications and effects of mercy killing, even apart from religious considerations. We do, indeed, appreciate the pity for people in unfortunate conditions of life, which is so prominent in the literature favoring mercy killing, but we wish to point out that the subjective feeling of unhappiness is mostly far less than it is pictured. The financial advantages accruing from killing the unfortunate and helpless are likewise considerably less than they are assumed to be. But what would be the effect on society as a whole if such killing were legalized, even within definite limits?

Three classes of people are, as a rule, mentioned as possible candidates for "mercy killing": (1) those incurably diseased or wounded; (2) incurable mental defectives; (3) unconscious persons who could awake only into a life of great suffering.

Here lies the real moral problem of euthanasia. Only such as consider suicide permissible can discuss the advisability of euthanasia. For those who consider self-destruction forbidden by an elementary moral law or by the tenets of their Christian faith, euthanasia is altogether out of the question. Especially the Christian knows that he possesses his life as a good entrusted to him by God, the Master of the whole creation, and that suffering is a trial.

But even the advocates of euthanasia find it difficult rationally and convincingly to justify the fatal interference with the life of any of their fellow men. The diagnosis of a disease or wound as incurable is not always easy, so that mistakes are well within the realm of possibilities. At times even the approach of death cannot be ascertained with certainty. The absence of breathing, of the heart beat, or of the eye reflex is not a sure sign of impending death. In a number of diseases, e.g., epilepsy and diabetes, there occur states simulating death, from which the patients may return to life. What is incurable today may be curable tomorrow, so that it would be unbearable for a physician to think that he had caused the death of a single patient unnecessarily.

Some cases of disease can be diagnosed as incurable with practically 100 per cent certainty. But the lives of such patients can be rendered bearable by sedatives, large quantities of which may rightly be administered under the given circumstances, without too much regard for the harmful secondary effects since these are unintentioned, though foreseen, and justified by the proportionate good obtained. For instance, an incurable sufferer from cancer or tuberculosis may be given sufficient doses of drugs to make him feel comfortable even though this interferes with his proper nutrition and reduces his resistance against the disease.

The complaints of sick persons and their frequently voiced desire for death are mostly not the expression of a serious and permanent determination, but of a momentary mood. People in good health often do the same thing. If in such moments a physician were ready to carry out the expressed desire, everyone would be horrified and would protest that he did not mean it that way. Neither do most of the sick mean it that way.

The suffering of the sick is often misunderstood because it is supposed to be the same as with persons in full health. The weakening or complete lack of consciousness at the end of fatal diseases renders many disturbances much easier for the patients than they appear to the healthy observer. Even the difficulties of the gradually ebbing respiration, which are so upsetting for those about the deathbed, are no torture for the dying. The same applies to other phenomena of approaching death. In cases of cancer of the throat, which renders eating impossible for some time, people often say that the patient starved to death and suffered excruciating pangs of hunger; it is a matter of fact that such patients feel nausea against all food and experience no hunger.

The supposed sufferings of persons seriously injured, e.g., by traffic accidents, often impress the onlookers profoundly. But here, too, the situation is not such as to warrant a reversal of the traditional practice of saving, if possible, the lives of the injured. A physician who happens to be present without the necessary equipment cannot do much more than see to it that the injured man is brought to a hospital speedily and without unnecessary movements. He may also close large blood vessels if such have been ruptured. But he will not be able to induce painless death. A physician arriving with the necessary equipment has all the sedatives required to soothe the pains of the injured man without killing him, for in such cases the medical practice is to use drugs very freely. In many instances the person involved in an accident is unconscious and is thus saved from pain by nature itself. Moreover, the injuries are often found, upon examination, to be considerably less serious than they appeared to be at first sight. How many persons would be needlessly killed if euthanasia were permitted! No physician would wish to face the reproaches of the relatives of persons unnecessarily put to death in the first excitement.

But worst of all would be the complete collapse of men's trust in the medical profession, a loss never to be compared with the occasional small advantages deriving from euthanasia. The physician's duty is to save life. In this lies the honor and glory of his profession, with which the idea of putting incurables to death must never be associated. Even if the law should permit him to do so, a physician could never consider himself free in conscience to perform the work of an executioner. It is a common experience that the sick readily take medicines but begin to feel hesitant at intravenous injections and even refuse to allow a needed operation to be performed. Yet they know that in our hospitals everything is done to cure their ailments. With what suspicion a patient would regard the physician's needle if it were lawful for him to put supposedly incurable people to death! Few persons would venture to consult a physician. The effectiveness of the healing processes would likewise be seriously curtailed by the fears and suspicions on the part of the patients.

Equally unrealistic is the demand for the death of the incurable mental defectives as an act of mercy. In fact, few of them feel any suffering at all, and most of them, in their contentment and their wish to live, surpass the average healthy person, who has to face the difficulties and cares of life. The mental defectives are spared these experiences. It is not true, then, to say that the idiots themselves would ask for their death if they knew their condition. Neither need we think that most parents would agree to such a procedure. True, sometimes these creatures are the offspring of degenerate parents whose consent cannot be urged as a justifying reason. As a rule, other parents show special love and tenderness toward such unfortunate children of theirs. Then, too, father and mother might not agree in the matter, and it would be difficult to decide whose wish should be respected. The suggestions that public welfare boards and similar organizations, which are interested in keeping their expenses at a minimum, should be empowered to decide on the life and death of the feeble-minded in their charge, offends most crudely every sound moral feeling.

The financial advantage resulting from the killing of mental defectives is commonly overestimated. If their death should be legalized, it would have to be restricted to complete imbeciles. But of the present inmates of institutions for the feeble-minded, only 10 per cent at the most belong to that class, so that these institutions would have to be kept open even in the absence of this 10 per cent. And then, what would be the economic gain for a country with a population of about 100,000,000 if it were relieved of the expense of supporting 2,000 or 3,000 idiots? Furthermore, the sciences of medicine and psychiatry profit greatly from the study of these defectives while they live. Thus, even from a crude materialistic standpoint, the care for these unfortunates is not useless. Lastly, all confidence in these institutions would be destroyed if it ever became the practice to do away with the incurable defectives. And since no institution or official office is beyond the possibility of abuse and corruption, a plausible case might be made out against a person disliked for one reason or another and so at least a few people would become the victims of horrible crimes.

Still less intelligible is the demand to kill unconscious persons who would awake only into an existence as hopeless cripples. Obviously only victims of serious accidents can be intended. It certainly would be monstrously irresponsible simply to presume the consent of such persons to their own death. There is scarcely a person overtaken by an accident who does not feel that he has to settle some matters of his soul and of his earthly affairs. Even if only explicitly desired euthanasia were permitted, the killing of a person without any such request would be nothing short of a crime. A civilization which once reaches the point where those incurably ill in body or mind, and the unconscious victims of serious accidents are deliberately killed, is not likely to stop there. Soon will come the desire to dispose in a similar way of the aged and those regarded as useless parasites on the family and society, with the result of an almost complete lapse into a condition resembling the savagery of degenerate barbarians.

Life is man's highest earthly good; its protection must ever remain the noblest obligation of the state. Here no exception can be allowed even at the cost of a few undesirable consequences. Only the inexorable refusal of exceptions guarantees real protection and confidence. The case is similar to that of marriage and divorce. There can be no doubt that the permission of divorce outside the Catholic Church favors the origin and growth of the tragic conditions which cause the breakdown of so many marriages. The inflexible rule of the Catholic Church, which allows no remarriage while the former partner still lives, is, of course, a source of suffering to some. But their suffering redounds to the happiness of untold thousands. A superficial view may thus lead us to the belief that it would be a good thing to put incurables to death. But the sacrifice involved in their continued existence and care proves a blessing for society as a whole because of the implied assurance that the aim of the medical profession will always be to aid nature and preserve life.

Where life obviously is about to end, the physician need not counteract the course of nature. In this point the medical practice has changed a little of late. It is no longer regarded as a physician's duty to arouse, by camphor injections or other analeptics, the life which is certainly about to expire. Where such aids will help a patient to pass successfully through a crisis, the medical stimulants are in place. Such and similar changes in medical practice are possible, but no changes by which the physician would be turned from a preserver of life into a death-dealing official. Medical ethics cannot emancipate itself from the general law of morality which is grounded in human nature itself and explicitly revealed by God. Suffering, sacrifice, and death cannot be banished from the world. Their presence constitutes the tragedy of life. This tragedy cannot be avoided by obtaining a few small advantages. For the Christian, this tragedy is truly overcome: behind and above the troubles of life stands the divine figure of the Savior who has conquered suffering and death, and reaffirmed the old commandment, "Thou shalt not kill." Christian ethics allows the sacrifice of life for the sake of higher goods and at the hand of rightful authority constituted by God as the executive arm of His punitive justice. Selfish advantage is unholy and cannot justify the destruction of human life.

X

Duties Toward The Dead Body

The burial of the dead has at all times been not merely an act of practical utility but an important concern of the family, society, and religion. The study of the tombs and funeral customs of ancient races is a fruitful source of information about the cultural life of past ages.

A dead body has indeed no rights like a living person. But all the former relations of the dead person with the living world assert themselves once more as though in a last flare-up. The corpse is not a waste-product to be disposed of quickly for the sake of public hygiene, but requires reverent treatment as the remains of a former member of human society. The memory of the deceased calls for an external manifestation of the esteem and respect paid to him in his life. Besides the desire of honoring the dead, the funeral rites are intended also as a touching expression of love for the deceased. The place of religion in this is obvious. But it is a historical fact that the part of religion in the funeral rites never aimed chiefly at consoling the bereaved family and relatives. The spirits of the deceased were often dreaded by the living, and certain religious ceremonies strove to induce them not to return. In general the religious symbolism in the funerals was concerned with the relations of this life to the next.

Nature itself indicates what should be done with the dead body. Death initiates the process of its dissolution, which is grievously offensive to our sensibilities. Hence man wishes to hide from his eyes what he cannot prevent. Burying is essentially an act of hiding. Burying is the most obvious and natural way of disposing of a human corpse. The dissolution which has set in

140

according to the laws of nature and not according to our will, is left to the forces of nature. It is quite unnatural for man to hasten the body's dissolution, which he resisted with all means at his disposal a short time before. But this is done by cremation.

History tends to establish more and more convincingly the fact that burial of the dead in the ground was the oldest form of the funeral. The desire to bury at home soldiers who died in foreign lands, may have given rise to the practice of burning the corpse because it was easier to transport the ashes. Later the burning of the dead appears as the funeral of the rich because of its greater display. Cremation of the dead may also have been promoted by the religious belief that fire effected the passage to divine immortality; e.g., Hercules went to the gods through death by fire, and the phoenix rises rejuvenated from its own ashes. In Rome cremation is first seen toward the end of the republic and was practiced only by the rich. Also among the Germans cremation on the funeral pyre is later than interment and is based on a religious myth. Nowhere do we find cremation the result of ordinary practical convenience.

If the ancient funeral pyre was mainly the expression of a religious belief, it is natural that the Christian funeral should take a form which is in the best symbolic agreement with the Christian faith. Christ did not destroy but perfected the religious provisions and developments of the Old Testament. Now, the religious symbolism of fire such as the Greeks held was unknown among the Jews of biblical times. Only in exceptional cases were corpses burnt by the Jews. E.g., faithful men retrieved the bodies of Saul and his sons from the battlefield, burned them for easier transportation, and buried them under a tamarisk tree near Jabes, whence David had them transferred to the tomb of Cis (1 Kings 31:12; 2 Kings 21:12). The cremations mentioned in Amos 6:10 were sinful imitations of a pagan custom. Later kings who in various ways imitated pagan rulers may have preferred the funeral pyre. However, it is not quite certain whether the passages which seem to indicate this practice (Jer. 34:5; 2 Par. 21:19) do not refer to the burning of spices at the tombs. In 2 Par., chap. 16, the latter ceremony is clearly described; it is condemned in two passages of the Talmud.

Burial in a tomb has ever been sacred for the Christian on account of Christ's rest in the sepulcher. In the times of persecution death was for the Christian a liberation. The condition of the dead was compared to the state of repose and sleep. At that time the living were looking for the second coming of Christ so that they hardly could think of burning the body which they knew was to rise again alive. Moreover their high esteem for the body as the temple of the Holy Ghost forbade its destruction by fire, all the more so as fire was not regarded as a means of union with God, but as an element of supreme punishment. Still the Christians had no dogmatic objections to cremation of the body. The martyrs who faced execution by fire were not troubled in their minds about their participation in the general resurrection of the dead. Still, wherever possible, the early Christians provided reverent burial in the ground for their deceased brethren because its symbolism agrees better with the belief in resurrection, whereas cremation contradicts it.

Religion always seeks to express in sensible forms the spiritual content of its doctrines. So it is natural that the Church should prefer interment for the reasons just set forth. For the same reasons the Church is almost obliged to disapprove of such disposal of the dead bodies as has a symbolism opposed to its faith. Furthermore, the Christian knows that he remains united with the departed and that he can show his love by aiding them through prayer and sacrifice. Love seeks to preserve and recoils from violent destruction. Hence cremation of the dead could never seem an appropriate funeral rite except for heretics; in which case it symbolized the destruction of the danger of error and sin. Wherever Christianity spread, interment of the dead became the accepted funeral rite even against contrary customs. This situation prevailed throughout the Middle Ages, even during the Renaissance period despite its admiration for and imitation of the ancient civilization and philosophy of life.

The first attacks upon the Christian custom of burying the dead were made by men of the Enlightenment in the eighteenth century. In 1774, at Modena, Italy, a certain Scipio Pialotti published a tract favoring cremation. In 1790 a town of southern France conferred on a revolutionary citizen the honor of the funeral pyre according to the ancient Roman style and sent the ashes to the national assembly in Paris, which was greatly amazed at this peculiar gift. Still this event was not imitated even in revolutionary France. In 1822 Lord Byron caused the body of his friend, the poet Shelley, to be burned. This fact was likewise of no consequence. In 1849 Jakob Grimm spoke on the subject of cremation before the Berlin Academy of Science, although he did not believe in the possibility of reviving cremation after the centuries-old Christian tradition of burial. Nevertheless his speech marked the beginning of propaganda for cremation by individuals and societies. In 1870 Europe for the last time saw a funeral pyre when the Indian Rajah of Keljapur, who died during a visit there, was solemnly burned in Florence.

Cremations of the old kind are not only very expensive but entail so many inconveniences that they would be altogether intolerable in the countries of Western civilization. Hence a new way had to be found if cremation was to become acceptable. The chief requirement is the quick and practically complete incineration of the corpse. This is obtained by the use of a furnace constructed after the pattern of those used in the manufacture of gas. Here the body is not burned in an open fire but in an oven heated to an extremely high degree of temperature. After the invention of this device there was started a lively propaganda for cremation.[1] An important factor in the movement was opposition to the Christian religion, and the Catholic Church in particular. Freemasonry was, therefore, the principal

---

[1] The sanitary reasons that were urged against burial are discussed in Ruland, *Pastoral Medicine*.

promoter of the movement. The *Rivista Massonica* wrote in 1885: "Civil marriage takes the family from the Pope and the Church; non-religious lay instruction takes away the rising generation; the civil funerals and cremation at death will rob them of their last claims. Thus progress will soon have destroyed the Church and the papacy."

This short historical sketch shows why the Catholic Church had to take a stand against the practice of cremation. There is no reason to suppose that all who now favor cremation are positive enemies of the Christian religion. Nevertheless some of the original poison is still active in the movement. There exist now crematories in many cities of Europe and America. Perhaps one-third of all dead are being cremated where the facilities for it are available. Since in the promotion of cremation the antireligious motives are now relegated to the background, it is possible that less instructed Catholics may in good faith join societies which aim at defraying the costs of cremation. This may be the case especially in places where the bodies are not embalmed and therefore some people have a hysterical fear of being buried alive. It will then be a question of pastoral prudence to consider whether or not such persons should be left in their good faith. Perhaps the institution of cremation may become quite dissociated from its former antireligious aspect. And since cremation itself conflicts with no article of faith, it is theoretically not impossible that the Church will mitigate its law in the matter. It is also interesting that in Italy, where modern cremation and Freemasonry originated, the movement has considerably fallen off since the advent of Fascism. We see that once powerful movements are not necessarily destined to endure. They may be the fashion for a time and then disappear.

XI

Social Obligations

SOCIETY AS A NATURAL ENTITY

VARIOUS aspects of human nature and condition indicate that man is not a solitary but a social being. The fact that the human race is composed of men and women, the gift of articulate language for the exchange of thought, the individual's need of help from others, especially the dependence of the young, all point to society as the natural condition of human existence. Man and woman as husband and wife together with their children constitute the family with its common interest of self-preservation and improvement in which all must cooperate. Now, the simplest of family coherence requires an order to which the individual differences of self-interest must be subordinated. Such order demands authority and organization however primitive, from which spring the first formulations of justice and right. The man as the founder and strongest member of the family is the one most able to safeguard the existence of the family and to enforce effectively the necessary order. The founding of new families by the grown children without losing mutual contact and attachment gives rise to the clan and tribe.

From its structural point of view, society is constituted by a plurality of human beings permanently united under a common authority for the accomplishment of a common purpose. This common authority and purpose need not be explicitly recognized and formulated; it may arise naturally by the instinctive collaboration, so to speak, of many persons, as is the case in the family. A distinction is made between perfect and imperfect societies according as they are destined to provide for all the needs of their members in a comprehensive and vital sphere and possess the means for the achievement of their task, or require the assistance of other societies. The Church and the state are commonly regarded as the two perfect societies in the supernatural and natural spheres respectively. The family and all other societies depend on the Church and the state for their well-being. This distinction, however, is not above criticism, nor is it valid at all stages of cultural development. The Church alone is incontestably a perfect society because it was endowed by the divine founder with all the means for the attainment of its supernatural purpose (*Immortale Dei;* November 1, 1885). The state must divide its work for man's temporal welfare with the family, and is liable to fail in this task for reasons inherent in its very nature. On the other hand, the great patriarchal family, say at the time of Abraham (about 2000 B.C.), was a perfect society which needed no state.

The highest possible society in the temporal order is the union of tribes of the same race, language, and folkway as a nation. National consciousness is rightly called the driving power of national life. Only at a certain height of inner maturity of its historical development can a race become conscious of its own particular character and formulate its special mission in the family of nations according to its racial gifts and geographical position. A higher and more comprehensive form of political existence does not seem possible. The practical union of all human inhabitants of the globe in one uniform society appears to be an unreal abstraction. It may be real and significant only in the supranational and spiritual community of all men in religion and the Church which has supernatural interests, being indeed in the world but not of the world. For the rest, the mountains, rivers, and oceans separate mankind into many groups which, notwithstanding the basic sameness of human nature, are so formed and molded by a great variety of tangible and intangible influences as to result in distinct races with different spiritual assets and liabilities.

There have been loose associations of many national groups in the so-called world empires. But as a result of the very imperfect means of communication in former times, these separate groups lived their own racial and economic life to such an extent that they could not properly be called one state. Improvements in the modern system of communication would indeed permit a closer central organization. But this situation would bring the national differences into such close proximity that a uniform empire of the whole earth appears hardly possible. There is still less chance for a world-wide society built by the international union of social classes. Real good does come from the international collaboration of professional groups for the advancement of definite scientific projects. Quite different is the Marxian idea of the union of the proletarians of all countries. By proletarians may be meant, first, the industrial wage earners who possess no landed property; then, all whose economic position is insecure; finally, all socially discontended persons. The common denominator of all these groups is a negative factor which is an entirely inadequate basis for any positive social program, still less for the unification of international society. The grievances of the proletariat spring from defects that can be remedied only by basing the reform on the concrete realities of each country.

THE FAMILY

The most fundamental of all societies is the family because it is the original cell of all other societies. Both reason and faith teach us that the family precedes the state not only in temporal origin but also in rank, inasmuch as the rights and duties of the family are part of the natural law and require no recognition or sanction from the state for their validity. This does not mean that no positive acknowledgment of the rights and needs of the family is desired. On the contrary, the more the state protects the interests of the family, the more firmly established is its own foundation. But there can never arise a condition in which the state is justified in disregarding the family and replacing it with other and artificial institutions. In so far as the young start to be members of the wider society in the state, the civil authority has the right to make certain demands, e.g., by setting up standards in education, by aiding the family in the preparation of the children for their later part in the life of the state, or by relieving the family of such functions. Also in matters of public health, national defense, and the like, the state is entitled to certain claims, without thereby being hostile to the rights of the family.

All basic virtues of the good citizen of the state grow up naturally in the good family. There the child learns the essentially beneficent nature of society, e.g., the providing of the goods of life, the necessary security. The family is the pedagogically soundest school of cooperation, helpfulness, self-control, and respect for others even at the cost of personal sacrifice. It teaches regard for authority, the need of subordination and obedience.

MARRIAGE

History shows that the union of man and woman in marriage was everywhere surrounded with sacred ceremonies. For the Christian, marriage is a sacrament. The Christian teaching that marriage is a strictly monogamous and lifelong union is one of the strongest forces for the moral education and restoration of mankind. The good of the national society is served not only by the great number of its members but also and especially by their high moral quality. Civic virtue proves its worth much more in suffering and sacrifice than in pleasure and ease. The fidelity and perseverance demanded by Christian marriage is a source of strength also in other spheres of life.

Religion is the only source of such fidelity and perseverance. No utilitarian considerations, no ideal of population growth and service of the fatherland, can so much emphasize the high moral value and importance of marriage and the gravity of its obligations as the Christian religion accomplishes by its teaching and practice. Marriage as a sacrament makes demands and also gives the strength to fulfill them. It is, therefore, in the state's own interest to show public respect for the religious celebration of marriage.

But since marriage has also certain civic and legal effects, it is natural—and compatible with the view of the Church—that the state should require a civil registration or declaration. A law requiring that the civil act precede the Church ceremony need not be considered hostile. The state's interest in the matter is not exactly the same as that of the Church. Thus it may justly desire that the civil requirements be first satisfied in order to avoid conflicts and confusion. The modern state must be tolerant toward persons of all religious denominations and toward those without any religious beliefs. But for the sake of public order it is obliged to register the marriages which are being contracted. Hence the uniform requirement of a civil marriage ceremony is not to be roundly condemned, so long as no obstacle is placed to the fulfillment of the religious requirements.

Marriage impediments are natural facts or legal restrictions which either temporarily or permanently render the marriage contract invalid or illicit. Both the Church and the state are interested in marriage and its consequences. Since the marriage of a baptized person is a sacrament, the Church alone has the right to determine the conditions required for its validity and to declare impediments affecting the validity or licitness of marriage. The state has the right to enact laws which concern the civil consequences of valid marriage. Civil legislation, in the name of so-called social welfare, tends to encroach on the domain of the Church. The Catholic faithful need clearly to understand that the Church, as legislator with regard to the sacraments, alone has authority to regulate the marriage of Catholics.

DUTIES IN MARRIAGE

The natural bodily union is the basis of marriage. This union becomes spontaneously a union of souls except with men debased by a civilization gone awry. The union of soul is much higher and more important than that of the body, and through the sacrament of marriage is raised to the dignity of a supernatural community of parents and children. The duties of the natural order must always form the basis for the common life of married people. Permanent common residence is one of the essential and obvious obligations of married people. The choice of the residence is mostly contingent on the occupation of the breadwinner, who is usually the husband. Within certain limits there is, however, nearly always the possibility of selecting various types of houses in neighborhoods which have various advantages and disadvantages. Here husband and wife will have to come to a sensible agreement with proper regard for each other's desires. A problem of greater importance is the desire by one of the parties to emigrate. Attachment to the home country is no empty sentiment but possesses solid cultural and moral value. Again homesickness is no mere obstinacy; it affects deeply both the soul and the body and may lead to death. Emigration is, therefore, a problem on which husband and wife must freely agree. Much depends on the reasons for emigration. A married person need not consent to the other's desire to emigrate for the sake of adventure or without reasonable assurance of decent living conditions. If under such circumstances the one party insists on emigrating, the other is not obliged to follow, or may at least wait until the venture has proved satisfactory.

We may ask also whether a married person is obliged to leave the country when the other party has come into conflict with the laws at home and has fled abroad. The nature of the violation (political, criminal), its penal consequences, the character of the fugitive, the possibility of a livelihood, and so on, will have to be taken into account. The firmer the spiritual bond of love and fidelity uniting people in marriage, the more they will tend to remain together also in misfortune, even though the distress was caused by the fault of one partner.

Another essential obligation of the married state is that of rendering the marriage duty. It is most important to point out that the Christian religion, which is so often falsely accused of being hostile to wedded life, has restored the order of equal rights for husband and wife. The husband is not permitted to

come to his wife or neglect her in the fashion of Oriental polyga-
mists. St. Paul states the Christian law: "Let the husband
render the debt to his wife, and the wife also in like manner to
the husband. The wife has no power of her own body, but the
husband, and in like manner the husband also has no power of
his own body, but the wife. Defraud not one another, except perhaps by consent, for a time, that you may give yourselves to
prayer; and return together again, lest Satan tempt you for your
incontinency" (1 Cor. 7:3 ff.). Canon law admits a few exceptions. Adultery deprives the guilty party of the right to demand the marriage duty. This duty may be refused also when
the other party is drunk, insane, or afflicted with a serious con-
tagious disease. Other restrictions are demanded by the natural
law, e.g., abstention from the conjugal act some time before and
after childbirth. To do otherwise would endanger the health of
the mother,—in the case of approaching delivery it would be a
danger to the very life of mother and child—and thus be a sin
against the fifth commandment.[1]

In earlier periods of the Church sexual continence in marriage was sometimes imposed as a penance. There existed also
the custom of such abstinence on the eve of great feasts. Neither
formerly nor now is there an obligation to do so, but the practice
contains a piece of biological wisdom. We know from experience
that the children with the best physical constitution are born of
parents who practice marital chastity by sane moderation and
abstinence. However, the desire of being spared the natural
exercise of the marital right, must not be too one-sided and
exaggerated, especially not on the plea of so-called nervousness.
If the priest happens to learn of the existence of such a situation,
he should advise the person to consult a conscientious and experienced physician. Frequently this nervousness hides some
psychological aversion; sometimes a tendency to perverse sexuality, especially in the case of men. It is clear that unusually wide
differences in the ages of husband and wife prove unpleasant
in the long run. Such marriages should always be discouraged.

[1] Cf. Ruland, *Pastoral Medicine*, pp. 23 f.

It is a demand of the natural, moral, and religious order that the marriage act be performed in a manner that agrees with its natural purpose. Artificial interference with its nature and purpose is grievously sinful. This is the traditional Christian view which has again been emphasized in the encyclical letter *Casti connubii* of Pius XI. If the woman, as the passive partner in the marriage act, sincerely disapproves of its abuse which she tolerates only in the hope of its correct performance by the husband, especially after prudent admonition, she is not guilty of sin. It is hardly possible that married people in our day can honestly plead good faith concerning this great evil. Unpleasant as the subject is for the confessor, he dare not avoid appropriate questions about it when the penitent's words are a veiled hint at the presence of the evil. If the sins clearly appear to be occasional lapses from the penitent's definite efforts at moral correctness, absolution may be given. Penitents of really good will who, despite their efforts, occasionally fall into sin may usually be helped by having the doctrine of the *actus imperfecti* in marriage pointed out to them, and the essential difference between these and *onanismus coniugalis*. This can be done in two or three carefully and yet clearly worded sentences. Such advice should be given not as an encouragement of regular indulgence but as a means of relief in times of temptation when the moral fortitude is in danger of breaking down. The use of the so-called safe period in the same spirit is also permitted and may be suggested. True, the "safety" of the theory is not altogether certain but is highly probable. Information about its actual use should be given by a physician. The priest should point out to all the need of self-control and the fruitfulness of sacrifice in personal happiness and eternal reward.[2]

Although the sexual union is the basis of marriage, the latter is capable of a state far above the level of physical attraction. In fact, it is destined for such a state and often actually achieves

[2] The problem of birth control is discussed in Ruland, *Foundations of Morality*, pp. 148 f.

it. The high spiritual faculties, the cultural refinement and the supernatural elevation of human nature, if properly cultivated, will result in a spiritual union. A consequence of this Christian idea of marriage is the requirement of its absolute unity. Human existence in the form of sexual differentiation extends through the physical level into every aspect of human nature and life, even the deepest reaches of the soul and spirit; not in the sense that the whole human being can be reduced to the common and ultimate factor of male and female sexuality, but in the sense that even in the highest spiritual spheres of the mind and the emotions man and woman complement each other. This completion is basically attained, in the form prescribed by nature itself, in the lifelong wedded union of one man and one woman. The spiritual, moral, and religious character of the married state shows itself in numberless ways, calling forth, as it does, intellectual, emotional and moral efforts in the daily contacts and exchanges of husband, wife, and children. Marriage is not a stationary situation, but a condition of living growth destined to reach increasing maturity and permanent fruit in the happiness of man and the glory of the Creator.

Where marriage is impossible from necessity or is freely renounced for higher ascetical reasons, there is the danger of one-sidedness, which, however, can be overcome by spiritual striving and with the help of divine grace. Marriage being so sublime and vital a union, it can be contracted and lived in all its perfection only once. What is best and highest in us can be given only once. While from the merely biological point of view, polygamy is not absolutely incompatible with the male nature, the spiritual qualities of man agree only with the marital union of one man and one woman. The second marriage of a person whose partner has died is perfectly legitimate. In former centuries such marriages, especially of women, were looked upon as morally inferior. This view was too severe and rooted more in superstitious feeling than in ethical reasoning.

The most flagrant violation of the marriage bond is adultery.

In this point as in others, the Christian religion has restored the dignity of womanhood by condemning adultery on the part of the husband as much as that committed by the wife, in contrast to universally prevailing customs. True, the Christian ideal has never fully supplanted the old pagan view which condones the sin of the husband as a sparkling adventure and glorifies it in literature. The modern age has brought equality to women by excusing their marital infidelities likewise and making these infidelities the subject of fiction, the stage, and the screen. This unceasing flood of poison which corrupts the morals of society is the deepest cause of the degeneration and death of the nations by race suicide. This evil cannot be remedied by any eugenic legislation. Only the bulwark of a moral and religious revival, a moral consciousness rooted in the fear of God and living Christian faith, can stem this tide of immorality. We need a morality that is ready for sacrifices and self-denial and that, in the recognition of human weakness, looks to God for strength instead of boasting about autonomous moral integrity. Especially the prominent members of society must set a good example. Unfortunately the very opposite is the case. All who are concerned with the welfare, temporal and eternal, of their fellow men should work for the purification of the moral atmosphere by eliminating all influences that incite sexual immorality and destroy the sacredness of marriage through adultery.

The highest moral demand of the Christian ideal of marriage lies in its character as an indissoluble union. This inexorable position of the Church, which is so much attacked and misunderstood, is an inestimable safeguard of the dignity and sacredness of the marriage union. It forces those contemplating marriage to consider their own condition and the choice of their mate as a grave matter of lifelong consequences. On the contrary, the thought of the possibility of divorce makes for less seriousness, often for real levity, in contracting marriage. After marriage has been entered into, the knowledge of its indissolubility is a powerful help in the conquest of the difficulties which even the best are not spared. Married life is to be a ladder to heaven on which husband and wife are expected to ascend as father and mother to ever greater perfection. This ascent is not as easy as the bride and groom often dream it to be. In the grind of daily cares, every upward step is a moral task, often a toilsome one. The mind and the will must be unalterably riveted on the inescapable duties and not allowed to glance about for other apparently more desirable or convenient marital opportunities. For grave reasons the Church permits the separation of husband and wife without the right of another marriage. The divine law forbidding divorce may bring tragedy into lives of some individuals, but it prevents the ruin of many more marriages and saves many souls from the depths of uncontrolled lust. For the rest, suffering borne in the Christian spirit is a source of much merit and spiritual joy.

MAN AND WOMAN IN SOCIETY

Recent ethnological research has produced some unexpected theories the correctness of which depends on the question whether the phenomena discovered represent aboriginal conditions of mankind or later cultural regression and degeneration. There have existed primitive mother-right cultures in which the woman as the mother of the family was invested with all authority over the children and society as a whole. This is said to have come about by the—in reality extremely doubtful—ignorance of the necessary connection between sexual relations and birth. Under this type of social setup the mother was protected and was represented, not by the husband, but by her brothers. However this may be, our own social organization has been based on the predominance of the man throughout the millenniums known to history, and Sacred Scripture explicitly confirms this condition as the natural order.

Upon a purely rational consideration of the mental and physical constitution of man and woman, we are forced to conclude that the Creator assigned to the man the external representation, support, and protection of the family and society, while the task of the woman consists in the immediate care for the welfare of the family. This dual position of man and woman simply cannot be gainsaid. Women have not the same kind of rights and duties as men; they have different ones but just as important. But both possess the equal value and dignity of the human personality, which must be respected in the family and society. One of the most beautiful passages of the Old Testament proclaims the praise of the good mother of the family, where mention is made also of the beneficial influence of her work on the accomplishments of her husband and sons in public life (Prov. 31:10–31). As a matter of fact, history tells of women who, without official public position, have achieved great things in the Church and state. History is likewise witness of pernicious intrigues by scheming women, which brought ruin and destruction.

However, we would not do justice to the problem of the social position of women by viewing it merely from the viewpoint of the former housewife. Time has brought many changes. Not every girl has the opportunity to marry. There is a considerable surplus of women. Although the majority of the children born are boys, so many of them die in childhood that more girls than boys remain in the end. And the technical advances of our civilization have introduced changes in the work done by women in the house. Less than a century ago, women made many articles (e.g., soap, candles, linen, clothes) in the home, which are produced now in factories, and they did the usual housework without the mechanical helps now available. Grown-up daughters need no longer stay with mother and assist her to the extent this was formerly necessary. It is imperative, then, to provide for many young women opportunities of useful employment in the complex and variegated forms of work and professional services of our time.

In times when the privacy of the home was the general sphere of woman's activity, it was possible to limit the range of their scholastic studies. The fact that women were not taught certain subjects gave rise to the general assumption that they were incapable of learning these things. It is true that the recurring phenomenon of the monthly period is an actual handicap which, in the case of healthy women, renders professional work more burdensome but not impossible. It is also true that the refinement of our civilization and culture as well as the conditions of life in the city and in the exercise of the learned professions has led to an increase in these physiological disturbances. Thus women are at a disadvantage as compared with their male competitors in many fields.

In purely manual labor women can well compete with men, although the average woman is not physically as strong as the average man. The endurance of women workers on the farm and the amount of work done by them is ample proof of this statement. As regards intellectual and scientific work, there appears a real difference between men and women, even if they have the identical instruction and training. The girls are more ambitious and better at memorizing than the boys. Their judgment is better in matters involving emotion and intuition, but less keen in cool objective analysis and reasoning. While women surpass the men in the early stages of education, their achievements begin to fall below those of the men in the more advanced stages, especially as regards independent original work. Although women have been allowed to take up every branch of scientific study for many decades, the number of really great accomplishments by them is extremely small. On the other hand, women have proved particularly valuable in the sort of learned work that requires perseverance, conscientious attention, and willing acceptance of guidance. Greater abstinence from alcoholic beverages on the part of the women may have something to do with this.

As a matter of principle, no field of knowledge can be justly called forbidden ground for women. But since the great majority of women do marry and become mothers of families, well-balanced curriculums will have to be arranged for their higher education, to develop their womanly character, enable them to appreciate the things of culture, and prepare them for the practice of an appropriate profession, if this is desired. Prudent guidance is needed to prevent ill-considered experiments decided upon on the spur of youthful enthusiasm. Experience shows that many well-gifted young women feel greatly attracted to scientific and professional work, only to give it up after a few years in favor of marriage. The women who attain to the practice of a profession seem to be more successful in connection with charitable or other organizations and institutions rather than in private practice. The reason for this is not their lack of ability but the general attitude—perhaps unreasoned and emotional—of the public. However, this attitude is not to be roundly condemned, for the same society that does not favor certain activities of women accords them privileges and courtesies which the women themselves would not wish to lose. Where, especially in times of unemployment, women appear as competitors with men in offices and industrial positions, it would be no solution of the problem to require that the women wage earners marry and leave the positions to the men. The surplus of women would still remain. It would be a sad aberration, of course, if the wife were to seek outside employment, leaving the care of the home and the children to the husband. Such a condition was unfortunately forced upon many a family in recent years. Legislation requiring the same compensation for women workers as for men might be able to stop this abuse and prevent its return.

As persons who share the consequences of the weal and woe of the nation, able to appreciate the problems of their fellow citizens, women cannot be denied the right of participation in the political life of the state. In our time women have been given the right of suffrage, which makes them equal to men as voters. But since the moving minds in the economic, industrial, social, academic, and cultural world, from which on the whole the problems of the state result, are and will be men, it seems proper that men, not women, should occupy the executive positions in political offices. Demands by feminists in this matter are but the excessive swing of the pendulum away from that former condition in which women had no voice at all in public affairs. That women in control of the government would bring on an era of permanent peace and prosperity, is a vain hope. While women will have a more active part in the shaping of the life of society, they will not be able to attain absolute equality with men. Neither society nor their own advantage would be served by such equality.

XII

THE CHRISTIAN STATE

ORIGIN AND NATURE OF THE STATE

THE great patriarchal family was a social group capable of providing for its members all things needful for their temporal welfare. It was what is called, by an unhappy choice of terms, a perfect society. The purpose of such a society is the common good, for the attainment of which a common public authority is required. The need of authority was easily recognized by men, since they had but to transfer their experience in the family to the wider social group. Sacred Scripture and the oldest human beliefs regard public authority as divinely instituted. Man of the pre-philosophical state of thought expressed this conviction in sacred myths. The rulers appear as offspring of the gods; the lawgivers are likewise divinely guided in the writing of the political constitutions; against all violations of them or even doubts about them, terrible curses are uttered as a protection. These myths show that mankind knows nothing of "social contracts" in the formation of public authority. Social groups and states have been formed not by abstract persons stepping out of individual isolation and entering upon formal compacts. The real process was much simpler. States have grown in a living manner according to the character of the people, their culture, the nature of their historical experiences and of the territory where they settled.

St. Thomas enumerates three factors underlying the formation of the state: (1) the divine likeness of human nature, which includes the principle of central rational direction; (2) the metaphysical idea of order pervading all creation; (3) man's social disposition, which demands the acceptance of authoritative decisions for the common good. St. Augustine lays special emphasis on this last element; without it states would be merely gangs of robbers. Any progress in material well-being and also any advancement in the cultural sphere of science and art would be impossible if there were no larger social community beyond the family.

History has seen many forms of government, none of which is ordained as the only just one by the natural law or the positive divine law. The most obvious form of government of the state as the outgrowth of the great patriarchal family is the rule of one person, whether he is known by the title of chief or leader or duke or king or emperor or by any other name. In times of great danger there will always be a cry for a strong leader. St. Thomas regards monarchy, in its ideal form, as the best government, being the most perfect imitation of God's rule of the universe. Under other circumstances it is the rich landowners or merchants who obtain supreme control of the state. Again, we find the captains of the armed forces as the rulers or as the ones who set up and overthrow governments at their good pleasure. As education spreads among the masses, the people take more interest in the destinies of the state. The subjects now become citizens, who demand increasing participation in the making of laws that affect their own welfare. But, since great numbers of citizens cannot actually govern, they resort to government by representation, the representatives exercising partly an advisory function, partly legislative and executive.

At this point in the history of human society, a curious situation arises. The larger a nation is, the less chance there is for an individual's character and ability to be well known. The candidate for election must be made known by a political campaign. A small group of interested and influential persons appoints a candidate, who is then cleverly advertised and presented to the people as a desirable choice. The candidate must, of course, possess some oratorical ability, which he uses to promise a cure for all the ills afflicting the people. Various interests of an economic, political, or religious nature divide the people into op-

posing groups known as parties, each of them claiming to have
the best program. The people are now called upon to make an
intelligent choice. Thus arises the appearance of government by
the people, whereas in reality the outcome of the election is to a
very great extent the result of skillful management. Thus the
masses of the people have little or no influence on most laws that
are enacted and in fact are not the real rulers. The actual rulers
are always a few men whose identity and methods become known
sooner or later.

Racial temperaments differ in their attitude toward government. Some races have a lively interest in all public affairs, while
others desire simply to be let alone. Accordingly the former may
insist on a democratic form of government, and the latter will
prefer, for the direction of political affairs, a more authoritarian
type of government. No form of government is the only possible
and morally permissible one for all conditions. Hence none can
claim the moral right to exist forever. It is intelligible that every
government considers itself a permanent institution. Such an
attitude is a healthy sign of confidence in its own worth and
accomplishment. The actual developments we may well leave to
the future, which will bring the necessary corrections at the
proper time. Christian ethics forbids insurrection against lawful government or its violent overthrow. The world is not always
consistent, since it makes heroes out of successful revolutionists
and punishes the unsuccessful ones as traitors. Since governments
exist for the common good and since uncertainty is definitely
detrimental to the common good, Christian ethics recognizes as
legitimate a government set up by revolution if it is firmly
established and if there is no hope for the return of the former
rule. Using this principle in the light of events which have shaken
the world in the recent past, we may perhaps say that a government that is too weak to assert its authority and thus fails to
fulfill its task loses its right to exist. It may be in the interest of
the common good that the weak is replaced by the strong, disorder and uncertainty by order and certainty of direction. A
government must possess the power to enforce order for the well-

being of the citizens. If it loses this power and if there exists another strong force capable of governing the state, this other force may rightfully step into the place of the collapsing regime.

PURPOSE AND OBLIGATIONS OF THE STATE

The state as the larger society must offer to man those greater opportunities of earthly development which the family cannot provide. Thus the purpose and the obligation of the state are found in the needs that led to its formation. They are essentially of the temporal order. Man's eternal concerns belong to a different sphere, where the Church is competent. The state is bound not to interfere with the work of the Church, but positive measures for promoting the care of souls are not the state's business. Ultimately the state, like every other creature, must serve the glory of God, but it does this indirectly by allowing no immoral institutions and, on the positive side, by the honest accomplishment of its earthly tasks. We should also note that the state serves the common good, not private interests. Individual claims are satisfied if no one is excluded from the general social benefits of the state and if all have equal opportunities for the attainment of their just personal aspirations.

National and external security is the first indispensable condition of the welfare of a nation. Hence the state must possess power of a sort that, by its very existence, discourages harmful encroachments from without and within. What constitutes adequate defense preparation for a particular country depends on many factors which it is for the government to appraise. On the part of the citizens there exists the duty to assume that just portion of the real requirements of national defense. The state must also provide sufficient police protection for internal peace and security.

The advantages of our modern civilization have made life very complicated, requiring a proportionately large amount of organization and administration. In view of this need, the pertinent regulations of the civil authorities bind in conscience unless they conflict with the natural law and the positive laws of God and the Church. The multiplicity of functions demanded of the government necessitates a vast array of officials, especially of the civil service type. The common good depends in an inestimable degree on the moral integrity of the government officials. To assure this it is eminently imperative that they receive an adequate salary. Their idealistic conception of public service which is often appealed to and extolled must not be taxed too severely. Enthusiasm is not a permanent mental attitude, nor does the most gorgeous celebration in honor of civil servants feed, clothe, and house a family. He who best knew the human heart, taught us the petition: "Lead us not into temptation." The reduction of salaries is always a convenient method of public economy, but also a dangerous one. Moreover, the right selection of officials and the assignment of their work needs careful attention. It must not be that some are overwhelmed with work while others develop a sort of omnipresence on festive occasions. The importance of having contented civil servants who honestly and efficiently discharge their duties cannot be overestimated.

The administration of the law is of equal importance. The healthy life of society in the state presupposes the confidence of the people in the just administration of the law, not only in the crude material sense that the officers of the law are above bribes, but in the sense that the interpretation and application of the laws are objectively just. The law itself will always remain the surest support and norm of judicial procedure and decisions. But since the specific provisions of the law cannot embrace all possible situations of life, judgment by analogy or general discretion have considerable scope in the administration of justice. The tendency of the modern state is to free the judge as far as possible from the rigid prescriptions of the law and have him accommodate his decisions to the sound sense of justice on the part of the people. This is good to a certain extent, beyond which it is difficult and dangerous. An authentic expression of the sound popular sense of justice is nowhere to be found. It expresses itself more often than not in a cry for vengeance which far exceeds just bounds and is otherwise distorted by ignorance of the facts and of the principles of right. There is also the danger that the judge may consider his own view as the popular sense of justice.

If the people's general sense of justice is to be made a principle of law, it must be used not only against the accused person but also in his favor. At any rate, the demand that no misdeed shall go unpunished even though there is no legal paragraph forbidding it, must be supplemented with the principle that no punishment shall be imposed from mere feeling without there being clear evidence of a real wrong committed. That all men are equal before the law should be a matter of course in a civilized state, and the existence of this condition should be demonstrated by actual examples for the sake of preserving among the public the confidence in the impartiality of the state. No private or racial or religious or party purposes and animosities must be allowed to influence either favorably or unfavorably the prosecution of a defendant. Equality before the law need not be, of course, cruelty where there is room for equity. Moreover, endless delays in the trials of giant frauds in high finance and big business are contrary to the sound popular sense of justice. The worst offense against justice is the lynching of real or supposed criminals by excited mobs, that disregard and violate the authority of the state.

Of like importance is the development and administration of civil law, which regulates the multitude of questions arising out of the many and often intricate ways of the economic life of society. The ancient Romans, with their special talent for legal reasoning, developed the civil law to a point of incomparable perfection. However, some of its principles, especially concerning property and the relation between creditor and debtor, are extremely harsh. The property rights of the individual are unduly favored to the disadvantage of the personal rights. We must not forget that the Roman law reflects the temper of another time and people; it is not sacrosanct and inviolable. There is room for more equitable principles. But the study of the Roman law will always remain the best training in legal thinking. The conditions of our modern economic and social life are so intricate that even honest and well-intentioned people may disagree on certain matters in good faith. Hence civil decisions by legally trained judges will be called for even in the best states. The most urgent condition for the welfare and prosperity of a nation in this respect is absolute certainty and assurance. Every uncertainty and fear of unpredictable changes has a paralyzing effect on the social and economic life of a nation. Even absolute perfection of detail in legislation cannot compensate for lack of certainty and stability.

Apart from the necessary legislation, experience shows that the economic life prospers best when the public authority interferes as little as possible with private life and private business. The selfishness of the unscrupulous individualist must be curbed, and the exploitation of the worker and consumer, especially as regards the essentials of life, must be prevented. But the adventurous spirit of private enterprise must not be paralyzed by excessive governmental interference. Industrial progress and technical inventions are not made by official command but by the responsible and joyful work of private initiative. The individual is, of course, rightly entitled to the fruit of his labor. Such work also serves the well-being of the nation and its prestige.

Another important task of the state consists in providing work for the able-bodied citizens, thus making possible the founding of new families. It is a sad consequence of our advanced civilization that, for economic reasons, the young people are not able to found families as soon as they reach physical maturity. The man of our Western world has raised his standard of living to a height which his income in early adult years cannot attain if at the same time he raises a number of children. Thus the number of children is limited, the population decreases and tends toward extinction, while less civilized races multiply and with a certainty will occupy the place of the dying nations. The increase of the population and its economic welfare are, therefore, vital concerns of the state.

A population of sterling value can issue forth only from the Christian family. In this respect it is most interesting to recall the "population" movement of the eighteenth century. Shortly before Malthus sent out his warnings against overpopulation, the question of population increase, known simply as population, had been widely discussed and made the subject of legislation. Great but quite mistaken hopes were set on the number of children born out of wedlock. Foundling homes, orphanages, and similar institutions were much favored by the state. It all ended in sore disillusionment. It would be tragic if a state should ever resort again to a similar policy and thus help to undermine the sacredness of the Christian family. It would indeed be criminal to recommend extramarital relations of the sexes, even apart from moral and religious considerations. It would be an insult to the married woman who has assumed lifelong duties, to make the unmarried mother her equal. It would be also an unspeakable folly from the standpoint of sound statesmanship. Only people who are ignorant of the moral and social misery of the children born out of wedlock can hope for any benefit to the state from promiscuous sexual relations.

One of the greatest advantages of life in the community of the state is the easy transmission of the cultural goods to the growing generation. The education of the children is, according to the natural law, primarily the duty and right of the parents. This right and duty requires no sanction from the state but precedes the state. Hence the parents can never be entirely relieved of this right and duty by any other organization. The educational work of the state is supplementary to the work of the family and must agree in spirit with the objectives of the latter.

Education is much more than mere information. Still, information is a necessary part of it. The child must learn at least enough to live and work in the community of the state as a useful member of society. Here is where the authority of the state obtains the right of legislating about education. In an ideal family the child would certainly receive all the necessary education and information, but there are few ideal families, i.e., families capable of performing an adequate work of education and information. Experience teaches that illiteracy grows alarmingly wherever there is no compulsory attendance at school. In nations whose population is not divided in matters of religious belief, the public school will reflect the religious spirit of the families. But where the population is religiously divided the problem is a difficult one. Two periods of religious instruction a week imparted by competent teachers over eight years of grammar school are certainly sufficient to convey the required religious knowledge to the child, whether the religion classes are held as part of the regular school program or not. We need not contest this point or the emphasis on the many contacts in civic life in which the citizens must cooperate irrespective of their denominational affiliation.

The main trouble is that the undenominational public school cannot effectively guard against positively irreligious influences or religious views that are contrary to the religious beliefs of the one or the other group of students. The Catholic Church as the guardian of divine revelation must consider such a system highly dangerous for her children. Aside from this consideration, the Church knows that the youthful mind can be well educated only under a system where a religious note pervades all instruction and where there is harmony between the spirit of the home and the school. How insipid and stale any instruction without religion remains is keenly felt by an appreciative reader of the otherwise splendid novel *Il Cuore* by Edmondo De Amicis, where the reader continually expects a prayer to God as the crowning of all the good and beautiful things narrated.

The religious school is to be preferred also from the psychological point of view. Uncertainties, problems, and doubts ill agree with the simplicity of the child's mind. Hence the child should not be jolted by differences of religious views and practices. The undenominational school, which is often demanded on the plea of civic unity, becomes the source of worse psychological conflicts in the soul of the child if the religious differences are made for the young a matter of daily experience. In the higher stages of education, where the students' minds are more mature, there is less danger on this count.

The wealth of the scientific and cultural accomplishments of the human mind is so great that it cannot be mastered by one person. Nevertheless these discoveries and achievements must be treasured, increased, and passed on to the coming generations. This cannot be done by printed pages but must be the fruit of the living relationship of teacher and pupil. Hence it is the duty of society organized in the state to further higher education and learned institutions. Higher education must be made possible also to the poor, not only to the wealthy as formerly. On the other hand, careful measures must be taken to prevent the unfit from crowding the schools of higher learning. No social class is less useful and positively more dangerous to society as a whole than the unsuccessfully educated, who failed to attain the goal of their ambition. They will discover the reasons for their failure in everything but their own defects either of intellect or of character. In its zeal for education the state must guard against the danger of making instruction and research subservient to preconceived ideologies. The truths of science and religion are not restricted by national boundaries but are valid everywhere. Scientific research is in need of generous public support, but also freedom from undue advice and coercion. The cultivation of neglected cultural treasures should indeed be urged and required; and the irresponsible brandishing of unproved theories which clash with the established tradition should be restrained. This is no restriction of academic freedom. University professors are neither infallible nor above passion. Serious and responsible research workers will hardly ever give occasion for criticism on this score. But the popularizer, who desires to peddle shocking novelties to the immature and half-educated, is the one who feels called upon to shout for academic freedom in the defense of his unholy business. There are those who are true scholars in certain fields where they maintain the proper reserve in their statements, while in other matters they are most unrestrained and reckless.

The cultivation of art is likewise of importance for the civilized life of a nation. Artistic creativeness is an elementary trait of the human being. The oldest remains of human activity show attempts at artistic decoration and in some instances works of considerable perfection. The Greeks and Romans, on whose intellectual accomplishments our whole Western civilization is based, have bequeathed to us an overwhelming amount of art treasures. Works of art rise out of inner experience, they cannot be produced upon command. The source of art is not always pure joy, but often pain and suffering. The great artist senses and divines something ultimate which exceeds his actual power of expression. True art seeks no ulterior purposes, although the artist desires that his fellow men understand and appreciate his work. True art is eventually recognized even though the recognition may come only after a considerable lapse of time. That sort of artistic activity which from the very outset addresses itself to only a small coterie and disregards the appreciative response of society, is an aberration. The fostering of real art cannot be waived aside as of no concern to the state, for art positively makes for the healthy growth of society. Certainly, architectural styles or works of music or poetry cannot be manufactured even though great events in the life of a nation may appear to offer the best inspiration. But works of art may be brought to the attention of the general public not so much by pedantic lectures as by making them the natural landscape and atmosphere of the people, and by restraining obviously immoral attempts at seduction under the pretense of art. It must be remembered that periods of great art are rare. If new films have to be exhibited each week, the safe prediction that most of them are trash can be made without much thought and with one's eyes closed. The same applies to radio broadcasts. Even the best intentioned attempt at patriotic education runs the risk of becoming pedantic and repulsive from the artistic point of view.

The state must help to bring about the right order of relationship between the professional and social classes. Division of labor, which is the first step toward civilization, leads to the formation of groups of various interests. The pursuance of these interests results in the fixing of rights and duties on the part of the various groups. The articulated structure of society in professional or occupational groups and social classes is the most natural, and its healthy development must be furthered by prudent statesmanship. Excesses, by which certain classes usurp so many rights that they become the oppressors of other social groups, must be prevented or curtailed. The caste system of India is an extreme instance of social perversion. In Europe the development has been away from the more marked division of the social classes, such as prevailed in the Middle Ages. The trend has been toward their gradual extinction. Complete abolition of all social distinctions was the ideal of the French Revolution. The inevitable consequence was the "liberal" reduction of society to individuals, and the construction of society on a negative basis, i.e., on the union of all who lack property, and provision for their needs in old age, according to the Marxist slogan: Proletarians of the world, unite! However, negative factors can never provide the foundation for a positive and vital functioning of society. Negative elements lead only to destruction. Destructive work requires neither thought nor skill. A child with a match can start a great conflagration.

When the general education of a nation has advanced to a certain level, the individual citizens feel personally interested in the internal and external affairs of the state. The government is, therefore, obliged to give to the citizens a truthful account of the current events and let them participate in the shaping of the policies to be pursued. There are various ways in which this can be done besides the familiar parliamentary system of the last hundred years. The exclusion of public opinion and cooperation in the present civilized nations is not feasible in the long run. The government must have the confidence of the citizens, and these must have the opportunity to express their attitude with regard to the affairs of the state. Differences of opinion and interests will always exist and lead to the formation of political parties. In reviewing the motives which have led to political parties among highly civilized nations at various times, one cannot escape a feeling of shame and anxiety at the political immaturity of the civilized human race.

Sound morals are the ultimate requisite for the healthy life of a nation. No progress of civilization, of science, or of the arts can prevent the downfall of a nation when its morality is decadent. A duty of responsible statesmanship is to maintain, protect, and foster good morals in society. In itself, morality is a private matter of the individual as long as the rights of others are not violated. Besides, a great part of the moral life is confined to the sphere of thought and inner dispositions, beyond the control of external human authority. Another great part of man's moral life, however, has immediate social consequences or is observed by others and has the effect of good or bad example. The general moral attitude of society is like the atmosphere we breathe, which encourages and strengthens the individual or weakens or poisons him in his moral life. Hence the state must take care to prevent vice and immorality from becoming a public influence. The measures must be neither too severe nor too weak. Let us take the case of intemperance. If an individual drinks to excess in the privacy of his home without inflicting harm on another person as a result of his action, it is of no concern to the state, even though there are evil effects on his family, his professional work, or his own health. Again, the total prohibition of the manufacture, sale, and transportation of alcoholic beverages is an unwarranted encroachment upon the liberty of the citizens, provokes their opposition, and thus defeats itself. Similarly, the enforcement of so-called voluntary patriotic sacrifices by spying upon the private life of individuals and families results only in arousing their natural sense of liberty and calls forth disgust and opposition in general. Of course we do not mean that the state can do nothing at all about it.

In the matter of alcoholic beverages the state can do much to prevent intemperance. Few people indulge in large quantities of alcoholic drink except in the company of others. This fact offers public authority various opportunities for the regulation of such drinking. In addition, the state may punish with special severity misdeeds committed as a result of intemperance and, on the other hand, it may favor with quicker promotion temperate persons, dismiss the intemperate from official positions, and by other such measures show its attitude in the matter. Other forms of immorality may be dealt with in a like manner.

Another important task of indirect protection of morality by the state lies in the problem of sexual excesses. Sexual purity is a religious as well as a moral ideal which cannot be enforced by police ordinances. The highest possible attainment of this ideal is most desirable not only from the religious viewpoint but also in the interest of the earthly society. The state cannot force people to live up to the demands of purity according to their condition of life, but it can and must act where the opposite vice appears as a force of public seduction, e.g., by suppressing pornographic literature and illustrations, impure stage and film productions, and the like. Sexual perversity must be punished, and young persons must be protected against all forms of seduction. Extramarital relations cannot be approved by the state; on the other hand the state has not the means to prevent their occurrence. For the prevention of greater evil, the state has often permitted the lesser evil of voluntary and partly supervised prostitution. Whether or not this situation actually was a lesser evil at any time cannot be decided here. It certainly does not seem to be a lesser evil now. But, even though it should be such, the state has the grave obligation of preventing public scandal, the molestation of the public, white slavery, and of seeing to it that as many victims of this vice as possible are brought back to an honest way of life. The state has a wide field for legislation in the interest of sexual morality by regulating the conditions of labor for women and children, for their accommodation in public lodgings, and the like.

The efforts of the state toward the promotion of public morality should be crowned by the good example of those in official government positions. According to the words of St. Paul, drunkards, gluttons, sexual perverts, and adulterers shall not inherit the kingdom of God; they should also be excluded from the government of the kingdom of this world. Whoever holds a public position is placed like a light on a candlestick and shines often much more deeply into the moral conscience of the people than he may wish to believe. The officials of the state must be irreproachable not only in such matters as bribery, honesty, and truthfulness, but especially in the matter of sexual morality and family life. Those whose character is marred with blemishes of this sort should be at once eliminated when their moral weaknesses come to light. The people are only too inclined to follow the example from above and thus excuse every licence, or to generalize the vices of individuals and discredit the whole system of government.

VALUE OF THE INDIVIDUAL PERSON FOR THE STATE

The considerations concerning the importance of good moral personalities for the state in the conclusion of the foregoing section suggest some reflections on the value of the individual person for society in general, for the state and the nation. We are here concerned with the individual and seek to determine his relation to the social group. Liberalism undoubtedly exaggerated the rights of the individual person. The social whole of the nation was considered merely as the sum of the individual citizens, and the authority of the state as a regulating agency constituted by the consent of all these individuals; the regulating power of the government having again as its chief, if not sole, purpose the creation of such juridical conditions as would secure for each individual the greatest possible freedom to seek and achieve his own individual advantage without respect for the nation as a whole. These ideas are largely on the wane now. It is again being understood that the social group is more than the mere sum of its members, having more comprehensive tasks than the individual, tasks that outlast the succeeding generations. But the pendulum seems now swinging too far in the other direction. It is true that the individual continues to live in this world only in his descendents and deeds for the future well-being of society and that only in these can he help to achieve the purposes which he believes to be providentially assigned to his social group or nation. It is also right that the individual should make sacrifices for the present and future welfare of his nation. Voluntary celibacy for the sake of restricting the spread of undesirable hereditary traits may be such a sacrifice. The more a person becomes convinced of the necessity of such sacrifices the more he will be ready to submit to the required restrictions.

The nature and just bounds of the restrictions which an individual may have to accept for the above-mentioned purposes cannot be described in general but must be determined in each particular case according to the principles of the moral and religious order. Every individual person has not only the right but also the duty to seek the eternal salvation of his immortal soul and he has the right to adopt that way of life which he feels in his conscience is the best suited to his needs. Nobody may be forbidden to follow his vocation to the religious life or the priesthood because the nation wants him to become the parent of many children and propagate desirable hereditary traits. Neither may a person be prevented from pursuing a reasonable amount of individual happiness of a purely earthly nature, especially as regards the choice of his vocation, the acquisition of cultural education, and the pleasurable enjoyment of life. Personal happiness requires some measure of personal freedom, the desire for which was placed in every human heart by the Creator. Freedom is a great good, and not every desire for freedom is a symptom of the taint of liberalism. It would indeed be an all too easy and thoughtless way of condemning differences of opinion in such and like matters to label them as liberalist.

Every person possesses certain qualities and faculties, the harmonious development of which gives him a special value and the right to his own particular way of life and happiness within the community of his nation. This personal value of his is his contribution to the living treasure of the nation. The greater the value of these individual contributions, the greater the value of the nation. It would be a fatal mistake to believe that we can disregard the rights of the free person and neglect the growth of independent individual characters, and at the same time expect to have a great and valuable nation capable of holding an honored position in the family of nations. Zeros added up produce no sum. This truth is neither liberalist nor antiquated, but an ancient and vitally young wisdom of life. Hence the young people of our day cannot be spared the hard school of obedience, discipline, and intensive application to study. Purely emotional attitudes and short-lived enthusiasms cannot take the place of the individual character of full value achieved by daily painful striving.

CHURCH AND STATE

The obligations of the state as regards the preservation and furtherance of religion are best set forth in a discussion of the relation between Church and state. We are not here concerned with states that cannot be considered part of the Christian world. We are dealing with the duties of states that have grown up in the Christian world and know of the Church as an organization founded by Christ for the eternal salvation of mankind. The ultimate purpose of the Church is supernatural and can be attained only by supernatural means. Christ has given His Church these means by the institution of the offices for the teaching, sanctification, and governing of men, vested in the priesthood. The Church is a perfect society because it possesses all those means that are required for the accomplishment of its end. From the apses of the old Oriental Churches the oversized countenance of the Pantocrator, on golden background and with the expression of calm seriousness undisturbed by earthly changes, looks down upon the succession of the generations who come to send their prayers up to heaven on clouds of incense. Thus Christ rules over His Church. The Church is Christ Himself mystically continuing to live in the world. There can be no ruler over the Church but Christ Himself as visibly represented by those chosen by Him and endowed with the appointed spiritual powers. All attempts at forcing the Church under the power of the state have failed sooner or later and have been condemned at the tribunal of history. Since the divine Founder gave His apostles the command to go into the whole world and teach all nations, it would contradict the nature of the Church to represent it as the natural development of the religion of one particular nation or to demand that it resolve itself in the mentality and folkways of any particular nation. Nevertheless it is possible for certain ecclesiastical religious practices to assume forms which agree with the peculiar character of different nations. This is true not only of popular devotions but also of the celebration of feasts and sacred seasons, the dogmatic meaning and liturgical foundation remaining always absolutely the same.

The purpose of the Church and the means for its attainment are not of this world, but the Church must fulfill its mission in the world and among men who are also members of the state. The two great organizations, the Church and the state, cannot disregard each other's existence. Positive cooperation of the state in the spiritual work of the Church is not necessary; the Church's freedom for the exercise of its mission is sufficient. This freedom includes first of all the right of persons to be members of the Church and of certain ones to dedicate their whole life to the service of the Church independent of all extraneous powers. Hence the Church must have the right to possess property. Furthermore, the dissemination of Christian truth demands not only a permissive but a positively benevolent and helpful attitude on the part of the state. The places of worship and all religious activities must enjoy the protection of the state. Of special importance is the early training of the Christian mind and conscience in the young. Hence the Church must have the right to conduct schools or at least to participate in the process of education according to the nature of its mission. Historically all education among nations was initiated and carried on by religious bodies long before secular society was interested in that work or capable of doing it. The state's interest in education is indeed justified and even desirable and necessary. But equitable ways of satisfactory cooperation can and must be arranged for the religious education of youth.

The Church has and needs the power of legislation and the power to enforce its discipline in its own sphere and by means proper to its nature. The state has no right to interfere with the legislation and administration of the laws of the Church. While the Church can hardly any more call upon the secular arm to carry out its judicial sentences, the state is bound to respect the rulings of the competent ecclesiastical authority wherever the temporal effects arising out of an internal ecclesiastical case are brought before the secular court; e.g., loss of benefices, transfer of property in the reorganization of ecclesiastical societies such as parishes, and similar matters.

The Christian religion in its genuine and perfect form of the Catholic Church has in its favor all the arguments for its claim to be the Church instituted by Christ. The entire Western world has gone through the school of the Catholic Church, and in it the nations have found and developed their own true selves. The many earlier contentions to the contrary have been shown by modern historical research to be misconceptions based on ignorance and passion. The Catholic Church has proved itself the greatest and never-decaying force of lasting cultural progress. The abuses which at various times so dreadfully disfigured the face of the Church were not the natural outcome of any unsound elements in the nature of the Church but the result of the unintelligent and sinful ways in which men, representatives of the Church and state and society in general, handled the holy things of God. For the Founder of the Church is God who, walking upon the earth in human nature, proved His divinity in word and deed. Hence disregard for and obstruction of the word of God by opposition to the Catholic Church in matters of her own sphere are certain to bring ruin. For such an attitude of indifference or hostility neglects and even rejects the life which God

Himself has come into the world to give to man in abundance. The Church and the state, the supernatural and the natural society of men, both intended by God, should cooperate in harmony and so promote the spiritual and temporal good of the individual person, which is the ultimate purpose of their existence.

XIII

CHRISTIANITY AND QUESTIONS OF PROPERTY

THE care of souls, as the term implies, being essentially a work in the realm of the spirit, apparently should have nothing to do with questions of property. Our Lord taught in word and by practical example that preoccupation with the material goods of earth may prove a serious stumbling block on the way to heaven. The apostles and many disciples of Christ throughout the centuries have followed and are following Christ's counsel of complete renunciation of earthly possessions. But for the general body of Christians this perfect imitation of the ideal of Christ's own poverty is clearly impossible. The possession and use of earthly goods is a necessity. The way of the soul is toward a goal beyond the earth, but it leads, at all stages, along the roads and lanes of the earth and is deeply steeped in the nature of earthly existence which cannot prescind from questions of property.

Certain forms of property and views concerning it existed wherever the Christian religion was introduced. To better understand the gradual development of a systematic moral and theological theory of property, we will be helped by considering it in a brief historical retrospect. Among the Jews of the Old Testament, property existed in the twofold form of common national ownership and private possessions of the individual. An important distinction, which in moral theology on the subject has not always been kept clearly in view and sometimes has been completely overlooked, is that between movable and immovable goods. Among the Jews as among all ancient races the private ownership of movable goods was taken for granted, but restrictions on the private possession of the soil for the benefit of the neighbor and the community were equally considered as a matter of course. From the time of their definite settlement, the possession of small farms was the Jewish ideal of ownership which was, however, greatly restricted in favor of the original family ownership. Supreme owner of the land was God Himself, the Jews being but guests and stewards on the soil owned by God (Lev. 5:23). At the beginning of every fiftieth year all landed property which in the preceding period had changed owners was to be returned to the original family owners. The prohibition of interest on loans to fellow Jews was a wholesome restriction on the ownership of movable possessions in favor of the community.

Christ's attitude toward property has been mentioned. Many of the first Christians were convinced of the early end of the world. St. Paul begged voluntary contributions for the benefit of poor communities. According to the Acts of the Apostles, there existed a sort of voluntary communism among the first Christians of Jerusalem for some time. We may assume the continuance of the eschatological frame of mind during the time of the persecutions. But disregard for earthly possessions from supernatural motives is by no means the same as denying the morality of private property. The early Christian literature contains no developed theory of property, but only occasional statements and fragmentary reflections. As regards their occurrence in homilies, it is well for us to remember that the literary taste of that time required emphatic statements, but the exaggerations were commonly understood and accordingly discounted.

In all questions of practical living, the early writers of the Church had to reconcile three separate elements influencing the Christians of that time: the practical conditions of their lives were determined by Roman laws and customs; their minds reflected the views and terms of the Stoic philosophy then current; their religious faith and hope were Christian. The Roman law greatly favored private property with very few restrictions in the interest of the community; the Stoics regarded private property as a departure from the original condition of common ownership; the Christian religion definitely subordinates man's use of the things of the world to the eternal concerns of the future life. The ordinary striving for and use of the necessaries of life constituted no problem, except among those embracing the eremitical and monastic form of life. But superfluous wealth is variously dealt with in the homiletic and ascetical literature, the pronouncements ranging from counsels of free renunciation to outright condemnation.

St. Ambrose, e.g., states that "the rich commit murder daily by retaining what the poor need"; or again: "to him that has nothing to eat belongs the bread which you possess in abundance." In evaluating sharply penned sentences like these, we must keep in mind that they do not allow us to draw immediate conclusions as to the actually spoken word and its effect. Besides, these words were addressed to a society steeped in Stoic thought, which condemned sympathy with the suffering as a moral weakness unworthy of the wise man. We find in the writings of St. Ambrose and the other Fathers of the Church also many passages which speak of private property as something lawful and willed by God as an occasion for the exercise of virtue.

The times and the internal and external conditions of the Church were too unsettled for the calm elaboration of a coherent theory of property. The Christians saw the crying inequalities in the distribution of the goods of the world. But they accepted them as the natural condition of a sinful world, a condition that was to be mitigated by personal charity among the followers of Christ. The thought of the solution of these problems in terms of social and economic reconstruction did not occur to them. The transcendent value of the soul and the equality of all men before God was the thought which held the attention of the Christian mind. The consequences of these truths, however, would be realized in the next world. For our existence on earth, the old tradition of inequality among men was so firmly entrenched in the human mind that even the most enlightened thinkers could not conceive, e.g., of the abolition of slavery. In fact, the existence of slavery made possible the ancient civilization with its great achievements in art and science. Without slavery the development of the material and cultural civilization of the ancient world would have taken quite a different course. It is equally certain that the Greco-Roman world would have perished from an eventual revolution of the disinherited and oppressed masses even if no invasion by the barbarian races from the north and east had occurred.

The spirit of Christian charity which did so much to relieve the social and economic inequalities in the ancient Roman world without abolishing them, brought forth even greater fruit in the form of pious and charitable foundations during the Middle Ages. The Christian Middle Ages were anything but hard in matters of private property, which was conceived as a stewardship under God as the real owner. There were no restrictions of a legal kind on the amount and use of movable possessions, although these were as a rule very modest. Limitation of such goods was dictated only by the demands of Christian charity. As regards the immovable property, distinction was made between the high domain vested as a rule in the ownership by ecclesiastical and secular princes, and the domain of use enjoyed by the subjects or feudal serfs. Through various circumstances the feudal rights to the use of land often became actual property rights.

The density of the population was never very great in the Middle Ages. Only within the walls of the towns were the dwellings very close to one another, leaving only narrow lanes and often only one large square for the market. Outside the walls there was room aplenty, and so we need not wonder that the owners of the land had to submit to a number of restrictions for the benefit of the community or neighbors or travelers. The income of the feudal lords as well as that of the serfs and tradesmen was mostly derived from the fruits of the land. The city dwellers—the cities being all small towns—worked on the farm and raised cattle. The artisans produced wonderful objects, but their work was done only upon orders received from individuals according to their private needs and desires. Commerce developed slowly from primitive beginnings because of a lack of good and safe roads. Money was simply a medium of exchange and a kind of accumulated property. Its use as an element of production as in modern capitalism was not known even though some traces of capitalism already existed.

PRIVATE PROPERTY

The justification of private property has as its primary basis the endowment of man with reason and freedom of the will, faculties by which he is capable of responsible action. Of all earthly creatures, man alone is a historical being, i.e., he need not start his culture all over again with each new generation, but his achievements for further development he is able to pass on to those coming after. He is able to control his living and inanimate environment, thus harnessing and organizing the forces of nature for higher purposes. This superior position of man, which renders him capable of private property, is not a mere luxury but a necessity, for only through the possession of property can he unfold and rationally employ the qualities inherent in his nature.

Ownership consists in the exclusive right of possession of an object. Even the brute animal to some extent needs the possession of objects to the exclusion of other animals for the preservation of its life and instinctively exercises this attitude even where it is useless and senseless. Man needs the right to private property for the development of his moral personality as well as civilization and culture. As a matter of history, there has been no other form of possession than private property, a fact of some weight in view of the thousands of years of human history known to us; and no other form is conceivable if we wish to remain realistic instead of indulging in utopian dreaming. The principles governing the exercise of the right of private property may vary, of course, and actually do vary. For the rights and wishes of one man are limited by the rights and desires of his fellow men.

Much has been written on the titles to ownership, i.e., the ways and circumstances which give any particular person the right to possess as his own any particular object. Whatever may have been the origin and early history of man, in the beginning occupancy or seizure must have constituted the original title to ownership. Whoever first claimed an object must have urged this temporal precedence as a just title to ownership, and the others must have recognized this title because they would have to use it for the justification of their own acts of occupancy. The application of this title to ownership has naturally become less widespread and less frequent, but it will always be of practical value in hunting, fishing, the taking of wild fruits, and possibly of unclaimed land. Objects irretrievably lost or freely abandoned are without owners and may be claimed by others through occupancy.

Labor as a title of ownership organically grows out of occupancy, which often requires considerable physical effort and thought as well as costly and well-designed preparations, e.g., in deep-sea fishing, the catch of large animals, and the like. Man's intensive occupation with animals and plants taught him that the work of domestication, protection, and artificial improvement yielded richer fruits. Naturally man claimed these as his own as the result of his skill and effort. When outright seizure became less frequent and the acquisition of property by personal industry more common, man came to see in work, mental as well as physical, the best founded title to private property. However, labor cannot be regarded as the primary title of ownership, because it presupposes the ownership of the material. In our modern civilization, labor has become a source of property in a way quite different from that which gave rise to the theory of labor as the only title to ownership. The worker of today is not the owner of the material nor does he wish to be the owner of the finished product; he simply offers the services of his physical and mental faculties for the production of goods and desires an adequate compensation that enables him to acquire the things of his own choice. That it was obviously wrong to look upon labor as a commodity to be bought at the lowest price, we shall see later.

Less important as an explanation of the origin of private property are the so-called legal and contract theories. The legal theory asserts the lawful power of the state to grant and withdraw the right to private property and to regulate it in every respect. Our answer is that mankind and private ownership are older than the state. The contract theory would have us believe that private ownership is derived from the tacit agreement of men, by which they allow one another the private possession of goods. But history offers not a trace of such a contract, not even in the vaguest form of mythology. Yet so momentous an institution of man's existence should have come to the fore in human consciousness. There is also the logical difficulty that men should have renounced their claim of ownership in favor of the individual before anyone possessed anything. Lastly, there is the theory of evolution which simply states that in the history of man private ownership happened to originate and entrench itself but is liable to disappear just as it came. This is no explanation at all, but an unfounded assertion which contradicts the universal fact of causes and reasons behind all developments in the world.

In the divinely established order of the world private property proves to be the most natural form of ownership because it is the one most conducive to the welfare of the individual and the cultural progress of society. It is the most effective incentive for well-planned and responsible work. Interest in work which requires sustained effort and careful attention cannot be secured in the same degree where the work is a collective enterprise and its fruits are distributed among the individuals by the authorities. The attitude of labor might be stated as a minimum of effort and a maximum of reward. Neither could the disadvantage deriving from discontent over the assignment of less desirable work be eliminated by frequent changes, because every kind of work requires a certain skill and practice as well as personal inclination and talent. To a certain extent all these things are actually experienced wherever work is being done under conditions that reduce the personal interest of the worker, so that the proper efficiency must be obtained by increased supervision. The fact that many publicly owned and operated enterprises are in continual need of subsidies whereas like enterprises yield profits under private management, is significant.

Private property is also a solid guaranty of social peace and security. The division of labor and wide distribution of private property help to make people realize the necessity of peaceful cooperation and subordination. In times of social stress it is always the ones who have nothing to lose because they possess nothing that join the ranks of the rebellious and work destruction without a plan for positive reconstruction. Private property aids man in overcoming times of scarcity and distress by allowing him to provide for such eventualities. Private property strengthens the family, which is the most natural and basic form of all society. The common enjoyment of the family's possessions keeps alive the interest and mutual affection of the individual members, whereas the impersonal assignment of goods from the treasury of a collective group would tend to loosen the family ties and contribute to the disintegration of society.

From the point of view of their ultimate value and destiny, all men are equal and have equal rights. However, men differ widely in their personal abilities, ambitions, and moral character. These differences greatly influence their attitude in the matter of property, its quality and quantity. He who is not seriously concerned about the acquisition and preservation of property or who is not able to perform work that brings greater profit will soon be outdistanced by those of a different temper and different talents. Thus it is evident that even in the most just society there will be differences in the distribution of earthly possessions. The existence of such differences is not in conflict with the spirit or explicit doctrine of the Christian religion. However, every man is entitled to the opportunity of holding or acquiring that amount of earthly goods which enables him to live and work in accordance with his faculties and to reach his eternal destiny.

The actual distribution of the earth's goods often shows inequalities which ill agree with our sense of justice. The economic changes are so frequent and intricate that they are beyond the control of many individuals and result in most regrettable situations. It cannot be the task of supernatural religion to rectify those situations by legislation or judicial decisions. The ultimate and complete compensation for all inequalities will be effected by God Himself in the next world, as our Lord clearly teaches in the Sermon on the Mount and the parable of the rich man and Lazarus. Christianity helps to remedy the economic inequalities in this life by stressing the effective practice of the virtues of justice and charity. These are not a matter of counsel but of strict obligation.

The actual regulation of the problems involved in the distribution of property pertains to the state. This task constitutes a fertile ground for state legislation. The perpetual changes and unforeseen developments call for new enactments and repeated revision of the laws. The question whether the state has the right to set an absolute highest limit of personal private possessions has not yet been decided and is difficult to decide because there are so many modes of possession. The question would have to be decided affirmatively if individuals or groups were to use their extraordinary wealth clearly to the disadvantage of society, e.g., by a decidedly irresponsible use of a monopoly. Christian morality recognizes the right to private possessions, but teaches also that there are higher goods than material wealth and the right to it. Life is such a higher good. In the case of extreme necessity, where a person's life is endangered through want of its material sustenance, such a person is permitted to appropriate and consume a sufficiency of the goods of others for the support of his own life. This principle of Christion ethics shows that the state has the power to institute regulations that will prevent such emergencies in the life of individuals or of large groups of people.

WAYS OF ACQUIRING PROPERTY

The ways of acquiring property may be conveniently divided into original and derived, or primary and secondary, modes. To the first group belong those by which are acquired objects that never had an owner or that have ceased to be anyone's property. The second group embraces the different ways property passes from one person to another.

We have seen that man's right to own property comes from his superiority by which he is able to seize and use the things of the world in a premeditated and purposeful manner. Of course, man can control only small individual objects. The world as a whole or even its larger portions man can merely behold and admire. The seizure for possession may be physical or symbolic; the former being always effective and unequivocal, while the latter may be only an empty gesture as when, e.g., a polar expedition sets the flag of its country on a block of ice, unless the nation is prepared to maintain its claim effectively and always. Wreckage cast by the sea on the shore has always been regarded as nobody's property and may be appropriated by the finder. In ancient times even the survivors of a wreck could be made the property, i.e., the slaves, of their rescuers. Whoever discovers antique valuables in circumstances clearly indicating that they cannot belong to a living owner may consider them as his property. However, most countries have special laws concerning such finds, and it may be prudent to obey such laws. There may even exist an obligation to comply with the pertinent regulations of the public authorities, especially if a proper reward is provided, because the cultural concerns and the decorum of a civilized nation are promoted by the preservation of such treasures for the benefit of the public.

Of much more importance than the discovery of lost treasures is the search for the treasures of nature under the surface of the earth. The right to landed property is practically everywhere measured in terms of extension on the surface of the earth with a right to as much ground below and space above as are generally used for building or agricultural purposes. This is, in fact, the only portion of landed property which the average owner can effectively control. The mineral treasures of the earth lie mostly at so great a depth that the ordinary owner of the land above them cannot effectively claim them. Hence they are subject to the occupancy of those who have the means of reaching and extracting them. In ancient times and throughout the Middle Ages up to the modern industrial era, the mining industry was mostly the right of the state or the crown. Among the Romans private individuals could own and operate mines. At present the laws of the different nations on this subject vary. Usually the owner of surface rights cannot prevent others from acquiring the right to exploit the contents of the earth below it at certain depths.

The finder of an object which appears to have been lost by its rightful owner does not acquire any right to the object but has the duty of keeping it in trust until the owner is ascertained. Much, of course, depends on the value of the lost object. If this is so slight that the owner can hardly be supposed to be concerned about it, e.g., a small coin or the like on a busy street corner, the finder may keep it. In general, the obligation to preserve a lost object for the owner is not an obligation of justice, but of charity. Once we have taken a lost object in trust we are obliged to bestow on its safekeeping as much care as we would employ for the preservation of a like object belonging to ourselves. We should make a reasonable effort to discover and inform the real owner. The same rule applies to objects that may be of no value at all to the finder but of great worth to the loser, e.g., notes, drawings, family papers, and the like. In many countries the laws provide easy ways of discharging the duties of the finder and guarantee even an appropriate reward. Those following the course prescribed by the law fulfill their moral obligation. However, the mere lapse of the time legally good for the recovery of found property would not entitle the finder to claim the object as his own if the real owner should appear within a reasonable time. This is especially true if the real owner would

suffer considerable harm from the loss and was merely too awkward or inexperienced in the ways of claiming his property.
On the other hand, the public seems to be careless in searching
for lost articles, as can be seen in the offices of the public con-
veyances where usually an extraordinary number of useful
articles accumulate which are rarely claimed. Hence in the case
of ordinary objects we may assume that the owner has given up
his claim when the legal time has passed without an inquiry
being made.

In this connection it may be well to discuss a problem which
at first sight appears to be of the nature of an ordinary purchase,
although it involves a number of other factors, such as the acquisition of unclaimed values, the barter of human interest and
attachment, venturesome financial risks, and the like. We refer
to the buying of genuine antiques, objects of art and of historical value, e.g., statues, carvings, pictures, clocks, coins,
books, and similar objects. Things of this sort occasionally happen to be in the possession of persons who do not know their
value and who neglect them. The expert collectors of such objects naturally desire to secure these at the lowest possible price
and to this end conceal their knowledge of the real value until
the purchase is accomplished. Evidently such conduct is not
always morally correct. To arrive at a satisfactory decision a
number of questions must be answered. It makes considerable
difference whether the owner's lack of appreciation of such objects is conditioned solely by his ignorance of their value or
whether he would remain equally indifferent if he knew it. We
must also consider what is likely to become of these things if
they are not given proper care by an intelligent owner, and the
fact that the buyer has also but limited means at his disposal.
Of course, falsehood in such transactions is morally wrong because it here becomes intentional deception. If the purchaser
will have to spend a considerable sum for the restoration or
preservation of the object and if, in addition, he intends to keep
it for himself, he certainly does not commit sin by offering a
comparatively low price, especially since objects of this kind

have no commercial value in the ordinary sense of the word. However, if such an object should possess an extraordinary value which soon would become sensationally known, it would be certainly sinful to buy it at a disproportionately low price made possible by simulation and concealment of its real value. The sin will be the greater the poorer the original owner and the lower the price paid.

Hunting presents another complicated problem. Generally speaking and prescinding from the conditions prevailing in civilized countries, it is true that the beasts of the forests and fields are *res nullius* and may be seized by anyone. But since the ground on which the animals live is mostly someone's property, the owner of the land must be granted a privileged claim to the game. Hunting in the jungle or uninhabited steppes differs widely from hunting in densely populated countries. The Roman law regarded wild animals as *res nullius,* but gave the landowner the right to forbid anyone to trespass on his property for the purpose of hunting. Thus each owner of land had the exclusive right to hunt on his own ground. This is still the situation in Italy. In the northern countries of Europe where the land belonged to noblemen who leased it in smaller parcels to the farmers (high and low domain of feudalism), there was made also a distinction between high and low hunting rights. The feudal lords were interested in the growth of a good stock of large animals for the exercise of their hunting sport, both of which proved a burden for the farmer whose fields suffered from them. Small animals were free to be hunted by the farmers on their fields. But the conviction of the people that wild animals were nobody's property and the farmers' desire to protect their crops led to conflicts with the claims of the noblemen, who punished such transgressions with extreme severity. This is the background for the traditional doctrine of moral theology that the laws regulating hunting do not oblige in conscience.

It may be said that the laws regulating hunting are not binding in conscience if they are clearly unfair and discriminatory, and if the game animals are wild beasts in the true sense of the word. But in most civilized countries this is no longer the case. The game animals are neither domestic nor simply wild, but grow up in the freedom of the fields and woods, yet their existence is in many ways controlled by the public authorities. Game wardens feed these animals in winter, protect them against dangers, and improve their living conditions. Often special types of animals best suited for a particular environment are introduced and nurtured. All this care for the animals of the hunt is deliberately undertaken and carried out under the competent supervision of specialists and at considerable expense of the public. It is, therefore, just that hunting should be exercised only according to the rules laid down by public authority, which are also for the common good. The laws against poaching are under such circumstances not mere *leges poenales,* but bind in conscience. In countries where individuals can rent their exclusive hunting grounds and by the payment of the rental fee defray the expenses for the proper care given to the wild game living there, poaching is doubtlessly an offense against commutative justice.

The original owner of pigeons or swarming bees has the right to claim them as his own even though they may have made their home on the property of another for some time. If the owner is known, he must be given the opportunity to retrieve them. If he renounces his claim or neglects to take appropriate steps, he loses his title to them and anyone succeeding in capturing them may rightly consider himself their owner. Fishing in inland waters is subject to the same moral considerations as hunting, while deep sea fishing may be compared to hunting in the jungle. The nations bordering on the sea claim the zone within a few miles from the land as their territorial water. The rest of the ocean is open to all.

Another original or primary mode of acquiring property consists in prescription. Prescription may be acquisitive or liberative according as a person by it obtains the full ownership of something formerly not his own or is freed from the obligation of parting with something which is owed to another. Prescription consists in the *bona fide* and undisputed use of something belonging to another or the *bona fide* and unchallenged non-fulfillment of an obligation over a certain period of time by the lapse of which the object actually used as one's own becomes one's property and an existing yet unclaimed obligation is extinguished. The time required for prescription varies according to the nature of the things concerned. The periods of time involved are usually determined by civil or ecclesiastical law. Where the time prescribed by civil law is very short, the effect of prescription cannot be admitted in conscience when soon after its lapse it is proved that the object in our possession belongs to another or that we have an obligation which we have not yet satisfied.

Accession is another title of original ownership. It consists in the increase of the value of an object either by natural processes or by human effort, whether or not the increased value can be physically separated. E.g., fruits growing on a tree can be separated from the tree; the improvement on plants by cultivation or the training of an animal cannot be separated from the original object. The main principle here is that accession belongs to the owner of the original object, but just compensation may have to be made to those whose efforts caused the increase of value.

The passage of possessions from a deceased person to a new living owner by inheritance connects the titles of original ownership with those of derived property right. For by the death of the former owner the possessions become *res nullius*, their assignment to a new owner being determined, however, by the will of the former owner or through his natural relations with other members of society. The morality of inheritance is denied by those who deny the morality of private property. If private property is immoral, the handing on of property by one deceased to another, they argue, is still more immoral because the beneficiary does not earn the new property, and it seems incongruous that a dead person should be allowed to make de-

cisions binding on the living. We answer that the whole of nature
is pervaded by the law of heredity. In a very special manner, the
cultural progress of man is dependent on the continuous passage
of the achievements of former generations to the succeeding
ones.

In comparison with the history of the human race the life
span of the individual is extremely brief. Thus some have
thought that the importance of the individual might be discounted altogether and all value be placed in the succession of
the generations as a whole. But each generation is worth only as
much as the individual persons composing it. By regulating the
orderly passage of property right from one individual to another in the succession of generations the interests of society
are best served. With his death the individual is not so eliminated from society as if he had never been but he affects it yet by
his deeds and accomplishments or at least by his example. The
work and personality of some persons become powerful forces
only years after their death. E.g., the Augustinian friar Mendel
was practically unknown to the world of science while he made
his now famous experiments. Now Mendel's laws of heredity
are the outstanding feature of modern biology.

The importance of the individual for society requires the personal transmission of possessions by individual inheritance. If
the state would freely dispose of a person's possessions after
his death, there would be little incentive for active and creative
work. The pleasures of the moment and the squandering and
reckless use of the goods in their possession would be the goal
of most people. On the other hand, interest in the well-being of
the next of kin or of such persons and institutions as have a
special appeal to the character and ambitions of an individual
are a powerful incentive to responsible work and wise thrift.
Especially the thought of helping such beneficiaries of natural
attachment or of one's own free choice gives a conscious purpose
to the life and work of the people. Besides, it is also just that
those who were in close and helpful relations with a person

should be benefited by the fruits of his work first of all and in a preferred degree. This is true particularly of his own parents and children.

The aberrations of the human mind and the perversions of the heart being very liable to trouble the questions of heredity, the state has established laws which guard the equitable distribution of the goods left by a deceased person. While leaving the greatest possible freedom in disposing of his property, the law generally provides that children or the nearest kin be given a fair portion of which they may not be deprived without serious reasons. The laws of the state, furthermore, provide for the disposal of property left behind by persons who die without having made a last will. The ownership of earthly possessions being a stewardship over a portion of God's creation, it appears that there exists a moral duty to make a last will. This duty should not be postponed too long since nobody is certain about the time of his death. But nobody will die a moment earlier for having made his last will. Much confusion and trouble and enmity can be prevented by a fair will made in good time. Care should also be taken that the laws governing the making of valid wills are observed, especially when bequests are made to pious causes; otherwise all good intentions will avail nothing.

Generally speaking, nobody is obliged to accept provisions of last wills in his own favor. Occasionally such provisions involve duties connected with the inherited rights. Therefore a person should first consider whether he is able personally and according to his state in life to assume and carry out the obligations contained in his share of a will.

By far the most frequent manner of acquiring and giving up titles of ownership and rights is the contract. A contract may be defined as the mutual agreement of two or more persons about their respective rights and duties concerning objects or actions. Valid contracts oblige in conscience by virtue of commutative justice. A first requisite for the validity of a contract is that the contracting parties are capable, both naturally and legally, of making a contract. The natural capacity consists in the sufficient maturity of a person's reason and his freedom to act. To assure the rights of all in this matter the state has fixed a definite age at which a person becomes legally capable of entering into contracts. For the safeguarding of the rights and the administration of the affairs of young persons below this age, the state requires, in default of the parents, the appointment of guardians. The priest may often have occasion to help in the appointment of capable and interested guardians. In this work he will find the greatest assistance in the family division of the diocesan charities and in such organizations as the St. Vincent de Paul Society, the Big Brother and Big Sister Societies, and similar socially active organizations of Catholics. The same applies to the appointment of guardians for persons who, through mental disorder, are not competent to look after their own personal and economic affairs.

There are various other restrictions according to a person's position in society, which must be carefully determined before contracts are made. E.g., whoever deals with married persons in matters of property should first find out the rights of the husband and wife concerning the property in question. Persons belonging to religious orders or congregations are also subject to various limitations. The status of ecclesiastical institutions, before both the law of the Church and that of the state, requires attention regarding their right to contract obligations, transfer property, accept bequests, and the like.

Another requisite for the validity of a contract is that its object must be possible and morally good or at least indifferent. Contracts which violate justice or any other moral quality are null and void. Lastly, contracts must be concluded in a manner which expresses the agreement of the parties concerned. For certain contracts the Church as well as the state prescribes definite forms that must be observed under pain of nullity. For many other contracts popular customs have developed a variety of forms. Written and oral agreements in one and the same contract should be avoided because these are likely to confuse the matter and lead to dissension.

MONEY

Barter is probably the original method of commerce. Only the great patriarchal family, which provided for all its own needs, could exist without even this primitive exchange of commodities. When, through division of labor, the individual talents of men were employed for the production of a limited variety of goods, there resulted a surplus of certain kinds of commodities and a lack of others in the different social groups. The exchange of commodities, or commerce, began. The direct exchange of goods could take place only on the most primitive level because often the ones who offered the things sought had no need for the goods offered in exchange. Thus it became necessary to find goods which were most likely to be accepted by all on account of their general usefulness. Such were cattle and grain. These served as a medium of exchange because they could be used in various quantities as a standard for measuring the value of other things. But this medium proved too cumbersome, and another was sought that could represent all values and could be accepted and easily handled by all. This is the history of the origin of money.

The essential qualities of money are its character as a general medium of exchange and the possibility of its easy transfer from one to another (currency). The origin of money dates back to the remotest past of the human race. It is even older than the organized state. Its general acceptance was not imposed by some public authority but grew out of the need for it felt by the people who met for the barter and sale of their goods.

The description of the functions of money is much easier than the determination of its nature. The great controversial question is whether money has a value in itself, i.e., whether it is a commodity like the goods of use which are exchanged in commerce, or whether it is merely a symbol with an economic function tacitly recognized by all. The fact is that money can serve no other purpose than that of securing other goods. Historically it seems that primitive races used as money small pieces of leather on which different values were indicated by various signs, the differences of value being probably also emphasized by small corresponding variations in the size of the leather pieces. Thus it seems that money was a pure symbol in the beginning. Aristotle, who was among the first to discuss the nature of money, calls it a sign, i.e., a symbol.

The practical development of money soon turned to the use of rare metals, especially gold and silver. The reason for this is easy to see. When states in the strict sense of the word began to be formed, the public authority was naturally interested in controlling the general medium of commercial exchange. This medium had to possess the qualities of durability, measurability, and divisibility. These requirements were best met by the rare metals. Their rarity and beauty gave them a value apart from their economic function and aroused men's desire to possess them. As highly treasured objects they were well suited to represent the value of expensive commodities. The divisibility into large and small pieces rendered easy the measurement of large and small values. Their resistance to the deteriorating influences of the weather assured their owners of a durable possession with which they controlled the market at all times and could exert their influence on all who needed a generally accepted medium of economic exchange, i.e., the whole mass of the people in the state. The state could impress the sign of its sovereign authority on these pieces, thus creating the coin. The coin made of rare metal is more than a mere symbol as long as men see a real value in such a metal.

To expedite the transfer of large sums of money, another purely symbolic token was created in the form of paper money. Other symbols of value for limited uses in the form of stamps and the like came into existence in the nineteenth century. The paper money was not intended as a new form of currency but merely as a convenient substitute for the gold and silver ingots contained in the vaults of the state treasury; these ingots are supposed to guarantee the value of the currency in circulation. The credit of a nation was said to be sound if the owner of paper currency could demand from the state its exchange for a coin of equal denomination at any time. Since practically all countries had adopted the gold standard, they were all expected to hold enough gold in their treasuries to satisfy all such claims by the owners of currency. It was calculated, however, that not all owners of paper money would ever make such claims at one and the same time. Furthermore, it was seen that the state had many claims to the money in circulation from taxation and by its undertaking of the postal service and other enterprises so that the government has the larger claim to the gold of the treasury. Hence the credit of a state with one-third of its circulating money covered by gold in the treasury is said to be sound since it is not expected to be embarrassed by the claims of its creditors under normal circumstances.

In itself the high value attributed to gold is an imaginary thing, for gold, despite its beauty and durability, has little practical use; whereas other materials (e.g., iron) are much more useful and necessary. Besides, the real credit and cultural position of a nation are determined by its valuable character traits much more than by the presence of dead gold in its vaults. The history of the first two colonial empires of Spain and Portugal, whose ships brought the gold across the ocean, teaches this clearly. The presence of the gold lessened the will to work and produced a multitude of restless adventurers. Unfortunately the economic thought and practice of the nations of the world have not yet come to an understanding of these facts. The economic life of the world is still predicated on the theory and practice of the gold standard. No matter how resourceful and productive a nation may be, its money is not recognized on the international market unless it is supported by gold in the treasury vaults. Such a nation may buy needed materials from foreign nations only if it can offer other desired goods in exchange or pays in the currency of other nations whose money is recognized on the international money market.

Within its own borders a nation without gold can establish its own legal tender for the efficient flow of its domestic economic life which will go on the more successfully the less the country depends on imports. Under the prevailing economic system, a nation without international financial standing is forced to satisfy its needs as far as possible from its own resources, and to withdraw from international commerce. No doubt such reorganization of a nation's economic life causes strains and calls for personal adjustments. But when the countries of the world realize the inadequacy of the gold standard as a basis for international commerce and put in its stead the vitality and economic potentiality of a nation, the exchange of goods will be easier and more natural, and the whole world will be happier.

The ancient sages who clothed their thoughts in the garb of myths seem to have been farther advanced in economic wisdom than our supposedly expert society, as may be seen from the ancient fable of King Midas, who wished that whatever he touched should be turned into gold and thus miserably starved to death. We ought to reach a point where everyone perceives that a ship which is used in the catch of herrings renders a greater service to the living men and women of the world than a costly diving apparatus designed to raise gold treasures from the bottom of the sea. After all, only a negligible amount of gold is applied to useful and decorative purposes, while practically the whole available supply of gold is kept in vaults.

The simplest and most obvious functions of money are those of a general medium of exchange and price index and accumulation of value. These are also the only functions of money in the simple economic system which is largely concerned with the exchange of goods produced and consumed within the limits of a small territorial unit. Value is conceived throughout in terms of concrete consumer goods and is expressed in figures of monetary units only for market purposes. The state best suited to this economic system is the city state of ancient Greece which Plato and Aristotle had before their mind in their reflections on economics. The political organizations and the economic life of the Middle Ages were in line with this thought and practice. The scholastic philosophers who lived in the business centers of their time and knew their conditions formulated their philosophical and moral considerations on the respective problems according to these experiences. The later Middle Ages show signs of a change in economic thought and practice toward the modern system, in which money is regarded as the real value. But the system of state and Church taxes continued for a long time in terms of natural consumer goods. This is well seen also in documents concerning donations, bequests, and foundations.

The Scholastics regarded money as an unproductive thing (*res sterilis*), the possession of which brings no profit (*nummus nummum non parit*). This is true if coins are kept locked in a chest. With this argument they sought to justify the ecclesiastical law against the taking of interest on loans not only for reasons of Christian charity but also on economic grounds. As a proof of the sterility of money, the theologians, by way of illustration, referred to what happens in the sale of wine. The use of the wine, they said, cannot be separated from the wine itself, because in the use (i.e., the consumption of the wine) the substance of the wine perishes. The same applies to money, they asserted. The use of money consists in its expenditure, by which it vanishes from the possession of its owner. Thus they called money *res primo usu consumptibilis*.

This reasoning was sound, even under the old system of consumer goods exchange, only where such goods as perish in their very use (food, soap, etc.) were bought with the money. It was no longer quite true where the money was spent on tools and raw material for the production of new goods. It lost all its force as soon as, in the production and exchange of goods, the factor of credit played an important part, and the relationship of creditor and debtor was loosened up and became more elastic. This development requires some explanation. The buyer who pays cash becomes full owner of what he acquires, but his purchasing power is restricted by the limits of the cash at his disposal. If, however, the buyer is able to acquire a larger quantity of goods than he can immediately pay for in the well-founded hope of a larger profit in the near future, out of which he can pay the balance, the process of the distribution of goods is

speeded up and greater earnings made possible. Thus the economic life is enriched and enlivened by the credit factor. The
credit need not be given by the one who sells the commercial
goods but may come from a third party in the form of a loan.
In this latter case it is evident that the principle that *nummus
nummum non parit* is not true. Credit has its rational and moral
basis in confidence both in the objective commercial possibilities
and the subjective ability and reliability of the person who asks
it. We need not wonder that, in the complicated commercial system which developed out of the introduction of credit, there
have come into existence highly organized institutions for the
investigation of the trustworthiness of business opportunities
and enterprises.

When a debtor signs a note, by this document he is obligated
only to his creditor. The creditor has given up his money and
has thereby become economically weaker. He has given up "the
wine and the use of the wine," while the debtor has received
"the wine and its use.." The creditor can obtain the repayment of
the loan only from his original debtor. The transaction remains
restricted to the two original parties (including their legal heirs)
and is of no wider economic consequence. The situation changes
considerably as soon as the promissory note is released from this
narrow relationship and passes into the stream of general business as a sort of money having its own value. Let us take as an
illustration the case of a mining company that wishes to expand
its capacity by installing new equipment. To obtain the required capital, the company solicits the participation of new
creditors. No notes are made out for the benefit of those who
are willing to invest their money in the enterprise, but a large
number of notes are printed and sold by investment bankers to
persons who will probably never become personally known to the
officers of the company. The sale of such notes is possible only
when the investment brokers are satisfied that the company is a
reliable and profitable enterprise. Whoever buys such a note
gives to the company the use of the wine. But he himself has not
become economically weaker or poorer. The miracle of the

separation of the wine from the use of the wine, which the
Scholastics thought impossible, has taken place. He has retained
the wine in the form of the share (to use the technical term for
this sort of note) which he can change into legal tender or other
values immediately or as long as the share enjoys the confidence
of the public.

The same effect, although in a limited degree, is produced
by the issuing of a note known as a draft. The vacabulary used
in the writing of drafts indicates that the country where this
practice originated was Italy, whose business centers (Venice
and Genoa), together with the cities on the lower Rhine and of
Flanders, were world powers even at the end of the Middle Ages.
The draft is a document in which the debtor promises to pay a
specified sum on a certain date, usually at the end of a three
months' period, to anyone who presents the note. The obligation
to pay exists independent of any connection with the transaction
that caused the draft to be issued. In the case of an ordinary bill
for goods delivered, the amount to be paid may be reduced or
payment be refused altogether on account of defects in the goods
or their complete rejection, etc. No such contingencies can affect the binding force of the draft, which may, therefore, be
circulated like ordinary money on conditions that each owner
signs his name to it before passing it on and by his signature
guarantees the stipulated payment together with all other pre-
vious owners. The credit extended to the draft is also based on
the confidence in the solvency of the original debtor and all the
others who have signed their name to it. The safety of drafts
as means of financial investments is also guaranteed by very
strict laws against fraud in the matter. The draft has become
indispensable for modern industry and commerce, and it does
not hold any terrors for the experienced financier or business-
man. But private persons who know little about these things
should make it an absolute rule for themselves never to sign,
accept, or give a draft.

The existence of different currencies in the different countries made it necessary for the merchants trafficking in international commerce to square their mutual accounts. No uniform and permanent standard for this work could be set up because money possesses no absolute unchangeable value even where it was given almost the complete status of merchandise in the form of gold and silver. In the use of these metals as money there clings to them always the subjective factor of confidence in the country issuing the money and assigning to it its value for domestic trade. This confidence is subject to fluctuations in the conditions of the several countries. War and peace, good and bad crops, and many other factors have a varying influence on the confidence in the money of a country. The values accorded to paper money, stocks and shares, etc., may even fluctuate more than the value of the gold. These changes in the value of money had to be considered in the squaring of the mutual accounts of the international merchants. So it came about that these merchants assembled in designated places from time to time for the settling of this matter. Toward the end of the Middle Ages one of these places was Bruges, a town in Flanders, where the merchants of Genoa met with other merchants in the house of the Van Der Burse brothers. Thus the institutions and places of the money market have come to be known, in many languages, as the "Burse." With the increase of international commerce, these meetings were held ever more frequently and were assigned to the great trading centers of the world.

In these modern money markets all kinds of notes and certificates representing money values, such as international currencies, stocks, and bonds, are being bought and sold. The basis for their commercial value is the confidence in the economic strength of the countries and industrial or commercial enterprises whose notes are being exchanged. Since the very latest events may influence these values, the money markets are in the closest touch with news of the world which is brought to the notice of those trading there in the speediest manner made possible by modern inventions. In turn, the prices at which the notes are being bought and sold on the basis of the news received, are flashed round the whole world and determine the flow of the whole international commerce.

The same sort of market activity has been extended to merchandise with a standard so well known that the goods need not be present for the fixing of their price. Moral theology calls such goods *fungibles*, i.e., goods which can be replaced in the same quality and quantity even though the original goods have been consumed. Commodities which can be so negotiated are, e.g., all kinds of money, natural products like cotton, coffee, and metals, and industrial products conforming to specified standards. The herring was the first merchandise or commodity to be made the subject of such trading, which has become possible only as the result of the speedy means of modern communication and transportation; but its roots reach back to the late Middle Ages.

The fact that these commodities need not be present, renders the market transactions independent of the place and time of their occurrence. The crops of grain in Canada or of coffee in Brazil can be estimated months before they actually exist; a catch of fish can be reported by telegram; the possibilities of mining industries can be calculated years in advance. On the basis of such information the prices of certain goods on the world market can be calculated or approximately estimated well in advance. Sales can be concluded and the dates for the delivery of the goods and the payment of the price fixed. The possibility of settling commercial deals long before their actual execution is good for the producer, the merchant, and the consuming public. Hence it is morally indifferent, like any other technical device of communication and commerce. The moral factor appears with the use made of these technological means. All human institutions can be abused, but the abuse does not render the institutions themselves evil.

The fixing of prices is the purpose of the money markets and commodity markets. Since not all factors involved in this business can be definitely measured, but are only estimated with a certain probability, the ability to appraise, i.e., prudence, plays a considerable part. But only a step separates prudence from shrewdness, which is less seriously troubled by questions of honesty and is likely to resort to little tricks such as half-truths, rumors, exaggerations, even outright lies and frauds. Business men who suspect that such methods are being used by their competitors feel, of course, free to retaliate in kind, and so an immoral element is introduced. Another danger lies in the need of quick decision, which is willing to take a certain risk when a good opportunity for the conclusion of a business deal offers itself. When carried to excess, quick and courageous decision becomes foolhardy daring, which is no longer guided by sound reason but is incited by the passion of greed. Thus an activity which is in itself legitimate may come to assume an immoral character. But to treat of the problems of the money and commodity market merely as a corollary to the question of ordinary betting and wagering, as is still done by many present-day moralists, indicates a lack of understanding and appreciation.

The misuse of prudence and courage by which they are turned into dishonest shrewdness and reckless daring in matters of the market is known as speculation. Financial speculation is not interested at all in the economic processes and results underlying the transactions of the market, but looks forward to quick and large profits. The speculator sells his own bids according to the possibilities of financial gain resulting from the fluctuations of the market from low to high prices (bull market) or from high to low prices (bear market). Thus any number of transactions may take place between the original bid and the actual execution of the real business underlying it. What is worse, entirely imaginary values that never can or will really exist, are bought and sold. This is gambling, to which whole fortunes are sometimes sacrificed and which has a definitely evil effect on the domestic and international economics of the nations. "Playing the stock market" in this way is immoral and hence sinful.

A certain venturesome participation in the fortunes of the stock market by experts who have legitimate industrial or commercial interests at stake may be justified. For ordinary persons who, without any other concern, are interested only in fortuitous profits, it is certainly sinful to invest risky amounts of money in such ventures, for it may be said with nearly full certainty that they always lose in the end. The ruin of families and suicide are not infrequent consequences of such gambling.

The money and commodity market which we recognized as an ethically justified institution is often credited with a greater importance than it actually possesses. Under the purely liberalist system of capitalist economics it was a necessity. This system has undergone various modifications in the different countries of practically the whole world. Its function as an aid in the planning of business for the future is now accomplished in various degrees by other means according to the recent economic developments in different countries. These developments affect first of all the domestic economic situations prevailing in the several nations. But since it is neither possible nor desirable that industry and commerce should be conducted on an exclusively national instead of an international basis, there will always be some room left for the operations of the money and commodity market.

The foregoing discussion suggests another economic function of money. Money buys the means of production and commerce, thus making possible the creation and expansion of economic enterprises. Money is the fulcrum of the economic process. In this capacity money is known as capital. True, capital includes also the real estate and equipment needed in industry and commerce. But these things are now looked upon as productively invested money, i.e., capital. Here lies the chief difference between the former economic thought, which was in terms of concrete goods, and the modern capitalist thought and practice, which are predicated in terms of money. Modern economics proceeds from money, counts in terms of money, and seeks profits in the form of money. Money has become more than simply a medium of exchange.

The older economic system recognized two sources of production: the raw material and human labor. Now there has been added a third factor, namely, capital in the form of actual

money and in its invested form of the means of industry and
commerce. The prominent position of the money factor marks
the change from the crafts to industry. The crafts do business on
orders actually received and perform the required work as a
unit. Industry does business by producing a supply in the expec-
tation of demands (stimulated by the supply) and performs the
required work in as many separate units as will aid speedy production. Time is an important factor in the capitalist system.
The quicker the process by which the money invested in the
manufacture and in the purchase (in case of the merchant) of
goods is returned as cash, the greater will be the profit over a
period of time. The industrial aim of speedy production for the
sake of a quick turnover of money leads to a certain neglect of
the elements of excellence and beauty that characterize the work
of the crafts.

The division of the manufacturing process into many separate
functions by different workers tends to despiritualize the work.
Man has an inborn desire to create and to enjoy his creation.
This joy, which comes to the craftsman who has succeeded in
producing a beautiful article, is missed by the industrial worker,
who becomes the better skilled in his partial performance the
less his heart and mind crave satisfaction. But thus all his attention is given to the clocklike precision of his work timed to
the rhythm of the machine.

In direct proportion to the exclusion of the ordinary worker's
chance to participate creatively in the industrial process, the
planning and guiding of the thousand and one separate actions
toward the eventual total product becomes of paramount importance. This planning aims also at the least expense of production, i.e., the least possible requirement of material, time,
and thus also of wages. The capitalist system embraces, then,
besides the factors of material, work, capital, and time, the factor of intelligence in the form of ingenious organization. The
engineer who does this work of organization rightly receives
a considerably higher remuneration than the ordinary worker.
The technical organization of production must be supplemented

by the organization of the distribution of the finished product. It is for the commercial expert to find the best market and the best ways of transportation, the best manner of payment and the quickest method of obtaining the raw material. The importance of the commercial organization is well expressed by the fact that the sales directors receive a higher salary than the engineering directors, although an outsider might suppose the latter's work of invention and the practical application of highly intricate technical schemes more important. But it seems to be a law of this world that the inventor earns the praise of the coming generations, whereas the merchant reaps the more tangible fruits for his personal enjoyment.

THE MORALITY OF INTEREST

Under the old system of economics, loans of money or of natural goods (e.g., grain for food or seeding purposes) were made almost exclusively to persons in distress. It is natural that the human feeling of neighborliness and the religious duty of charity should have forbidden that a person's distress be made an occasion of profit. The Jews were explicitly forbidden by the Law to demand interest from their fellow Jews. The business world of the Roman Empire, however, was strongly marked by capitalist trends and practices. Plato's and Aristotle's discussions of the subject were based on the economic life of the small city state where business consisted largely of the exchange of goods for immediate use or consumption. The Stoics also condemned the taking of interest. Cato compares it even to murder. Apart from the rhetorical exaggerations of such statements, the Stoic attitude which was spread among the masses of the people may be explained by the fact that extremely high rates of interest were being demanded, which under the Roman law led to the ruin of the independence of many a free citizen and brought about his reduction to slavery. Christ, who made charity His special command and its fulfillment, the sign by which His disciples would be known, admonish His hearers to seek no profits from loans to a poor neighbor (Luke 6:34).

Throughout the first Christian centuries there prevailed the idea of the loan as a help extended to persons in need. The Scholastics took up this tradition and gave it a philosophical basis in Aristotle's theory of the sterility of money. Thus they arrived at the conclusion that the taking of interest was not permissible. This theory was then made a general law binding all Christians by the canonical legislation of the Church; the Council of Nicea (A.D. 325) had forbidden only the clergy to accept interest. The canonical law prohibiting the taking of interest probably kept many Christians from making loans because, at the best, they could recover only the amount actually loaned, which they might have had opportunity to use profitably in the meantime. Since canon law obliges only Christians but not the Jews, of course persons seeking loans found willing lenders among the Jews. Thus the law of the Church forbidding Christians to take interest has undoubtedly, though unintentionally, helped the Jews to obtain their powerful position in the financial world.

Although the Scholastics taught the theory that money was sterile and that time could be neither bought nor sold, the fact that a different economic system was growing up in which these principles lost their meaning, was perceived by the theologians living in the great commercial cities. To satisfy the authority of the Church and of the great doctors on the one hand, and to face the realities of life on the other hand, a number of reasons and exceptions were introduced by which the general prohibition of interest was in many ways nullified. It was seen that, by loaning his money, the creditor deprived himself of the opportunity of gain. A compensation for this loss of gain or damage sustained was, then, regarded as justified. Moreover, the risk involved in letting others use one's money for the promotion of a commercial enterprise was considered worthy of financial compensation. The compensation obtained on such titles was but another name for interest. The intended evasion of the Church's law was evident in the use of the *titulus poenae conventionalis*. Loans which by their very nature could be intended only for long terms were made for impossibly short terms without interest in order to satisfy the law of the Church. After the lapse of this short term, a certain sum of money was demanded as a penalty for not complying with the time stipulated for the repayment of the loan. The penalty payment amounted to the profit from interest covering the entire period of the loan, including the original short term.

The rigid adherence to a theory which had long since been left behind by the development of the reality of life shows how much the canonists and moralists hesitated to think independently because they were overawed by the authority of the great doctors who in their day could not foresee the shape of later conditions Pope Benedict XIV recognized the above-mentioned titles for taking interest in his encyclical *Vix pervenit* (1745). He did not, however, modify the law against interest. Loaning money without interest to a person in distress, who does not use it for commercial purposes, is certainly more in conformity with the spirit of Christian charity. For many a debtor the payment of interest is a wholesome lesson of thrift and a useful reminder that the creditor expects the principal to be returned. Loans without interest are apt to be regarded as gifts or as something found (Ecclus. 29:4). The question of interest on loans has been regulated by the laws of different nations, and the Church recognized these laws as a just title to the taking of interest (*titulus legis civilis*). Thus the ecclesiastical law against interest practically ceased. When Rome was asked in the nineteenth century whether it was permitted to accept interest, the answer was given: *Non esse inquietandos, dum modo parati sint stare mandatis sanctae sedis*. The new code of canon law abolished the prohibition completely in canon 1543.

THE JUST PRICE

The price is the market value of the goods offered for sale. During normal times people trouble themselves little with the question of how prices are determined. They are all vaguely aware that the factors of supply and demand have something to do with it. Equally general and unburdened with serious thought is the complaint about the high prices, until people themselves wish to sell something. But when the prices of essential commodities become so high as to endanger the customary standard of living and the demand is made that the public authority fix the prices of these articles, then the difficulty involved in the determination of just prices is realized. Although Plato and Aristotle lived at a time when the Greco-Phoenician commerce was flourishing and had such modern institutions as the credit system, their views were based on the more primitive forms of trade which obtained in the rather self-contained city-states of Greece. They did not approve of commerce on a large scale and as a means of acquiring wealth. Only on a small scale and as far as it is necessary to bring the commodities to the consumer, would they call commerce ethical and honorable.

Plato's dictum that the tradesman knows the just price, points in the direction of the so-called retrospective or objective price theory which teaches that the just price consists of the cost of production, transportation, etc,, including the proper wages for those engaged in these processes plus a moderate profit for the merchant to assure his suitable standard of living. In this sense Plato advocates the fixing of just prices by the state. At first sight, nothing seems more just and easier than this. In fact, this seems to be the method usually employed by governments whenever the cry for public control of prices becomes clamorous. Under normal conditions, when the course of commerce is not dictated by extraneous regulations, the sales prices are and have always been arrived at by a different route. This fact seems to indicate that this latter way is natural and cannot be condemned outright. We see the law of supply and demand operative in the oldest time and continuously until now. An analysis of this law leads us not to the original cost plus moderate profit as the factors determining the price, but to the value of an object in the present and predictable conditions of the buying public. A merchant may be forced to sell at less than the original cost and may thus sustain a loss. On the other hand, he may be able to sell at a considerably higher price an article for which he paid comparatively little, but which he can replace only at a sharply increased cost. Apparently neither the retrospective nor the prospective price theories alone can do justice to the realities involved in the determination of the just price. The two must supplement each other at many points. Even Aristotle, who shares Plato's low esteem for the merchant's profession, does not believe in the sufficiency of the retrospective theory of the price. He sees the relation of the parties engaged in a sales transaction under the figure of the diagonals of a parallelogram; i.e., their relation is not one of mathematical equality but of geometrical proportion.

The Roman world in which the Christian religion first took root was favorable to commercial activity and had a highly developed economic system. Big trade was regarded as highly respectable, and complete freedom in the negotiation of contracts was guaranteed. It was not before the reign of Diocletian that the excessive profits made by the middlemen called for government intervention in the fixing of prices. In view of the emphatic otherworldly attitude of the early Christians, it is natural that they should not have discussed commercial problems. Their ideal of the life on earth is the community of men in the religious union of the mystical body of Christ where the members help one another in such a way as to eliminate the two extremes of great wealth and pressing poverty. But they lived in the midst of a commercial society and could not avoid all contact with it. St. John Chrysostom's harsh word, that a merchant can hardly save his soul, reflects Christ's stern warning about the dangers of wealth, but it does not imply a condemnation of all mercantile activity. St. Augustine, with his delicate

sense for the fitness of things, appreciates the necessary and
beneficial aspects of commerce and states in his *City of God* that
the value of a thing is determined by its relation to the needs
of man. Thus St. Augustine, without elaborating a systematic
doctrine, expresses himself in favor of the prospective theory of
the just price.

The Scholastics, most of whom lived in the great commercial
cities and witnessed the lives and activities of successful and
respected merchants, recognize also the utility and respectabil-
ity of their work. St. Thomas says: *"Nihil utilitati communiter
deserviens est peccatum."* Duns Scotus and Buridan, a disciple
of William of Occam, give evidence of their understanding of
the nature and problems of commerce. They emphasize the freedom of subjective estimation of values in the sales contract, in-
cline toward the prospective theory of the just price, and teach
that the merchant's *industria, diligentia,* and *solicitudo* are also
deserving of reward. The price theory of Antoninus of Florence
is of importance even in our time. According to him the price
is to be determined by the general estimation of the value of a
thing: *communis aestimatio.* He distinguishes three prices:
pretium pium, the lowest price; *pretium medium* or *moderatum,*
the normal price; *pretium rigorosum,* the highest price. Later
casuists set the difference of these prices as 10 per cent above
and below the normal price. Sometimes they allowed considerably greater differences. The *pretium pium,* i.e., sale without
profit, could not be made obligatory but was advised in case of
really poor people or very intimate friends. The highest price,
however, played an important part. That time could be neither
bought nor sold was for the Scholastics an axiom like the unlaw-
fulness of interest, which they did not venture to give up in
theory. But they knew, as well as the merchants, that it makes a
considerable difference whether a sale is made on a cash basis
or on an agreement providing for deferred payment. Just as the
forbidden interest on loans was admitted into the economic
system by way of evasive titles, so the factor of the time element in sales on credit was introduced by allowing the *pretium*

rigorosum to be exacted from him who could not buy for cash.

About the middle of the sixteenth century a great dearth came over those nations which, in their desire for gold and adventure, had sent the ablest part of their youth into the New World and had neglected the production of commodities at home. There was a demand for civil legislation to fix price ceilings for the goods needed in daily life. Around the laws which were enacted there grew up a moral and theological controversy as to the obligation in conscience to observe the legal prices, because their defects were soon manifest. The complaints about the failure of the legally established prices read as modern as if they were written in our own day. We learn also that the consumer is interested as much in a sufficient supply of merchandise as in moderate prices. External interference with the healthy operations of commerce does harm not only to the merchant but also to the consuming public.

The economic life of our time has become extremely intricate, and long and serious studies are required to understand its operations. Not only has economics separated itself from the influence of the Church in the last few centuries, it has also become an independent science. Still we must insist on the principle that all human activity must submit to the dictates of sound morals. Moral theology will, of course, not arrive at ready-made solutions for all possible business problems, but it can undertake an objective study of these problems and judge them in the light of moral principles. It is high time for consciences to be again awakened to the fact that mere cleverness in business affairs is not the same as moral correctness. The fact of the social solidarity of men must again become a living thing in the mind of the people. They must learn that there are demands of social justice; that all who partake of the economic life of society either as producers or as merchants or as consumers have social duties; that negligence or injustice harms not only the individual primarily involved, but also the whole social body. All must realize, e.g., that neglectful habits, such as unnecessary delays in paying bills, are not mere private affairs but have an evil effect on the economic life of society. Honesty and helpful cooperation in our economic contacts are moral virtues, and the opposite attitudes and practices are violations of justice and Christian charity.

ADVERTISING

In the commercial exchange of goods, advertising, that is, bringing the objects for sale to the attention of the public so as to stimulate buying, is of great importance. Moral theology is interested only in the methods of advertising, because the action of making saleable objects known to the public is morally permissible, if the objects are intended primarily for good purposes although they may also be put to evil use. In the old-fashioned markets the buyers are attracted by the open display of the merchandise on the stands. Very old is also the hawking of the things offered. The superlatives used in their recommendations are recognized as mere efforts to attract attention and are, therefore, not sinful. Only very naïve persons will be deceived by them. In the show windows of a modern store and throughout the store itself, the display of merchandise has become vastly more impressive and effective.

The large newspapers and periodicals carry the advertisements now to the silent reader. In pictures and printed words the objects are now presented as useful and desirable possessions. The emotional appeal is here secondary, giving place to more persuasive language by emphasis on what is described as the objective quality of the merchandise. The material ingredients as well as the long experience and scientific work employed in the production of the goods are described and stressed so as to awaken the confidence of the buying public. It is, of course, important that the public be induced to consider the merchandise offered as more excellent than rival products. Thus, besides the stress on the objective good qualities, mention is made of weak points which have been eliminated, intimating thereby that rival products may suffer from such inferior qualities. According to the law and the accepted code of advertising, inferior qualities need not be revealed so long as the positive claims are true. Again, in stating the elimination of weaknesses or harmful elements there must not occur false statements and exaggerations which would cast unfair reflections on rival products. In this respect, advertising is probably kept within moral limits because the keen competition of the many concerns interested in the sale of their products maintains watchfulness over rival advertising and forces any undue methods to be abandoned. The same applies to advertising over the radio where, however, the purely emotional appeal comes very much to the fore.

Increase of sales is the purpose of advertising. Its effect must be the favorable impression upon the mind of the buyer regarding the objective value of the goods along with the desire for the goods advertised and even the conviction that they are a necessity. The desired result of advertising is thus an artificially created state of mind. The desire of material gain dictates the nature of the appeal. Advertising is essentially an appeal, not a factual statement, although it may be in the interest of the effectiveness of the appeal that it be factual. But evidently advertising, of its very nature, is beset by a ceaseless conflict between truthful information and false or misleading statement, frank admission and clever concealment. On the part of the emotions and appetites, advertising will always proceed on the narrow path that separates the decent from the indecent in its illustrations; temperance from immoderation palliated in euphemisms or promoted by the creation of new wants; morbid excitement from healthy interest in the radio entertainment. Ugly as may be the many posters which from every possible place tersely advise the public of its needs and of the best way to satisfy them, they are comparatively harmless.

Undeniably, advertising is an indispensable service in the present world of commerce. Articles that are not advertised do not sell. The great commercial firms have advertising specialists in their sales department. There exist advertising firms which organize and carry out advertising campaigns along all avenues by which the public can be reached. Many branches of science

and art concentrate their efforts on effective advertising. Many
a good product, whose manufacturer lacks the means of advertising, may thus be lost. Such is the tragedy of life even under an
economic system which tries to remedy the excesses of liberalism.
Industrialists and merchants seriously striving to uphold Christian moral principles cannot be denied the right to use the modern
ways of advertising. A certain glow of allurement and persuasion
for which there is little or no real foundation will always hover
around modern advertising. But this feature will be understood
by the public and is, therefore, not sinful. Actual deception or
other means that cause harm to the health of the soul or body in
the manner indicated above, make advertising sinful even though
it may be impossible to take legal action against it.

REAL ESTATE

The most sacred and important possession of a nation is the
land as that part of the earth where it is called upon to work out
its destiny. In the old Germanic code, landed property was subject to laws different from those applying to movable possessions,
whereas the Roman law treated both alike. In fact, the soil is a
different good from all the rest. It is not only the theater of human life; it is also the source of the sustenance of man's life and
activity. Hence the question how much and what quality of land
a nation calls its own, is of paramount importance.

In contrast to all other kinds of property, the soil has this
advantage, that it cannot be destroyed. It may be devastated
and the cultural work of man on it wiped out. If properly tended,
the land will again produce its crops and provide the settler with
things he needs for his life and work. Conversely, land has the
disadvantage that it cannot be increased like the products of
industry, although its fertility can be improved within certain
limits. The amount of the land does not grow with the increase
of the population, and after a time it may not be extensive
enough. The fear that the earth would soon prove insufficient to
feed the human race gave rise, in the nineteenth century, to the

pernicious social heresy of Malthus, which asserts that the population increases in geometric proportions while the fertility of the earth may be raised only in arithmetic proportions. The first proposition is true, the second is false. By intensive cultivation the soil can be made to yield fruit at geometrically progressive rates. Besides, there is yet so much uninhabited and unused land in the world, and the possibilities of providing for the needs of men by new discoveries and inventions are so great, that the future generations will still find ample room and sustenance. These considerations are not meant, however, to justify thoughtless and selfish laissez-faire practices in the distribution and exploitation of the land either in the domestic concerns of the nations or their mutual relations.

The question of landed possessions looms large in the internal and external history of the nations. The historical developments resulting from the quest of land and its use have decisively influenced the political vicissitudes and cultural advance, many of the successes and failures, of the human race. This undeniable fact argues strongly that the problem of the distribution, within and between the nations, and the use of the soil by private and public owners, involve a moral issue the settlement of which must be based on the reasoned demands of equity and justice. Wars of extermination, devastating revolutions, the collapse of civilizations, the moral and religious deterioration of men, have been largely though not exclusively the result of the unfair distribution of landed property. Shrewd and ruthless real estate speculation has produced the iniquitous tenement houses which from the very start were places of disease, immorality, and social hatred. The inequitable distribution of the agricultural soil was the ruin of ancient Rome, the reason for the desperate revolts of the peasants in the sixteenth century, and a contributing cause of the discontent and radical tendencies of the masses in many countries of our day. The rapacious or simply inconsiderate exploitation of the soil has impoverished many once flourishing districts and countries in the world with the result of great hardship to the succeeding generations.

In many countries where the correction of these evils was felt as an urgent necessity for the preservation of social peace and the sufficient material support of the population, enlightened and promising steps have been taken of late by the governments. In other countries private organizations under religious auspices have undertaken on a large scale the study and execution of like projects, which may yet prove of tremendous significance in this matter so essential for the creation of a Christian social order. We cannot here offer a detailed account of the work that is being done. For such information the reader is referred to the pertinent literature, which is easily accessible. Neither may it be feasible for the individual priest to take an active part in these movements, but he should appreciate and favor them as Christian morality put into practice. They relieve suffering, remove occasions of sin, and tend to provide that natural basis which is presupposed by the supernatural order.

XIV

The Use of Property

CONTRACTS CONCERNING THE USE OF PROPERTY

A LEASE is usually a contract by which the owner leaves the use of *immovable* property to another person. The conditions of the lease, such as the time of its duration and the rate of compensation, are agreed upon in the contract in the drawing-up of which it is important to observe the civil laws governing such transactions. From the moral standpoint care must be taken to determine whether or not the purpose for which the lease is sought is good or evil, and whether the probable abuse of the leased property implies material (i.e., not sinful or formal) or sinful cooperation on the part of the owner. E.g., a person who leases his premises for the sale of alcoholic beverages under legal conditions does not cooperate in the sin of those who happen to drink there to excess. Cooperation is formal and sinful if the purpose of the lease is in itself sinful, e.g., the establishment of a place of immorality, or for the storing of stolen goods, the manufacture of counterfeit money or of forbidden explosives.

The owner is obliged to make an honest statement about the condition of the property to be leased, but he need not point out obvious defects and limitations. Hidden defects which can be discovered only by the actual use of the property must be revealed. The rent to be paid must be just, i.e., not too high or too low. The same principles which apply to the just price in sales contracts must be observed here. A contract made in accordance with the sound demands of morality must be faithfully kept by both parties. The faithful observance of such agreements is the best ethical conduct. For a person to make unfair use of his social or economic position in disregarding his contractual obligations is an abominable crime.

The leased object must, at the expiration of the contract, be returned in substantially the same condition as that in which it was accepted. In the case of objects which naturally deteriorate by age or by normal use, the proper compensation is supposed to be included in the stipulated rent. Depreciation, however, which is caused by neglect or excessive and inconsiderate use and exploitation is to be compensated for by an additional charge.

In case of severe hardship on one party there may arise the moral duty for the other party to renounce the fulfillment of the contract either as a whole or in part. Such free relinquishing of rights acquired under the contract is morally higher than when it is forced by legal action of the suffering party. Sometimes the duties of charity, which, needless to say, are real obligations, may demand more than the norms of strict justice, although it may be generally stated that those who observe the laws of their country in these matters satisfy also the moral law. But in extreme cases of distress, e.g., on account of sickness or ruinous loss of property, charity may demand, absolutely and under pain of grievous sin, leniency or complete cancellation of the contracted obligations even though these could still be upheld under the provisions of the law.

The lease ends at the expiration of the stipulated time. It may come to an end even before that time upon the mutual consent of the contracting parties. It is terminated by the death of either party unless the contract provides that it shall pass on to the legal heirs. If the leased object, e.g., a house, is destroyed, the contract also ceases to be in force.

LOAN OF PROPERTY

A *loan* (or *hire*) is a contract by which the owner leaves the use of some *movable* property to another person. Life is full of situations in which a person is in temporary need of an object that at the moment he is unable or unwilling to acquire as his own either because he lacks the means for it or is prevented by some other circumstance, or because he does not consider its permanent possession proportionate to his need of it. Accordingly we must distinguish between loans made to an indigent neighbor which should be gratis as an act of charity, and loans granted to persons who borrow an object instead of buying it as a matter of well calculated business policy. In the first case, the loans should be made without financial considerations whether the objects loaned are consumed in their very use (e.g., bread) and are to be returned in kind, or are not consumed and must be returned identically the same. The same applies to loans made to a temporarily embarrassed neighbor or friend or any other known and trustworthy person. Even spontaneous feelings of friendly helpfulness and neighborliness will prompt such loans. Such were practically all loans, except loans of money, up to comparatively recent times; hence the provision in the traditional definition of a loan, that it must be gratis.

But it cannot be of the essence of the loan to be gratis in the case of a person who borrows an object, perhaps of considerable value such as costly machinery, because it suits his financial interests better, i.e., for business reasons. The nature of the contract is not changed by calling it *hire*. That the loaning of all kinds of articles is not always of the nature of helping an embarrassed neighbor but of helping him in a positively gainful undertaking and has even become an established institution of regular business for gain, is seen from the fact that there exist now whole industries which provide things that people ordinarily would not care to buy but prefer to borrow or hire whenever they wish to use them. The classified section of any large telephone directory contains scores of examples of such industries and businesses. The rent to be paid must be just, but it need not be based on some external or accidental title. The very contract of the loan is a business transaction in the ordinary sense of the word, in which the principles of *quid pro quo* is operative.

The principle that loans of money and of objects of use should be made without interest or compensation was and still is valid in cases of need requiring the help of Christian charity, or when they are made out of friendliness and neighborliness. But then it would seem that there is no contract involved in the strict sense of the word, although common decency demands that in letting another person use our property we should see to it that that person is really benefited and suffers no harm. And the beneficiary should likewise see to it that his benefactor will receive the loaned object in good condition and at the right time. In such acts of friendly accommodation the thought of contracting obligations in the strict legal sense is mostly absent from the mind of the persons involved; actually the understanding is that the question of legal action should not be considered at all. If in the case of insincerity legal action is taken and admitted by the law, the real ground for such action is the unjust privation of the lender of his property similar to theft or the breach of promise which may occur without any connection with the loaning and borrowing of goods. At any rate, the contractual loans which, as licit business deals, stipulate for compensation are now so commonly accepted that we cannot realistically define the loan as a contract which excludes the idea of compensation.

SURETY

Surety consists in the contractual promise to satisfy a creditor's demand on a debtor in case the latter is unable or unwilling to pay his debt. From the moral standpoint we should observe that it is sinful on the part of a debtor to obtain such a legally binding promise by flattery and misrepresentation when he has reason to doubt his own ability to fulfill his financial obligations. Again it is sinful on the part of a person to sign his name on such a promissory note when he feels that he is likewise unable to assume the financial obligations of the debtor in the case of his default. From the standpoint of practical experience it must be said that "going surety" is a dangerous and treacherous thing. It has been the cause of serious loss and financial ruin to many a goodhearted person. The statement usually urged, that the signing of the surety is only a formality and will never entail any real consequences, is false. For a person to put his signature on documents that may give rise to real obligations, is never a mere formality. Those who have no resources must not sign a surety obligation. Those who can afford to help should give a quarter or half of the sum involved as an outright gift. They know then that they are rid of their money and the matter is closed.

MORTGAGE

A real-estate mortgage is a contract by which real estate is offered as security for a large loan. The creditor receives a properly executed document entitling him to the stipulated payment of the principal and interest and to coerce such payment, if necessary, by the forced sale of the mortgaged property. Several such mortgages may be attached to the same piece of real estate, and their claims are considered in the order in which they were made. The first mortgage is the safest, especially if it claims only a portion of the mortgaged object. The holder of the second mortgage frequently becomes the owner of the mortgaged property in case of default, by satisfying the claims of the first mortgage and accepting the mortgaged object instead of the money owed. As in all like transactions, morality demands truthfulness and sincerity. The person borrowing on a mortgage must make truthful statements about the value of his real estate and his ability to pay. The creditor, on the other hand, must not without a serious reason seize upon an unforeseen and temporary embarrassment of the mortgagor to drive him from his property. The holder of a mortgage is under a grave moral obligation to refrain from forcing the sale or surrender of the mortgaged property except for serious and clearly equitable reasons.

DEPOSIT

Deposit is the agreed-upon or understood safekeeping of another person's property for a certain time. In general there exists no obligation to keep other persons' property in safety, except for the obligation in charity to prevent loss from coming to them, if this can be done without undue inconvenience. Whoever accepts objects for safekeeping even by such actions as the taking up of found articles or accepting packages of merchandise not ordered where the practice of such shipments exists, assumes thereby certain obligations. The first of these is that he keep these things with the same care as he devotes to the same sort of objects which are his own property. If in spite of proper care things kept for others are spoiled or lost, no compensation need be made to the owner. Damage resulting from culpable negligence involves an obligation of restitution. Accidental advantages that may result from the presence of such objects in a person's safekeeping may be retained, but their intentional use for personal gain, especially when there is any danger of their deterioration or loss, is not permitted. Nor may their natural fruits be appropriated without the consent of the real owner.

Merchandise sent for inspection without being ordered need not be returned, particularly when its return involves inconvenience and expense; but it must be kept in readiness to be surrendered when it is called for. Charity and enlightened self-interest, however, should prompt the speedy return of unwanted goods. Expert care and vigilance must be bestowed on the safekeeping of deposited objects which have been accepted for that purpose by an explicit contract, whether or not this service is rendered as an act of private accommodation, professional service, or public duty.

DONATION

Donation is the free transfer of property from one person to another with the mutual understanding that no compensation is to be made in return. The donor must have full ownership of the object and the right to dispose of it at his discretion. He must clearly understand the nature of the action and he must be free from inner constraint or undue external influences. This implies also that donations obtained on the basis of grossly false pretenses, such as imaginary stories of distress or good causes, or by threats, are invalid and cannot be retained. A donation may be morally illicit or more or less devoid of merit according as it conflicts with duties of justice or charity. Persons in debt should first satisfy these obligations before making large donations. If a person knows that close relatives of his are in distress, he should make them the beneficiaries of his generosity before expending it on strangers. The motives of donations determine also their moral value. Gifts made in the secret hope of gratitude shown in the form of immoral acts are sinful. Sensual affection as the chief motive of donations renders them always less perfect, even though no return of sinful thanks is expected. Donations made from the motive of public praise or fear of shame are likewise imperfect. Of higher moral value are gifts prompted by disinterested helpfulness to the promotion of humanitarian and cultural causes, or impelled by the spirit of penance and similar religious considerations. The highest motive is the detachment from earthly possessions and the exercise of Christian charity.

Gifts to the poor are known among Christians as alms. Almsgiving according to one's means is an essential part of the Christian life. Readiness not only to share actual wealth but to help the poor also by personal sacrifice is a sign of true Christian character. Almsgiving, prayer, and fasting belong to the Christian life in the form of the imitation of Christ. Ancient and modern braggarts pretending to be supermen would have us leave the weak and poor perish as not worthy of existence. But Christian charity sees in the poor, brethren in Christ whose distress we must alleviate. The Fathers of the Church are eloquent in the praise of almsgiving. St. John Chrysostom ascribes to it the power of diminishing even the pains of hell and calls it more effective than prayer. St. Ambrose would even have the sacred vessels of the Church sold if no other means of assisting the suffering can be found. These statements and the actual works of charity in the form of charitable and pious institutions founded and supported by alms throughout the Christian era demonstrate that men of true faith are also men of charitable deeds.

Almsgiving is indeed an act of personal virtue, an expression of living religious faith, but it must for all that be guided by prudence gained from experience in the world. There are many unconscionable persons who provide for themselves a life of leisure and comfort by exploiting the ill-instructed kindness of other people. The clergy are especially imposed upon by these professional idlers and beggars. Hence the priest must expect that a high percentage of the beggars unknown to him personally are of that type. And since it cannot be right that the money he is willing to give to the deserving poor should be squandered on idlers and liars, he should use discriminating judgment in giving alms. Small sums of money and food may be given away by the domestics without any inquiry. Larger amounts should never be given away without prudent examination of the petitioner. The priest should never allow himself to give large alms to strangers immediately. If they are deserving of help, this fact can in most cases easily be established by an inquiry upon obtaining their names and addresses. If they refuse to give this information for the purpose of investigation, they are evidently impostors. Alms should never be given to those who ask it in connection with confession, with the promise of turning Catholic, or under the threat of suicide. These circumstances are but artifices and no signs of real intention, but sure evidence of fraud.

If it can be so arranged, the priest should have witnesses present when he is talking to a person who asks for large alms. As any rate, he should be as reserved as possible in his statements lest an imprudent word of his may be turned against him and used as a means of extortion. Unusually large gifts may even give rise in the minds of malicious persons to suspicions as to the pure intentions of the giver, who in reality perhaps made a heroic sacrifice, though acting imprudently. These considerations show also the advisability of practicing Christian charity by contributions to the ecclesiastically organized charitable institutions which, by their professionally trained and religiously inspired personnel, do admirable work that the priest alone cannot do. Through the operations of the diocesan Catholic Charities, the St. Vincent de Paul Society, and other like organizations, many persons can be brought again to a position of respectable self-support who would remain forever in the condition of beggars if helped only with private alms.

Donations are free gifts which do not call for any gifts in return. But they demand a morally worthy attitude on the part of the recipient, i.e., a dignified expression of gratitude which must show itself also in a tangible form if at any time a former benefactor happens to be suffering need. In reality, benefactions are often a source of bitter disappointment which may paralyze a person's readiness to give. Such disappointments must, of course, never bring a person to the point where he abandons the practice of almsgiving. Christian helpfulness must be exercised in a Christian manner. Christ said that in doing good the left hand should not know what the right hand does. Publicity should not be sought nor should it be made an incentive to almsgiving. Alms should not be given in a manner that humiliates the deserving poor, but in a way that bespeaks the attitude of Christian respect for one another and helps the poor to endure their lot in this life with Christian fortitude.

The state, which has the right to regulate questions of property on the regular social plane, may also interfere with conditions on the level of begging if its frequency indicates a social disorder in need of correction. It may, therefore, create institutions that eliminate or reduce the necessity of begging from house to house. Donations on a large scale are also subject to regulations of the state, and these must be observed. Donations of immovable and movable goods are known as foundations if the giver expresses his will about their immediate and future use. The laws of the Church and the state concerning such foundations must be observed. The great accomplishments of the Church in the past and present depend largely on pious foundations. Also the growth and progress of many secular cultural achievements owe an immeasurably great debt of gratitude to these expressions of the religious spirit.

INSURANCE

Certain possessions are so unavoidably exposed to the risk of damage or destruction by the elements of nature that the individual owners, if unaided, are in peril of losing all their support of life and the possibility of rebuilding their economic undertaking. To these possessions belong transportation of valuable cargo on the high sea and on land, buildings, crops, and others. To restore such unpredictable losses men have banded together for the purpose of creating by regular contributions funds out of which the stricken individuals of their organization receive the means of re-establishing themselves. Such was the beginning of the now highly developed and diversified system of insurance. Seagoing ships were the first things to be so protected. The idea of insuring crops against hail was suggested by Defoe, the author of *Robinson Crusoe*.

The technical organization and operation of the insurance companies need not be discussed. But since the insurance policies are explicit bilateral contracts in which the terms of the insurance are agreed upon, it is necessary that both parties be truthful in their statements and that they strive for sincere clarity in the formulation of the terms. Especially in policies which are designed to be sold mostly among the masses of the people, false impressions created by the wording of the policies or the sales methods of the agents may verge on intentional deceit, although no fraud can be proved in court. In the insurance of highly technical objects and processes the principle *caveat emptor* may be employed more freely because there the contracting parties are expected to have expert knowledge of the matter. Compensation received from insurance companies by fraudulent claims must be restored, although the insured may deduct the amount of premiums paid with the interest thereon, less the clerical expenses of the company (cf. H. Davis, *Moral and Pastoral Theology*, Vol. II).

At the beginning of the insurance institution, religious objections were raised against it on the ground that it indicated lack of confidence in the providence of God. If this were true, then all attempts to provide for the future would be sinful, a view which is untenable in the light both of reason and of divine revelation. It is permissible to buy the protection provided by any of the many kinds of insurance now available, within the limits of one's financial resources. There may be even a moral obligation for some to take out insurance policies to protect their dependents against grave hardship. Fire and life insurance, sickness and accident policies, are widely held and of long standing. The dangers involved in the automobile traffic on the highways suggests that proper insurance at least with regard to the damage that may result to others from automobile accidents is a grave moral obligation binding on all who own and operate motor vehicles.

PARTNERSHIP

Partnership is the joint undertaking by several persons of a business enterprise which usually exceeds the economic possibilities of one person, e.g., mining, railroad operation, manufacturing. The contributions of the partners may be of the same or different kind, e.g., invention, real estate, mechanical or executive experience, capital. But in the partnership contract these contributions are all expressed in terms of money value. From the standpoint of ethics, the mutual relations are to be based on truthfulness and honesty. And the civil laws must be exactly observed.

From the standpoint of human prudence we should note that he who does not understand perfectly the working of such joint enterprises and can have no influence on their management should avoid partnership. Too many such undertakings are vitiated by fraud, and even the ones planned with honest intentions are liable to fail for unpredictable reasons and circumstances beyond control. The contributed money may all be lost and more may have to be paid over an extended period on account of the originally contracted liability long after the shrewd founders have succeeded in severing all connections or in avoiding liability under some technical guise of insolvency. Most large enterprises of this sort obtain the necessary capital by issuing stock, which is sold to the public. Those who have to handle money so invested should acquaint themselves with the pertinent laws and facts by consulting a lawyer specializing in this field. Priests should never be the founders or responsible directors of such undertakings. Neglect of this evident and obvious principle has brought bitter experiences on many occasions.

Large-scale partnerships are of great economic importance and usefulness, and indispensable at our advanced stage of material civilization. From the social point of view they suffer from the evils of absentee ownership under which the personal contact between employer and employee is lost and the only interest shown is the demand for increasing profits by the stockholders. Here lies one of the pressing problems now generally known as the social question. It is one of the points where industrial and economic organization has outrun the appropriate social and moral forms of human relationships. Countless organizations espousing different and conflicting views and programs are at present engaged in the struggle for supremacy in the creation of a new social order. It is the mighty task of our generation to see to it that the new social order shall be in conformity with the laws of the kingdom of Christ.

The stocks providing the money for the large commercial enterprises are bought and sold in the open market. Their values are subject to considerable fluctuations. Traffic in them, by playing the stock market, may bring great wealth quickly, but likewise sudden financial ruin. The practice of continually buying and selling stocks for the sake of financial gain is ethically wrong. As a rule, it ends also in financial loss.

GAMES AND BETTING [1]

The attraction of competition in social games is increased by adding the element of loss and gain. For such games to be

[1] See also Ruland, *Foundations of Morality*, pp. 358 f.

morally permissible the sum liable to be lost must be so small that it is insignificant in comparison with the economic situation of the players. If this amount is exceeded, the playing of games is immoral. Experience teaches that the passion of playing for gain may lead people to economic ruin and into the paths of crime. As a certain courage and moral strength is required not to follow general customs, so courage is also required to refuse taking part in games. It may become a moral duty to refuse to play games if too much time needed for professional duties or other obligations will be lost or if a person's economic condition does not permit such recreation. Sometimes unreasonable superiors force young subjects by moral coercion to join parties that play for stakes beyond their means, at which they almost always lose on account of their lack of interest.

The stimulating thrill and tension experienced in trying the seemingly endless possibilities of winning in games of chance exert a perennial attraction which few can resist even after many disappointments. For this reason various games of chance have been used since ancient times as a means of raising funds. In some countries they are used by the government for the purpose of obtaining money needed for public improvements. On a large scale these games of chance take the form of lotteries. Participation in such games is morally right as long as the money thus spent does not in any way endanger the economic security of the player. Since the profits derived from such games are mostly used for the promotion of good causes, the games fulfill a useful purpose and their playing is justified. In most cases people who play such games publicly with others or take a stake in a national lottery do so because this gives them pleasure and they spend no more money than they would use for other forms of recreation.

Another game that attracts by the element of uncertainty and the possibility of some gain, is betting. Betting is a sort of contest of the wits and is morally permissible if the financial stakes are kept within the proper limits as explained above and if neither contestant has as yet any certain knowledge of the

matter that is the object of the wager. If a person has definite
information on the matter, he cannot in fairness make a wager
with one whose view is based on mere conjecture and general
reflection, unless the latter insists on betting even after he has
been told about the ascertained knowledge of the other person.
Betting is in itself lawful, but when it is done for high stakes or
professionally in connection with sport events, such as horse
races or boxing bouts, it often leads to unfair and even criminal
acts designed to determine the outcome in advance. In this way
the public has often been swindled out of much money for the
luxurious support of criminals.

DISTRIBUTION OF PROPERTY AND THE SOCIAL ORDER

Private property is a necessity. Primitive man, still more man
on the higher cultural levels, needs the right to the free use of his
tools and primary material for the work by which he provides his
sustenance. The full and permanent right to the fruits of his labor
is likewise needed as an incentive to industry and perseverance
in planned labor for progress and improvement which are the
foundation of civilization and culture. If mankind were naturally
good and sinless, the growth of culture would have developed in a
unilinear direction; and this would have shown itself also in the
equitable distribution of property. Real history presents a different picture. Especially in the matter of property we find
great inequalities, which are a source of hatreds and enmities
under a variety of forms; a source that never dries up but that
at times pours forth torrents which threaten to sweep away all
rights and goods.

The ancient Greek philosophers recognized, as the source of
all moral evil, *hybris,* i.e., selfish and wanton immoderation, and
consequently held up as the chief virtue *sophrosyne,* i.e., reasonable contentment and moderation. The pernicious results of
immoderation—apart perhaps from the cravings of sex—are
nowhere as evident as in man's desire for property. Probably
never in the history of man was there a time when wise men,

philosophers and priests, lawgivers and statesmen, did not recognize the evil effect of greed on the character of the individual and the welfare of the community, and did not seek remedies in accordance with their outlook on life and their religious or political position. The two basic observations were: (1) that immoderate desire of possession disturbs the social peace and brings disorder into the individual soul; (2) that the remedy of immoderation and greed lies in limitation and renunciation.

All agree in this, and we should not regard all similar efforts of reform as traces of cultural contact or literary dependence. The idea of renunciation is found at all times and in all cultural patterns. The reforms differ only in the measure and degree of their rejection of private property and the extent of their insistence on renunciation, i.e., whether it should be restricted to their own person or a small circle of disciples, or extended to the whole nation or even to all men. Further, there is the distinction between movable and immovable goods.

The extreme forms of flight from the world and renunciation can be practiced only by a few together with some disciples and presuppose a favorable climate. There were hermits long before Christ, and after Him also among the Christians as a form of life aiming at the perfect realization of the Christian ideal. The founders of the eremitical life lived in lonely and barren desert places. But as soon as their disciples began to lay stress on work among their fellow men, they had to make a more extensive use of material goods. The community of possessions among the first Christians, mentioned in the Acts of the Apostles, was not a general obligation but a local attempt to realize the Christian ideal of detachment from the world. The otherworldly attitude of the Christian religion implied always a struggle against attachment to the world, but no systematic clarification of the whole problem. The eremitical and monastic institutions emphasized again renunciation of property as an ideal form of life. Communities with traces of socialism, such as the common education of boys by the state, existed in ancient times but had no influence on the Christian way of life. On account of the Christians' high regard for Plato, his political views influenced Christian thinkers. But the existence of private property was always regarded by the Christians and the whole ancient world as a matter of course. The Stoic view that only the wise man could make good use of earthly possessions and therefore had the only real right to them, was accepted by some of the great writers of the Church. According to them, the virtuous Christian takes the place of the wise man; he has the right to all goods and yet does not desire them.

We must not forget that among the ancients there was an institution which precluded all the difficulties that are the cause of our modern social problem. That institution was slavery. The ancient world had many more slaves than free men, and these disinherited millions performed all the hard work without the right to share in the fruits of their labor. Speaking from a merely economic standpoint, we should note that the slaves had to pay by their work for their original cost, which was often quite high, but after that they were no expense except for their food. When well organized, the work of the slaves represented pure profit which enriched their masters and allowed them luxuries which we can hardly imagine. The greatest slaveowners were the state and the ruling princes. Slavery was so old an institution that it did not occur even to the most enlightened sages to investigate and consider its justification. A few Christian writers made the unsatisfactory statement that the origin of slavery was due to Noe's intoxication and the sin of his son Cham: *nisi ebrietas fuisset, servitus non esset.*

Among the Germanic races that played the leading part in the shaping of the events and institutions of the Middle Ages, there existed a class of unfree people and vassals who could not make the same claim to the possession and enjoyment of the goods of the earth as their superiors. At the end of the medieval and the beginning of the modern era, the social inequalities resulting from the increasing wealth of the upper classes, became the occasion of bloody rebellions and insurrections on the part of the underprivileged, which were sometimes connected with heretical movements. At the same time there appeared theoretical doctrines for improving the distribution of property. They were clothed in the form of political novels after the pattern of Plato's *Politeia;* they were wishful descriptions of non-existent social conditions, utopias. The most famous of these are St. Thomas More's *Utopia* and Thomas Campanella's *Civitas Solis.* Programs for a thorough reordering of the distribution of property on the basis of secular science together with the call for a return to nature appeared only from the eighteenth century on. The principles of freedom and equality presented an entirely different situation from the conditions contemplated by earlier thinkers in whose plans slavery or vassalage were still an accepted part.

The authors of the later plans and programs were not in opposition to the state or the Church or religion, but counted on their cooperation. The existing enmity developed later. The desired changes were not sought by violence and revolution, nor was a simple exchange of position between the higher and lower classes intended. Socialist and communist elements were freely mingled, or rather not yet clearly distinguished. Socialism is now said to advocate the common possession of the means of production; whereas communism aims at the common ownership of the means of production and the goods of consumption, and seeks the realization of its ideas by violent worldwide revolution. The modern ideas, originating in France and England, were developed into a materialistic philosophy of life and history in Germany and then brought to the masses of the workers, who accepted them with a fanatical fervor as a new gospel and religion. Religion needs dogmas. Hence the new movement formulated a series of articles which were not proved, because they could not be proved, but were held as a common creed. When they were later subjected to critical examination, they were dropped as untenable.

One fundamental tenet held an exaggerated theory of the importance of economic conditions for the development of human history. All historical facts and situations were supposed to be direct reflections of the contemporary economic conditions.

The constitution of the state, the family, property, religion, law, and popular customs, all were thought to change automatically in conformity with economic changes. Another article of this creed was Lassalle's iron law of wages, stating that wages were inevitably destined to become continually lower because the supply of labor would always be greater than the demand for it by employers. This may have been the condition at the time of the crassest liberalism in industry. But as soon as labor became organized and was protected by the state, this law—if there is such a thing as an iron and unalterable law in human relations—no longer existed. Labor itself became a force and urged other factors than the mere relation of supply and demand. The excess value theory of Marx is another such tenet, which says that the exchange value of "work for sale," which is paid to the worker, is always less than the commodity value of the product. The difference represents the excess value which is accumulated as capital. Thus capital continually increases on the one hand, and the poverty of the worker on the other. This process will lead to a tension of intolerable strain, at which the existing society will collapse, whereupon the golden age of socialism will arise. The proletariat becomes the ruling class. All this is to take place with the inevitable force of a law of nature.

The masses that had received these doctrines with great fervor owing to the real grievances of their situation, desired action for the speedy arrival of the improvement of their lot in life. This required organization and political activity. In 1864 Lassalle founded the General German Workers' Alliance. The Social Democratic Party was founded in 1869. From now on the aims of the Workers' Alliance were united with the ideas of democratic liberalism. This introduced the element of hostility to the Church and religion in general, at least as a conscious factor. The slogan that religion was a private matter was only a means of deceiving the unwary. The party was in itself anti-religious and atheistic because of its purely materialistic basis. The party program was revised in many conventions; of these the most famous for their platforms were held at Eisenach, Gotha, and

Erfurt. Once its elected members were faced with definite problems in parliament, they were forced out of their purely negative position and came to dissension among themselves. This led to the disruption of the party into two groups, the moderate socialists and the radical communists. Both have given to the world painful demonstrations of their inability to make a paradise of this earth.

Marxist liberalism is a purely theoretical construction which lacks organic growth and historic foundations. The large number of its adherents is explained by the oppression from which the workers suffered. Liberalist economics regarded labor as a merchandise to be bought according to the fluctuations of the market. Liberalism was altogether blind to the need of integrating the economic processes with the life of the nations as communities. The individualism of the time considered the unmitigated struggle for existence as a natural condition. The moderations which might have been effected in this struggle by the observance of the Christian law of charity were rejected by the employers under the influence of the philosophy of the so-called Enlightenment. In the theory and practice of economics as well as in the conceptions of the origin and nature of law and social justice, all guidance derived from morality and religion was discarded. The leaders of society had little understanding of the situation of the workers and still less inclination to help. Thus the workers were pushed into an attitude of hostile opposition and readily followed any leaders who promised improvement of their lot.

The beginning of the nineteenth century is the time of the industrial revolution which transformed the ways of commerce, transportation, and communication, and had a profound effect on the private life of the people. The old ideas of space and time as factors in the work and life of men were changed. Even agriculture was no longer determined by the natural circumstances of place and season in the same degree as before. The machine brought about the unemployment of many a worker and despiritualized the work by reducing it to the fatiguing and monotonous repetition of some very small part of the production. Such methods of work presuppose, however, a high degree of organization by the engineering expert whose intellectual accomplishment dwarfs the part played by the ordinary laborer. The vastness of the modern industrial enterprises calls for the formation of corporations, which are impersonal owners. The supreme concerns of the directors of modern business are the creation of a market for the industrial products, the securing of raw material, the speedy transportation of the materials and finished goods, the quick turnover of the invested capital. All these are considerations of impersonal commerce and finance, which are likely to overshadow and eclipse the human problem of the worker. This was the case for too long a time, with the result of worldwide unrest and a cultural crisis, the end of which is not yet in sight.

As a criticism of Marxist socialism and communism, we should note that they do not seek the positive reconciliation of the classes participating in the economic life of the nation, but their division for the sake of a class struggle which is expected to end in a general collapse and worldwide revolution. The proletariat is to know no fatherland, but is urged to join the vast army of the discontented in the whole world. This idea is self-destructive because the workers of the different nations are subject to widely different conditions and therefore have different interests, not only by the ill will of the employers but by reason of the differences in the geographical locations, supply of raw material, and other natural economic factors. We must not forget that the industry of communist countries had some degree of success in competition with the industries of other countries, not by their generous accommodation to the needs of their international comrades. The fact that their economic processes were nationally determined no less than those of the capitalist countries, must not be overlooked. Whatever may be the form of a future worldwide economic system, it will always have to be regionally determined, and the conflicts in the needs of the different regional units will have to be resolved by mutual compromises requiring on all sides reasonable restraint instead of uncontrolled claims and demands, which characterize the attitude of the discontented masses.

The first and most essential step in the organization of an equitable economic order is the rejection by all social classes of the liberalist individualism and selfishness, and the acceptance of the attitude of Christian charity as it was proclaimed by Pope Leo XIII half a century ago. The spirit of solidarity rejects both the equalitarian organization of anonymous masses dictatorially controlled and the disjointed struggle of self-assertive individuals for economic gain. Solidarity recognizes the rights of the individuals and of the variously determined groups formed according to the demands of geography, occupation, etc. Reasonable limitation of one's own demands, sincere cooperation with others, and intelligent recognition of their contribution to the common welfare, are of the essence of the spirit of solidarity. True practical solidarity represents the realization of essentially Christian virtues and is impossible on the basis of the mere worldly wisdom of enlightened self-interest, especially in the equitable organization of international economics.

In view of the extremely complicated nature of the modern economic set-up resulting from the countless varieties of business, the practical application of the ideal of solidarity will require many different forms. It is not the purpose of this book to discuss the technical nature and value of the various suggested schemes, that are already partly realized. A good knowledge of these things can be gained only by a study of the literature devoted to these problems from the practical point of view. Sufficient guiding principles have been suggested here to enable the reader to see these problems in their right perspective. The lack of such a perspective is what warps many a study and renders it one-sided and misleading, despite its able presentation of much technical detail. Since true solidarity is an essentially Christian thing, the development of this spirit is indeed a concern of the priest. It is with this aim in mind that the priest should be sincerely interested in the social question. His mission must always be essentially religious and supernatural in character as was the work of our Lord on earth. But in the furtherance of the spiritual concerns of souls, he may well interest himself in the social question, imitating the divine Savior, who fed the hungry and healed the sick because He had compassion on the multitude.

WAGES

Modern business is based on money; it is ultimately a matter of finance. But every business enterprise needs workers, who handle not money, but concrete material and processes. Under the liberalist economic system these workers are not regarded as belonging to the enterprise as personal participants but as so many impersonal hands whose services are hired according to the law of supply and demand. A certain excuse for this attitude may be found in the fact that the subordinated character of manual industrial labor requires and establishes little or no inner personal relation between the worker and the enterprise, and renders possible frequent changes in the personnel. The situation of paid labor has markedly developed in this direction on a broad front as practically all services, such as domestic and farm help which formerly created intimate personal relations, are now rendered on a business and industrial basis.

It will always be requisite that the wages be proportionate to the work done. But what factors must be considered in determining the right proportion? The utilitarian liberalist calculates the profit to be gained from any business undertaking and pays labor accordingly. What happens to the worker apart from his actual employment is of no concern to the employer, especially since there are always other workers willing to sell the skill and strength of their hands. This calculation is false from the standpoint of religion, morality, human dignity, and social solidarity.

The mass of manual laborers is as much a part of the economic enterprises as are the capital and the management. Large businesses and industries need a stock of workers who consider the localities where they work as their permanent home for themselves and their families. A frequent labor turnover is economically harmful. Hence, even from the business point of view, it is essential that the workers feel contented and cherish the place of their residence as a desirable home for them and their families. Workers who derive from their employment sufficient means for the satisfaction of the normal human desires become spiritually attached to their work and hence are more efficient and faithful. In the long run, it seems that good wages are also good business for the reasons just stated and for the additional reason that good wages create a bigger market by increasing and spreading the purchasing power.

Furthermore, manual labor is more than mere physical or instinctive activity; it involves the worker's whole personality and affects his mental and emotional faculties. The worker is a man who is called upon to save his soul, he has a right to found a family and provide for his children as for himself conditions of life worthy of human beings. Dignified human existence certainly does not mean the largest amount of material possessions and sensual pleasures that may be possible economically, but it does mean a sufficiency of earthly goods which allow a person to be free from distressing want and to share in the respectable and truly desirable aspects of social life. It includes also the possibility for the gifted children of the worker to rise to higher professions not only by extraordinary effort or by accident but by a way possible within the ordinary means of the parents.

Another reason calling for wages higher than their merely material business value is the fact that the worker gradually spends his vital energies. Many types of work are in themselves injurious to health, others are necessarily a source of immediate danger to the body of the worker, all wear out his capacity for physical effort. Adequate wages for the worker whose energies are declining may, therefore, be demanded also as a compensation for the loss sustained by the more strenuous work formerly accomplished. This principle does not exclude the factor of the actual accomplishment in determining the just wage. Both factors must be taken into consideration. In the case of younger workers the prospect of higher wages for greater accomplishments will serve as an incentive to fidelity and self-improvement. Young workers who do a normal amount of work must, of course, receive normally adequate pay for their decent support.

The family wage for married workers with children deserves our particular attention although reference to the worker's family has been made in the foregoing remarks. Industry and commerce have a *raison d'être* only if they provide society with necessary and desirable goods. But since these goods are not and cannot be distributed gratis but must be bought, it is essential that the wage earners should be enabled to buy them. Society as a whole must be able to share in the fruits of industry, not only a few privileged classes, since the goods of the earth are meant for all. But society grows out of and consists of families; it is not a loose assemblage of unattached individuals. Hence it is a sound demand of social justice that the breadwinners of the families receive wages that will sustain the families on a level of frugal comfort. Adequate family wages are also beneficial to business not only as a means of increasing the public's purchasing power but as a factor of social and economic stability and order. The married worker who receives sufficient wages for the support of his family is interested in the prosperity of the enterprise where he is employed. He wishes to live in peace, and so his family becomes the cell of future generations of workers who take pride in their association with the place where their ancestors worked and prospered.

An adequate wage includes also the possibility of providing for the average amount of sickness, accidents, and other misfortunes which are the lot of man, as well as for the worker's retirement at the evening of his life. It may not be possible to save a large fund to be held in reserve for such contingencies, but it should be possible to carry such insurance as will prevent distress if and when these needs arise. This function of the adequate wage is of the utmost importance for the tranquillity and contentment of the masses of society. The feeling of insecurity and helplessness in the event of future emergencies is a source of terror and mental depression for normal people, just as the feeling of security makes for serenity of mind and efficiency in work.

These reasons show that adequate wages must be higher than the bare monetary value of hired labor in the total production cost of industrial goods or the rendering of commercial services. On the whole, the best method of giving the worker the proper wages consists in paying a fixed sum of money at regular intervals. Thus he is enabled to plan his own affairs independently of the decisions of others and to act as a free and responsible person. However, there may be enterprises and circumstances which render it more advisable to provide the wages in close connection with the regular or irregular changes in the fortunes of the industry or business. Various methods have been proposed and are being practiced here and there. The technical nature of these procedures cannot and need not be studied here. We need merely to point out that just wages are not at a uniform level but depend on many factors which can be determined only after careful study of the particular cases. Lastly, it should be mentioned that, where the methods of paying just wages may occasionally be of the nature of social welfare institutions, these must never appear or be conceived of as charitable gifts but as the best suitable arrangement for satisfying the workers' just demands. Ultimately the question of just wages, which will always be fluid and subject to changes and differences as an economic problem, will be solved only by the recognition of their mutual solidarity on the part of capital and labor and by the cultivation of the virtues of moderation and contentment. These virtues are of a religious nature; they are based on positive religious faith and are ordered by the laws of God the fulfillment of which is the only guaranty of real progress and true prosperity.

VIOLATIONS OF PROPERTY IN GENERAL

Private property is of divine institution as a part of the natural law. It is also protected by God's positive command in the decalogue: Thou shalt not steal. Stealing as well as all other forms of property violations is condemned and threatened with divine punishment in many places of Sacred Scripture. All are bound in conscience to respect the property rights of others as regards both the actual possession of goods and their unhampered disposal by the owners. Violations of property rights offend against commutative justice and entail the obligation of restitution. The injustice committed by offenses against property inflicts the twofold injury of material harm and personal affront on the owner and violates the public order of human society.

It is noteworthy that all races from the most ancient times on punished no crime, except adultery, with the same severity as theft and robbery. Persons guilty of violence or intemperance were more easily readmitted to society than the thief. In fact, the death penalty was frequently inflicted on those violating the property of others, especially in the case of repetition, even where small values were involved. It is likewise significant that such harsh laws continued to exist in Europe as late as the nineteenth century. Under more primitive conditions, only the property of those belonging to the narrow circle of the same tribe or race was, as a rule, so protected. The divine natural and positive law acknowledges no such restrictions. Offenses against the property of others violate the order established by the will of God and are, therefore, sins in the theological sense of the word.

The order of private property is an important institution in the life of human society. Its serious disturbance is, therefore, a grievous offense and, prescinding from the question of subjective moral responsibility, a grave sin. On the objective side, the gravity of the sin is determined by the amount of material harm done as well as certain accompanying circumstances. Usually regarded as a serious matter is that amount which is enough to deprive the person concerned of his accustomed sustenance for as short a period as one day. This principle allows considerable differences in the amount involved according to the economic situation of the injured person. However, there is a definite limit beyond which violations of property constitute always a grave matter regardless of the wealth of the person or institution harmed.

The reason for the establishing of such an upper limit is the common good of society, which needs security of the property of its members for its very existence. Besides, each individual member suffers positive harm in direct proportion to the frequency and gravity of the violations of property committed against anyone in society because the devices and organizations required for their prevention and prosecution add to the cost of the things we need every day. This burden on society and its members results not only from actual violations of property, but also from the expense involved in the protection of property against potential violations of this sort.

The gravity of the injury by offenses against the property of others is increased when actual violence or premeditated fraud is used against the victim. The same is true when a person is maliciously deprived of something for which he has a special personal attachment or the lack of which proves greatly embarrassing and amounts to serious insult, e.g., the stealing or robbing of his necessary clothes. Similarly, the sins against property are rendered more grievous if contempt for the owner or for the law of God is signified either explicitly (e.g., by insulting inscriptions or notes left behind) or implicitly by sacrilegious theft and desecration of sacred places.

PARTICULAR VIOLATIONS OF PROPERTY

Theft is the secret alienation of property from its owner against his will. Theft is so typical of all violations of other persons' property that the seventh commandment forbids them all by the brief precept: Thou shalt not steal. It is in the interest of the public good that no secret transfers of property against the will of the owner should be permitted even though the thief might make better use of the objects concerned than the rightful owner would do. Where this latter situation exists on a large social scale, we are forced to admit that the owners of excessive property have come by their possessions in a socially harmful manner, and the state is obliged to arrange for the just distribution of the goods among the population. Private authority and secret methods cannot be allowed to effect such changes. In cases of pressing need and especially of extreme necessity, the consent of the owner is justly presumed and those suffering such want are permitted to take as much of another's property as is sufficient to tide them over their critical predicament. In general, thefts committed out of real need may be judged with greater leniency than thefts practiced by persons for the purpose of living beyond their honest means. For example, domestics whose healthy appetite is measured by miserly employers according to their own inability to enjoy a full meal because of their inactivity and the frequent taking of little "snacks," are allowed to take a sufficient amount of food secretly. If at all possible, the matter should be openly discussed and corrected. But where there exists no real necessity, thefts by members of the household should be judged more severely because in the home there should prevail an atmosphere of perfect trust and security.

Thefts committed by pathologically affected persons may have to be excused partially or completely. It has long been known that some persons suffer from a morbid craving for stealing articles which often are quite useless to them (cleptomania). But this craving occurs rather seldom as a permanent condition. Formerly it was believed that this was a privileged disease of the "idle rich" and was resented by the common people. Recently psychiatry has discovered that such is not the fact, especially for periodically recurring forms of cleptomania. On the borderline of this disease complex we find the morbid stealing of articles for collection purposes. Here it seems that the persons doing this sort of stealing must be credited with sufficient responsibility to hold them guilty although the motives in some cases are lost in the subconscious. Nevertheless it appears that the one-sided concentration of a person's desires on the collection of certain types of articles may so grip his mind that the voice of reason and the demands of conscience are stifled. It has happened that great scholars or otherwise important and respectable persons were apprehended in the act of appropriating to themselves from libraries and art galleries pieces of art or whole books or illustrations out of rare volumes. The accumulated treasures of the large stores exert an almost magic spell upon the visitors, especially women who, often after considerable genuine purchases, steal useless trifles. Statistics have shown that most women shoplifters were under the influence of menstruation at the time of the theft. Various processes of sexual development seem to influence offenses against property. We find thefts as a sort of compensation or primitive reaction at the time of excited adolescence, and also in connection with pregnancy and the change of life (the menopause).

Occult compensation is the secret appropriation of property by one who has a clear right to it but cannot obtain it otherwise without grave inconvenience. One condition for the lawfulness of occult compensation is that others be not suspected of theft. Under ordinary circumstances, occult compensation should be recognized as justified very rarely. Nevertheless, times of distress are often exploited at the expense of those who need employment in order to earn a bare living; occult compensation may then be permissible. Overtime work is sometimes demanded with serious inconvenience to the manual laborer or office worker and with no compensation forthcoming, despite the obvious understanding that such work should be paid for. It will be difficult for the confessor to judge each case accurately. He will have to point out very clearly the circumstances permitting occult compensation and admonish the penitent most earnestly to be on his guard against self-deception. But unless injustice on the part of one practicing occult compensation can be established beyond doubt, the penitent cannot be obliged to make restitution.

Small thefts repeatedly perpetrated at the expense of the same person may eventually result in grave matter. If the thief's intention is to steal a large amount by small installments, this evil intention makes the sin grievous.

Fraud is an act by which a person is made to agree to the

surrender of his property through deception. The owner's consent to the loss of his possession is only apparent. In reality the owner does not freely give up his property, but is deprived of it against his will and without his knowledge. The deception practiced on him adds to the malice of the sin. The great social harm done by fraud is evident from the countless laws enacted, the mental efforts made, and the tremendous expenses incurred for the prevention and prosecution of fraud. It can hardly be imagined how much mental energy and material resources could be released for positive cultural work if they were not claimed by the unproductive struggle against fraud. The roots of fraud are greed and the abuse of mental superiority. Just as the physically weak—individuals and nations—are likely to become the victims of the powerful, so the simplicity and confidence of some stimulate the criminal dispositions of others into scheming for the purpose of unjust enrichment. The enumeration of all possible and real frauds would be as useless as it is impossible. The tests for the sinfulness of fraud are the same as with theft. A series of individual acts of fraud committed against many different persons may constitute for the deceiver one grave sinful action, e.g., in the use of short weight, the sale of adulterated food.

Robbery is the forcible and unjust seizing of the property of another. The use of physical violence which involves the danger of serious bodily harm and mental shock make rapine also a sin against the fifth commandment. Robbery is, of course, always grievously sinful.

Extortion consists in forcing a person to yield his property by threats of evil consequences in case of refusal. It is a crime which has grown to alarming proportions in recent times and is popularly known as blackmail. Generally the victim is threatened with the publication of unpleasant facts about him. Often the helpless person is frightened with grossly distorted fancies of more or less harmless facts. The victims of extortioners never have peace if they yield to the latters' demands; they lose their entire possessions and frequently end their lives by suicide. Whoever has to advise prospective victims of extortion should counsel absolute refusal. They should secure witnesses or written proofs and, armed with these, prosecute the blackmailer, since the crime of extortion is severely punished in all countries. The gravity of this sin is evident.

Usury, in the modern sense of the word, is the demand of excessive interest on loans. Evidently nobody borrows money at excessive rates unless he is constrained to do so an account of his need and the impossibility of obtaining the loan at just and reasonable rates. Usury, then, is the exploitation of another's distress for material gain. This is clearly sinful. But such was the situation in former centuries in the case of every loan, because money had no productive value then. Hence the term "usury," in the writings of the older moralists, denotes simply "interest." This use of the word in present-day moral treatises is confusing and requires unnecessary explanations. (See *supra*, pp. 210 ff.)

The spirit of the former ecclesiastical law against interest must still guide us. If an honest and able person is forced by untoward circumstances to borrow money, any rate of interest or pressure for speedy repayment beyond the normal possibilities of his situation, are unlawful and usurious. Even an able, industrious, and thrifty person may be able to secure (e.g., from a farm or small business) only a small surplus for the reduction of a debt and the payment of interest. The Christian lender of money must take account of such facts and content himself with interest and repayment rates that may fall considerably short of the legal limit. Not the letter of the law but the spirit of charity is the decisive test of what is right and what wrong.

Usury which is forbidden even by civil law is being practiced under many technical evasions, and other forms flourish through the inadequacy of obsolete laws. Greed is inventive of many devious ways by which the obvious purpose of protective laws is circumvented. Specialists in law and finance are required to unravel the ingenious mazes of business complications designed by unscrupulous usurers in their preying on the need of others for their own gain. Formerly various monopolies were sources of usurious gain, but these are now largely restricted and regulated by law.

Besides the violations of property for the sake of personal gain, there occur countless other *property offenses not aimed at personal profit*. While the former spring fundamentally from the excessive desire for possessions, sometimes mixed with the pangs of real need, the latter proceed from different motives. Such appear to be envy and revenge or mere wanton malice in the case of acts of destruction. There is also the damage resulting from mere negligence, laziness, and the omission of obligatory vigilance and care. In case of negligence and omission the responsibility for the resulting damage may vary between grievous guilt and almost complete innocence, according to the degree of blameworthy inattention, the gravity of a person's duty to preserve another's property, and the ordinary or extraordinary nature of the cause of the damage. Vicious acts of injury which spring from envy, revenge, or sheer reckless malice or disregard for the rights and well-being of others are soon grievously sinful even though the actual damage resulting from these acts may not be very serious. They are the more grievous the more destructive the damage is which is intended, foreseen, and actually inflicted.

From among the many possible ways of doing harm to others by destruction, arson may be singled out for special consideration because of its frequent occurrence and the peculiar psychological motives underlying it. The destructive crime of arson must not only be punished severely as a deterrent, it should also be understood psychologically. After setting aside the cases of revenge and insurance frauds, there remains a considerable number of psychologically strange cases. There should be mentioned first of all the feebleminded and infantile person who, like a little child, enjoys playing with fire without consideration of the possible serious consequences. He may bear this urge in his subconscious mind whence it suddenly emerges and is carried into action. Young persons suffering from homesickness and painfully aware of the impossibility of returning home, such as soldiers, inmates of orphanages or penal institutions, may be liable to resort to arson as a primitive reaction to their emotional strain that may have a subconscious sexual basis. It is hard to decide to what extent such psychopathic defects diminish or even exclude moral responsibility.

The right of ownership has now been accorded also to the authors of *works of the mind,* and the property rights arising out of them are protected by *patents* and *copyright.* The protection consists in the legal prohibition of any reproduction of patented or copyrighted inventions or products in the form of articles or processes, and of literary, musical, artistic, or scientific compositions in the form of texts or public performances, without the permission of the owner of the patent or copyright, and also compensation if that is demanded. Of course the legal provisions about registration and so forth vary in different countries. The institution of the patent and copyright is of recent origin. Formerly and especially in ancient and medieval times, references to authors whose works were quoted at great length were hardly ever made and nobody would have thought of giving a suitable compensation for the use of quoted material. It is now a task for the critical student of the literature of those times to trace the first appearance, development, and path of transmission of thoughts and theories by the comparative study of the texts. Today it is a matter of professional ethics to acknowledge the sources expressly consulted, particularly when any part of them is reproduced verbatim. Knowledge that has become the general ground and atmosphere of any particular field need not be explicitly referred to its originator, but may be freely used as a general basis for further work.

Attention must be drawn to the practice of privately copying plays, songs, etc., for public performance by amateur groups. Limited as their funds may be, it does not seem right to deprive the authors of the just profit from the use of their work. As a rule, different rates are set for professional and amateur performances, and these conditions should be complied with. We cannot expect gifted authors to devote their energies and time to the creation of cultural works if we do not consider them worthy of our moderate support even while we enjoy the fruits of their labor and look forward to more and better artistic creations.

The popularization of scientific works is permissible, for it constitutes a new work which, moreover, does not harm the sale of strictly scholarly books because the two types of literature are addressed to different classes of readers. Due credit to the scientific authors must be given, and if the text of the popularization as a whole or in large sections reflects the original works closely, express permission for its publication must be obtained and compensation made if it is demanded. The transposition of literary or other works of art from one genre into another, e.g., in the dramatization of a novel, the development of a plot into a story or drama, and the like, is to be judged similarly. In these matters also the copyright laws will have to be respected, especially where they have been applied to particular cases by judicial decision. There are so many delicate factors involved in this matter that often a right decision can be rendered only after a careful examination and upon a maturely pondered total impression of each individual case.

Popularization of a praiseworthy nature is the preaching of good sermons. The best material for solid sermons and religious instruction is to be found in scholarly treatises on theological subjects. In the oral delivery of sermons it is not necessary to mention the sources even though whole phrases are taken verbatim from them. But when sermons are published in print some definite acknowledgment of the sources is required, particularly if the latter have been used very thoroughly.

Practically the same rules as in the case of the copyright apply also to the patent rights concerning inventions. In this field much injustice is being done. It can safely be said that no inventor whose work is not backed by strong financial powers and interests ever derives any material profit from his work. By shrewd little alterations on an invention the patent rights can be evaded. Frequently, too, the inventor's resources do not allow him to renew his patent rights often, with the result that those interested in the exploitation of the invention wait for the expiration of these rights and reap the fruit of the inventor's work without cost. Most inventors have died in poverty, while those who commercially exploited their work grew rich.

XV

Restitution of Property

Repentance of the sin of injustice must include also the practical will of correcting the disorder caused by the violation of commutative justice. The restoration of the just order by which to the ones injured is returned what was unjustly taken from them, is known as restitution. Restitution is a demand of sound reason; the one who has injured the just rights of others cannot expect pardon of his sin if he refuses to correct the unjust condition created by his act although he is able to do so. When Zacheus received our Lord into his house and the divine grace touched his heart, his first thought was to make ample restitution of his injustices (Luke, chap. 19). Unfortunately, not all sinners are so eager to rectify the injustices they have committed. It is not so much by outright refusal as by continual postponement of the required restitution that many penitents evade this obligation. True, absolution from the sin is possible and must be given where there exists the right disposition of the penitent *hic et nunc,* i.e., the serious resolution to make restitution. This may be broken later like any other resolution. But where such breaches have occurred several times, there is reason to doubt the sincerity of the promise. Some actual efforts toward restitution may be taken as signs of good will, whereas their omission argues lack of seriousness.

Violation of the right order of commutative justice may occur without formal guilt and yet entail the obligation of restitution. A frequent case in point is the unintentional exchange of articles of clothing in public places or at meetings. The gravity of the obligation of restitiution depends on the value of the thing concerned. There is no obligation if the efforts and expenses connected with the return of the article exceed its value. In various ways things may come into the possession of persons who are not their rightful owners although these persons may consider the objects their own in all good faith. For the solution of the countless questions arising out of the obligation of restitution, moral theology has set up a number of helpful principles.

(1) *Res clamat domino,* i.e., if the rightful owner of an object is known, it must be returned to him. (2) *Res fructificat domino,* i.e., the fruits deriving from an object belong to the owner of that object. Distinction is made between *fructus naturales,* coming from the object without human intervention, *fructus industriales,* which are the result solely of human effort in connection with an object, and *fructus mixti,* which are in quality and quantity the result of the object's natural productivity but essentially improved and controlled by human effort. (3) *Res naturaliter perit domino,* i.e., if an object perishes from intrinsic causes or due to circumstances beyond human control, the loss is the owner's; if the loss is due to the fault of another person (unjust sale, consumption, or neglect), this person must restore to the owner the equivalent of the lost object. (4) *Nemo ex re aliena locupletari potest,* i.e., fruits essentially deriving from an object belong to the owner. Fruits secured from an object by its accidental relationship to circumstances, especially if this relationship was brought about by another person without any violation of the owner's rights, belong to this person.

Possessor bonae fidei is the person possessing an object not his own in the honest belief that it belongs to him. The sincerity of this conviction mostly rests on the title by which the object was acquired, e.g., purchase, donation, finding, inheritance. As soon as the possessor in good faith recognizes his mistake and knows the identity and whereabouts of the real owner he must return the object to him and cannot dispose of it in any other way. If the rightful owner is unknown, the *bona fide* possessor must deal with the object according to the rules applying to a finder. If the object cannot be returned immediately, it must be held in safekeeping according to the rules applying to such action. If the object is consumed by the possessor while he is in good faith, so that neither its equivalent exists nor any definite profit from its possession and consumption, nothing further need be done.

Possessor malae fidei is the person who takes or retains an object as his own although he knows that it belongs to another. Such is also the finder who makes no effort at all to discover the owner of the found article. The possessor of an object in bad faith is obliged to make good the whole damage of which he is the responsible cause. He must return the object itself or its equivalent if the original one no longer exists or is no longer under his control or cannot be restored except at a proportionately grave inconvenience. The obligation to restore the object itself is the greater if this object has a value which allows no equivalent valuation, e.g., a piece of art. If the *possessor malae fidei* cannot restore an object in person without exposing himself to the danger of being apprehended, he may use the help of third parties, e.g., the confessor or other reliable persons and organizations. Besides the return of the object or its equivalent, restitution must be made also of the profits which were lost and other damage suffered on account of its absence. E.g., he who steals the instrument from a musician who is about to give a concert must return not only the instrument but also the remuneration which would have come to the musician if the concert had taken place: *lucrum cessans*. Here belong also the fruits which naturally grow out of an object, as set forth under the principle; *nemo ex re aliena locupletari potest*. Other damage, *damnum emergens,* actually suffered may consist of the deterioration which would not have occurred if the object had remained with the real owner, and of the greater expense for the repair due to rising prices, and the like.

Possessor dubiae fidei is one who has positive reasons to doubt whether an object which he acquires or already holds is rightfully his own. Persons having such justified doubts must make

reasonable efforts to clarify their title of ownership if an object
of some value is involved. It is sinful to acquire objects while in
doubt about the rightful owner. When, e.g., children give valuable things as presents, there exists good reason to doubt if they
have the permission of their parents. Hence parents should never
permit their children to keep such presents without first consulting with the parents of the children who gave the gifts. Objects that are offered for sale by strangers far under the normal
price are likewise suspicious. The solving of a doubt in one's
favor under such circumstances is an obvious excuse designed
to hide bad faith. When reasonable doubts about the righteousness of one's possession of goods arise later, the investigations
concerning their true owner must be the more intense the greater
their value and the probability of finding the owner and the
more serious the loss may be felt by him. If there is scarcely any
hope of success or if the investigation is inculpably delayed so
that it becomes practically useless, there exists no obligation of
restitution, not even *ad causas pias*. Such restitution may be advised for the calming of people's conscience, but it cannot be
required. If the real owner should happen to become known,
however, restitution must be made. If after a proper search the
doubts still remain, the possessor may consider himself the true
owner.

If *unjust harm* is the basis for the duty of restitution, not only
the direct damage inflicted but also the resulting *lucrum cessans*
and *damnum emergens* mentioned above must be restored. But
only moral guilt in the violation of commutative justice gives
rise to this obligation. New inventions by which industrial processes are revolutionized, the expansion of a business which puts
other business enterprises in the neighborhood at a disadvantage, etc., are not acts of injustice although many persons and
organizations may suffer harm. Furthermore, an unjust act must
be the direct effective cause of the damage. It is not enough that
it is an indirect cause as a link in an accidentally concurring
chain of causes, unless such concurrence is foreseen and intended. In genuine doubt whether one's unjust action is the

cause of another person's damage, there is no obligation to make restitution unless conditions of uncertainty have been purposely created.

Culpable omission of the necessary attention and precaution likewise induces the obligation of restitution. A person driving an automobile which is not in a safe condition is responsible for the damage from an accident owing to the faulty condition of his automobile. A landlord who, after a night which brought sleet, has not yet rendered his sidewalk safe for pedestrians at 5 o'clock in the morning is not responsible in conscience for the damage suffered by a passer-by at that early hour. Again, if a burglar comes to grief because of his ignorance of a dangerous spot on the premises which he has invaded, the owner has no obligation to make amends. Sometimes civil law requires compensation even in such cases in order to force people to eliminate all sources of danger from their premises. But before an obligation to make compensation has been imposed by a court decision, no such obligation exists. The safety regulations of the state concerning industrial and commercial plants and the various public services oblige in conscience because they are a necessity. Their omission or neglect constitutes a sin against the fifth commandment. Those who are not able to sin because of the lack of reason, e.g., small children, feebleminded or insane persons, are not obliged to make restitution. But in such cases the obligation often rests with the parents or guardians.

Cooperation entails the obligation of restitution under the same conditions as in the case of unjust action, i.e., if it constitutes a morally responsible act which directly and effectively influences the harmful action of another in a matter involving commutative justice. E.g., bad example is an incitement to evil-doing and may be grievously sinful, but it is not the direct cause of the consequent evil deeds and does not entail the duty of restitution.

The most explicit manner of cooperation consists in commanding another to perform an act. Command presupposes the relation of superior and subject, and the superior bears a greater responsibility for the act than the subject who carries it out. The law of God permits no one to accept an immoral command. Still the subject is socially the weaker party and psychologically somewhat dependent on the superior. The Latin term *iussio* includes, besides command, also order by contract to perform an act. Here the two parties are on equal terms, and the one accepting the order to do harm is more responsible for his evil deed than the one who obeys the sinful command of his superior. The one who engages the sinful service of another is responsible not only for the harmful act but also for the evil consequences even though he has not intended them, because these can never be separated from an evil deed or limited according to one's wishes. No definite limits can be set, e.g., for damage by arson or explosion; any attack on the bodily integrity of another may prove fatal. The person who hires another for harmful acts is not responsible for the harm done by the hired person beyond his order, and the latter accepts the risk of all penalties that may be inflicted on him for his criminal deed. If the sinful order is recalled in sufficient time to prevent its execution, there is no obligation of restitution, nor does approval of a single act after the deed has been committed involve this obligation, because it had no influence on its commission. Yet frequent approval and praise of wrongdoing has the effect of encouragement. Tacit approval and praise by screening and sheltering are the breeding ground of fraud, thievery, and other kinds of crime.

Cooperation by active participation in evil deeds may take place in all degrees of near and remote, necessary or merely facilitating, aid. The more remote, perhaps even forced, the participation is, the more it is material in character and hence not subject to the obligation of restitution. Close and necessary participation, except under the compulsion of very grave fear or through complete ignorance, is always formal and involves the obligation of restitution. There is an extensive ground between formal and material participation where certain decisions are very difficult. Counsel as a mode of cooperation is also hard to evaluate. The theoretical statement that counsel involves the

duty of restitution to the extent of its real influence on the commission of a harmful act, is indeed easy. But how can a person
determine the degree of its effectiveness? Many persons follow
only the advice which they welcome as a confirmation of their
own desires. Of greater importance is the question of professional advice regarding acts that are harmful either to the one
seeking the advice or to third parties. Wrong advice given, in
a professional capacity, out of culpable ignorance or negligence
oblige the counselor (e.g., confessor, physician, lawyer) to restitution. The degree of culpability will largely decide the extent of
the duty of restitution. In the case of persons normally conscientious in the fulfillment of their professional duties, this obligation will have to be interpreted mildly. Whoever has given a
harmful advice must correct it if there is yet time to do so. If
the correction is not accepted, the party who may be harmed
must be warned so as to diminish or prevent the evil.

Restitution because of a person's consent to a harmful act
or decision, e.g., by his vote in elections, can hardly ever become
very effective. Nevertheless it has happened before and will
happen again that prominent persons withdraw their endorse-
ment of movements and actions and oppose the causes they
promoted before. Of little importance is the duty of restitution
on account of cooperation by flattery, because its influence can
be determined only very indistinctly. The opposite of flattery
(censure and reproach) may have a more clearly discernible influence on the actions of others and thus become a tangible form
of cooperation. E.g., frequent and biting reproaches of cowardice
may drive persons under the influence of alcohol, or persons of
an excitable character, of little will power, or low intelligence,
to rash actions of extremely harmful consequences to themselves
and others. Cooperation by omission (*mutus, non obstans, non
manifestans*) may call for restitution on the part of those who
are in justice bound to prevent harm in their respective capaci-
ties as parents, guardians, watchmen, and so forth.

Obligations of charity do not involve the duty of restitution
if by our failure to fulfill them others come to grief. We need

not repair the damage suffered by a person whose lost property we could have taken up and brought to his attention, although we may have sinned by our failure to do so. Often our fulfillment of duties of charity, e.g., by warning people, would be regarded as unwarranted interference and would be repaid with ingratitude and perhaps abuse. Where no such danger or other serious inconvenience is likely to present itself, we should be helpful to others and prevent avoidable harm from coming to them. The confessor is not considered bound to make restitution when he, without being asked by the penitent, omits to point out the latter's obligation to make restitution, even though the confessor's omission may be due to ignorance or negligence.

SPECIAL CASES OF RESTITUTION

Life is the highest earthly good for it is the foundation for the enjoyment of all other goods. But true and full life is healthy life. Hence *unjust injury of health* is an attack on one's life. Of course, life itself cannot be restored at all, and health only within certain limits. Unjust injury to a person's health or destruction of his life calls for the restitution of all damage which can be restored. Besides the obligations imposed on the criminal by the law, he who killed another person must support the dependents of the murdered person. Economic damages to distant relatives or to creditors of the murdered person need not be made good by restitution unless these damages were directly intended. The same is true of the harm done to insurance companies or other institutions which have to pay pensions in connection with the unjust injury or killing of a person. According to the opinion of most theologians, he who kills another in a duel is not obliged to make restitution, because the one who lost his life, they say, exposed himself to the danger of death. Some make an exception in the case of a person who accepted the challenge under duress, i.e., moral coercion. But, then, these ought to make restitution who forced the unfortunate one into accepting.

In the case of injuries by wounding it is the medical and hospital expenses that must be restored together with the loss of income due to sickness. The law often awards also a certain sum as a compensation for the suffering inflicted. The theologians do not recognize the obligation of such an indemnity, on the ground that health cannot be expressed in terms of money. We should say, however, that such a compensation is justified as a means to obtain some enjoyment which may counteract the psychological shock and thus help the restoration of health. Besides, such payment is an appropriate token of recognition of the injustice committed and of atonement for the personal offense.

Sexual sins with unmarried women do not call for restitution if the latter freely consented. But if the act had its natural consequences, the care for mother and child is not a matter of restitution; it is a new natural obligation. Restitution of all resulting damage must be made when the other party was morally or physically forced to suffer the sinful act. The best form of restitution is the marriage between the seducer and the seduced person if there is well-founded hope that their marriage will be a happy one. Where this does not appear probable, the future of the seduced or oppressed person must be sufficiently provided for. If from adultery a child is born into a family, there exists the obligation of restitution for the support of the child and for the reduction of the inheritance that will be suffered by the legitimate children of the family. The woman need not confess her adultery outside the sacrament of penance if the misdeed remained secret. It may be in the interest of all concerned that the secret be kept. Restitution must then be made also in secret and indirect ways. If the man involved in the sin does not contribute, and the penitent woman has no other means, she must fulfill her duty of restitution by extra application in the care of the home and thrift as regards her own person. Where husband and wife give each other permission for extra-marital relations, as occasionally happens in our present degenerate society, the sin of adultery remains the same; but there is no obligation of restitution.

The morality of *tax evasions* and the problem of restitution can be best understood by a brief study of its history. On this point we have positive statements of Christ and the apostles. Christ answered the question whether it was permitted to pay tribute, i.e., taxes, to Caesar, with the famous words: "Render to Caesar the things that are Caesar's, and to God the things that are God's" (Matt. 22:2). St. Paul says: "Be subject of necessity, not only for wrath, but also for conscience' sake. For therefore also you pay tribute. For they are the ministers of God, serving unto this purpose. Render therefore to all men their dues. Tribute, to whom tribute is due; custom, to whom custom; fear, to whom fear; honor, to whom honor" (Rom. 13:5 ff.). St. Peter also admonishes the Christians to be subject to human authority (1 Pet. 2:13). In view of the harshness of the Roman tax system and the abuses connected with the collection of the taxes by the publicans who were commonly considered sinners, this strictness of the words of Scripture is significant. Scriptural exegesis as well as the Fathers of the Church, including the great St. Augustine, teach that the taxes to be paid to the state are a matter of conscience.

In the chaotic times of the migration of the nations the conditions of civil order were severely dislocated and upset. In place of the well articulated order of the Roman state, there appeared primitive social forms under which tribute in natural goods and personal labor service were demanded. Extra contributions and work were demanded and obtained by force for special projects. Indirect taxes in the form of road tolls and bridge tolls were exacted. The law in all this was the arbitrary will of the powerful ones who exploited the weak. It was at that time the Church began to raise her voice against unjust taxes. But it was the teaching of the Scholastics that the payment of just taxes is an obligation of conscience. St. Thomas proves this obligation from reason and revelation. But the public authorities are admonished not to exact higher taxes than the reasonable needs of society require.

At the time of the decline of Scholasticism the treatment of moral theology and its practical application were taken over by the students of canon law, who handled the problems largely in a casuistic fashion. Thus there was developed the theory of the *lex poenalis* which does not oblige in conscience. The contrast between the arbitrariness of the ruling classes, the extravagance of the princes, and the privileges of the nobility on the one side, and the oppression and exploitation of the lower classes on the other, makes the tax laws appear as *leges poenales*. At least the indirect taxes are declared to be such. The obligation to pay taxes is derived from the *iustitia legalis,* not from commutative justice. The obligation of restitution, however, is based on violations of commutative justice. In view of the gross abuses at the time of the princely absolutism, it is quite understandable that many theologians felt justified in approving the general persuasion of the common people that the tax laws, by which were meant primarily the tolls and customs, were unjust and did not need to be observed in conscience. The somewhat mitigated doctrine that the very doubt of the justice of a tax released a person from the duty of paying it, led to the same practical result. After all, anyone may doubt the justice of any tax.

The nineteenth century brought to an end the absolutism of the princes, the abolition of the social privileges, the participation of the people in the government, and the reorganization of the finances of the state. The state assumes many tasks, such as the promotion of cultural works, the welfare and public safety of the people, and the defense against external enemies. Hence the state must have the right to demand the necessary means from the citizens. It cannot be denied that in general the modern state applies the principles of justice in the distribution of the tax obligations. Justice requires the exclusion of special privileges and the universality of the obligation to pay taxes in relative proportion to the economic situation of the people. Hence we may no longer, in contrast to the past centuries, presume that the tax laws are unjust. Rather, moral theology must start out with the presumption that the existing order of taxation is just and its details reasonably adjusted to the actual economic conditions of the different classes of the tax payers. The moral basis for the individual's obligation to pay taxes is his life in the community of the state and his enjoyment of the many benefits deriving from organized society.

Legists are not agreed on the juridical nature of offenses against the tax laws. Some class them under the heading of fraud, others would keep them as a special class and have them treated separately. At any rate, we cannot continue to call the tax laws mere *leges poenales*. In view of the existing persuasion, however, our judgment will have to be lenient on the question whether an actual tax evasion was a grievous sin, and whether restitution has to be made. But the old view must eventually give way to the recognition that taxes are a necessity and their payment a moral duty.

METHODS OF RESTITUTION

He who possesses goods which are not his own is in the first place obliged to make restitution. If he fails to do so the duty devolves on those who participated in the unjust alienation of the goods from their rightful owner. The order in which the accomplices, if there are any, in the unjust action are obliged is (1) the one commanding or ordering it, (2) the one carrying out the order, (3) the one lending positive assistance, (4) those aiding in a negative way (*mutus, non obstans,* etc.). If the possessor of the property to be restored is not implicated in its unjust alienation, he has the right to seek compensation from the guilty ones for the loss he sustains by the act of restitution. Those who take part in an action which brings harm to others are bound to make restitution to the extent of their effective participation. The obligation of restitution binds also the heirs; but they may refuse the inheritance as a whole if they are unwilling to assume this obligation. He who is the effective cause of the whole damage is also bound to make complete restitution of the harm done; i.e., the one doing the harm in his own name or the instigator by commanding or ordering or advising such action for his own gain.

If those who actually carried out the harmful deed are compelled to make restitution or do so of their own accord, they are entitled to compensation from the instigator.

The rightful recipient of the goods to be restored is their rightful owner if he is known with certainty and can be reached. If he is dead, his lawful heirs take his place. If neither the original owner nor his heirs can be reached, restitution can be made to the poor or to pious causes in the spirit of the owner, if there are indications of it, e.g., by giving alms to the needy of the owner's home town or to a charitable institution to which he showed favor. Debts cannot be settled by donations to the poor but must be paid to the real creditor in the first place. Other people's property held in trust may not be used for the payment' of debts without the consent of the owners. This has been done of late by many savings banks and other such institutions which hoped to tide themselves over a crisis in this way and replace the savings afterward—a plan which mostly miscarried. A debtor who foresees his bankruptcy in the near future is not allowed to dispose of his possessions to the disadvantage of any creditors. He may act in good faith if he satisfies poor creditors by paying them at a preferred rate. It is also wrong for him to put property aside for his own use or that of his family before filing the petition of bankruptcy. After filing the petition, he must follow the laws of the country in the matter.

The right manner of restitution requires that the unlawful possessor not only give up all unjust gain as explained before, but that the rightful owner receive his property either in its exact identity or at least in a form which corresponds best with his needs. Cash money appears to be the best substitute for the original object; less commendable are commodities because of their limited utility; least apt of all are articles of luxury. It is necessary to point this out because some authors state that, for the sake of secrecy, restitution may be made in the form of presents. If direct personal restitution may involve the risk of revealing the identity of the one who did wrong, he should make use of persons or organizations that know how to handle such delicate matters. In the case of awkward and helpless people, the confessor may act as intermediary, but then he should be very careful lest the identity of the penitent become known. He may transmit the object to a priest who lives at a considerable distance and direct him to communicate with the rightful owner. If possible, he should choose a means which leaves him in the possession of a document proving the execution of his trust.

The *possessor bonae fidei* may leave the object where it is at the time when he learns of his error and simply notify the real owner. The unjust possessor must bring the object to the place where its presence may be expected to agree best with the real owner's wishes. This probably is in most cases the residence of the owner or any other place where the object will be quickly discovered and taken by him. Restitution should be made as soon as possible and not postponed without good reasons. A year should be regarded as a rather long delay. The danger of revealing one's identity may excuse and justify a certain delay. E.g., an employee may wait, if necessary, until he has another position and make restitution from a distant place. Each case will have to be studied in its own circumstances and handled accordingly.

RELEASE FROM THE OBLIGATION OF RESTITUTION

The first and most obvious ground for the release from the duty of restitution is condonation by the real owner. Condonation may be explicit, or implicit if the owner's conduct plainly shows that he is not at all interested in things such as would have to be restored. Condonation may be presumed when the owner's situation so changes that restitution would appear foolish. Compensation may end the obligation of restitution when the persons involved owe each other an equal amount, a condition which often obtains in the business world. Self-help by the owner also extinguishes the duty of restitution. Prescription according to the law of the land may end the duty of restitution on the part of the *possessor bonae fidei*. Real impossibility on the part of the unjust owner also closes many a case of restitution, for nobody need deprive himself and his descendants of the necessaries of life.

As to the release from the obligation of restitution by composition through the authority of the Pope or the Sacred Penitentiary, the following must be said: As long as the real owner is known and can be reached, he alone has the right to receive restitution or to renounce his claim. The Pope and the Church cannot dispose of the property of Catholics or even of other people. Non-catholics have sometimes fantastic notions about the powers of the Pope. These false notions must be corrected wherever they are met. Only when the real owner cannot be found or reached, do goods unjustly held become the property of the poor; they belong to the goods destined *ad pias causas,* which are counted among the possessions of the Church in the widest sense. Of these the Pope has the right of disposal and thus may condone part of the debt to a repentant sinner. The Apostolic See has generously pardoned those who acquired property unjustly taken from the Church at the time of the secularization. The obligation to make restitution does not cease with a person's entrance into the religious state. In fact, a person under this obligation cannot licitly enter the religious life unless the religious community assumes this obligation or shows the petitioner a way of satisfying it as a member of the community.

Conclusion

THE cares about earthly possessions are not only the content of a great part of men's lives, they also influence to a considerable extent the conscious and unconscious motives of their whole moral life. Questions of property are uppermost in man's search for earthly happiness. This is the heart of the social problem, which becomes the more urgent the more clearly the conviction dawns upon the minds of men that excessive differences in the distribution of the goods of the earth, whether in the hands of individuals or of groups or of nations, are not a necessity of inalterable fate, but that an equitable share of all is desirable and possible. The actual realization of this ideal, within limits, is not the direct concern of the Church, although the Church both in the remote and the most recent past has prepared the way for the reasonable and morally noble solution of this important question.

Christ has compared the work of His Church to leaven which, starting from a small spot, gradually permeates a large mass of flour and changes its nature. In this way the principles of justice and charity must permeate the thoughts and desires of mankind. It is the task of the Catholic priesthood to further this penetration of humanity by the Christian spirit. The fact that this process takes place in silence and relative obscurity does not detract from its paramount importance. Justice alone cannot solve the pressing problems. Charity will have to contribute the element of equity in the reconciliation of the clashing interests. It will be the silent contribution of the priesthood toward the solution of the social problem that the leaven of Christian brotherly love never lose its vital force; while the large visible form of justice will be molded by the strong hands of the state.

Another task of the priesthood in regard to questions of prop-

272

erty will be the quiet but ceaseless battle against the overesti-mation of the things of the world. Among the greatest represent-atives of scientific scholarship and culture the cry has become loud for a better appreciation of suprasensual and metaphysical things, even of positive religious faith. Without the soul-shaking events of a worldwide cataclysm, it may take many years before this attitude will penetrate the masses of the people who are captivated by the dazzling achievements of technology and live on the meager and thin diet of a materialistic outlook on life. Hence there is little room for God and religion in the hearts of men. But the fact that the human heart is without rest until it finds its repose in God cannot be gainsaid; it is a reality. All wealth and material comfort are unable to satisfy the deeper yearnings of the human heart. Hence the priest must have com-passion on the people and help them to free themselves from the shackles of the worldly mind. The cry of the soul for God must not be stifled. There is no more ignorant and inexperienced view than the belief that the times of supernatural faith, of religion, and of need for priestly ministrations are past. No, they are not past; in the new era they are going to have a greater part than ever before.

To the extent that the most refined technical discoveries and devices will become a matter of daily use, they will lose their spell of the marvelous and their fascination. The human heart will not find its satisfaction in them, but will be impelled to look beyond the material sphere to the realm of the spirit, where man will recognize his true home prepared for him from the begin-ning of the world. A philosophy of life which is determined by the eternal values of the spirit will renew and spread the recog-nition that in our dealing with the goods of earth we are but stewards of God, who will call us to render an account, He the only and true Master of all possessions: the Author and Keeper of all morality.